To my beloved Frankie and our four children
Rosemary, Laurence, Lucy and Naomi –
Whom I suspect would have preferred me to write a thriller!

Contents

Introduction

The title of this work *Approaching God* is ambiguous. Does it envisage us approaching God or God approaching us? We shall see. But first of all, and in order to formulate a response, we must consider some of the ways in which discussion about God can arise.

Reflective discussion about God occurs in various contexts of human thought and scientific endeavour. For example, it is involved in a subsidiary way in various human sciences such as psychology, anthropology, sociology and political science. It is addressed more centrally and fundamentally in philosophy of religion, in metaphysics and in theology. It is with these central domains of discussion that this study is principally concerned.

Of course all of these reflective discussions about God presuppose, in various ways, the lived, pre-philosophical religious affirmation of God. The affirmation of God (or gods) occurs primarily in the context of lived 'religious' experience and worship which enacts a conscious resolution of one's existential quest for ultimate meaning and value in one's life. Here God is typically invoked, in a self-conscious, self-involving, practical and pre-philosophical way, as the sustaining providential source and goal of human life – a God-for-humans apprehended, affirmed and worshiped as correlative and corresponding to deep human exigencies, hopes and desires.

In philosophy of religion, this pre-reflective lived experience of religion is made the subject of philosophical reflection. Phenomenology of religion is one very influential contemporary form of such philosophical reflection. It is, as we shall consider in greater detail, a form of philosophical reflection which concentrates attention exclusively on phenomena, which have a bearing upon religious experience, as they give themselves to human consciousness.

But the affirmation (or denial) of God occurs also in the context of detached metaphysical reflection about the nature of ultimate reality or being. Here discourse about God unfolds in relative abstraction from any specific self-involving significance for human existence. Interest is focused on the issues of God's objective existence and intrinsic nature and the role that these play, if any, in a detached impersonal investigation of the ultimate foundation of the entire order of being – rather than on his salvific self-involving significance for any individual person. His relationship with human selves can be a particular project for, rather than a definition of, metaphysical enquiry – unlike religion and phenomenology of religion which are defined by this relationship.

Thirdly, there is the reflective discourse about God which arises as a theological elaboration of what God himself has allegedly revealed about himself and his relationship to things other than himself and to human existence in particular. Here one typically has a reflective elaboration of a salvation history – a systematic recapitulation and development of the revelation of an historical accomplishment of a divine intention.

One could say that each of these three kinds of discourse about God exemplifies a different way of seeking to achieve fundamental and dependable knowledge about everything. They are each animated by what one might call a distinct first principle or animating concept from which a coherent account of everything is unfolded. These three principles can be designated as (1) human consciousness; (2) being; and (3) God himself. 'One can seek to know how things are, or how they appear to consciousness, or how God sees them.'[1]

There is first the viewpoint of self-conscious awareness, attentive to everything as it appears to and has a bearing upon human consciousness. This is the perspective, one might say of the self-conscious incarnate subject who seeks to situate and make sense of everything with reference and as co-relative to her conscious awareness. Religion, as a self-involving quest for ultimate meaning and value for ones life is a pre-philosophical lived expression of this viewpoint. Phenomenology provides its most characteristic contemporary philosophical elucidation.

From the phenomenological first-person perspective of viewing everything as it appears to conscious subjectivity, God is described as a phenomenon corresponding to or originating a specifically religious form or dimension of human consciousness namely the conscious quest for a self-involving relationship with that which constitutes the ultimate meaning and value of one's existence. Through phenomenological description and analysis, which accord primacy and ultimacy to what is given as appearing to human consciousness, one seeks to attain a comprehensive, intersubjectively verifiable, perspective on everything, including the affirmation of God, which characterizes the specifically religious form of human consciousness.

The second perspective, from which a comprehensive system of knowledge may be initiated, is that of a metaphysics of being. Here, at least in the realist tradition, the animating first principle is the all-embracing affirmation of being. This affirmation and the subsequent exploration of everything precisely as a manifestation of being – of that which exists – unfolds as a systematic objective presentation of the various categories, structures, interrelationships and gradations of all that is affirmed to exist, and affirmed to exist as more than just an object of human consciousness. From this perspective, God is envisaged as the most profound and perfect expression of being, existing in a more ultimate way than any of the finite beings of our experience including our conscious selves.

The third perspective which aims at a comprehensive system of knowledge is theology. Here the animating first principle is God himself and the saving truth about himself and everything else which he has graciously revealed in the course of human history. This ultimate account of everything, faithfully elaborated in the light of God's revelation, provides a theological system of knowledge. The truth of this theologically elaborated knowledge is affirmed in virtue of the divinely accorded gift of faith in God and his revelation.

This book offers a study of these three approaches to an all-inclusive system of valid knowledge. In each case they are often represented as the uniquely appropriate means of attaining some understanding about the existence, and nature of God and of our coexistence, and that of everything else, with him.

The first three chapters examine individually each of these approaches in their distinctive bearing on the affirmation of God. The discussion of phenomenology is principally concerned with the innovative thought of the French-phenomenologist Jean-Luc Marion. The chapter on realist metaphysics is a personal representation of the metaphysics of Thomas Aquinas. This may appear as rather unfamiliar material to contemporary sensibility and some readers may perhaps be satisfied, in the first instance, to devote their attention to the concluding summary of the chapter. However, I thought it important to try to present this metaphysical approach in some detail and as cogently as possible in view of its frequent dismissal by phenomenologists as a discredited philosophical endeavour. Indeed the core of the book is a dialogue between the views of Marion and Aquinas – although the chapter on theology introduces Karl Barth into the equation. Barth's repudiation of any role for the metaphysical pretensions of traditional 'natural theology' corresponds closely to the equally trenchant repudiation of such metaphysics by phenomenologists such as Marion. This consideration bears directly upon an important issue in contemporary theological discussion. This is the issue of whether phenomenology, such as that espoused by Marion, might provide a positive role for philosophy in a Barthian approach to theology which dismisses the philosophical claims of traditional metaphysics as a form of idolatry?

Chapters 4–6 discuss various comparisons, compatibilities and relationships, which can be held to obtain between these three approaches to God. Chapter 4 devotes particular attention to Hegel's heroic but ultimately unsuccessful undertaking to elaborate an all-embracing unified system incorporating all three approaches integrally into a remarkable speculative synthesis. Chapter 5 devotes particular attention to a comparison of the phenomenological and metaphysical approaches. Chapter 6 discusses the way in which these two philosophical approaches relate to the theological with particular reference to two foundational beliefs of Christianity, namely, that God created us and that God loves us. Then, by way of general conclusion, The final chapter considers the manner in which these various approaches, and their mutual relationships, might be best understood in order to achieve an effective insight into the broad significance and implications of an affirmation of God. It gives final expression to the same few recurrent considerations which are developed progressively, and with increasing insight and conviction, throughout the preceding chapters.

The book has emerged from a long process of reflection on issues in philosophy of religion. This began about 50 years ago when my philosophical attention advanced from an early deep interest in the natural theology developed by Aquinas in the thirteenth century to a consideration of the development of contemporary philosophical atheism. This took the form of an enquiry into why although until around the seventeenth century it was assumed that the unbeliever was the odd, alienated or estranged person – 'the fool who says in his heart there is no God' – today it is widely assumed, at least philosophically, that it is the religious believer who is out of date, estranged and alienated. How did the philosophical relationship between the concepts 'atheism' and 'alienation' become reversed? This led to a book entitled *Atheism and Alienation* involving a discussion of both the elaboration of modern scientific method and the development of philosophical thinking about human subjectivity from Descartes, through Kant, Hegel, Feuerbach and Marx, to twentieth-century existentialism.[2] It involved a philosophical reflection, not so much on the existence or nature of God, as on the issue of the coexistence of finite and infinite, of human subjectivity and God.

After a period of philosophical distraction in university administration at Dublin and Florence, I returned to the topic addressing it now from the more metaphysical concept of 'creation', the fundamental relationship alleged to obtain between finite and infinite – between humans and God. This consideration gave birth to a book *The Sense of Creation* which sought to examine, as given within experience, certain 'ciphers' of the asymmetrical relationship which is characteristic of the doctrine of creation, that is, the non-mutual relationship of radical dependence of creatures upon God.[3] Such experiential ciphers of this asymmetrical relationship, which become apparent through careful description of various speculative and moral human capacities, help to make sense of the idea of creation, which in turn helps to make sense of these somewhat paradoxical features of our experience.

This book *Approaching God* revisits these issues of the existence, nature and coexistence of finite and infinite, of humankind and God. It seeks to compare an objective metaphysical approach to such issues with that arising from a more 'subjective' phenomenological perspective. Here my early interest in the decidedly metaphysical natural theology of Aquinas is brought into dialogue with a more recent interest in phenomenology of religion so effectively represented in the thought of Jean-Luc Marion. Each saw their philosophical endeavour as serving a significant methodological role in the theological elaboration of Christian Revelation. And so, although the book is essentially a philosophical work, I was led to venture beyond a comparison of philosophical perspectives to envisage their bearing upon and influence by a theological approach. It is suggested in the concluding chapters that the irreducibility and complementarity of the two philosophical perspectives is confirmed and possibly required by certain theological considerations of central significance in Christian Revelation.

Phenomenology

Religion

This chapter considers a particular philosophical approach to God, namely, a phenomenological account of the God of religious belief and experience. It may be called an exercise in philosophy of religion.[1]

Our ordinary pre-philosophical lived conception of religion is a rather broad one. It signifies in a general way the distinctive set of conscious relationships between us and a higher sacred reality or God. These include inner beliefs, sentiments, desires, prayers, etc. and outer professions, symbols, myths, rituals, cult and regulation of personal and social life inasmuch these are valued as mediating or embodying valid relationships between us and the sacred or, more specifically, between us and God.

Religion is at once theoretical and practical, a life of belief and practical engagement which nourish each other. It is profoundly self-involving – no mere detached assertion of a factual state of affairs. In professing my belief that I possess my being from God, I profess my radical dependence upon him. The God of religion is worshipped rather than just affirmed – a God of pre-philosophical culturally conditioned belief, conviction and worship, rather than a philosophically derived conclusion. As Henry Dumery remarks: 'We should not speak of a God peculiar to philosophers, but of a God that religion worships and that philosophy must take into consideration, as it does any other value.'[2] And again: 'One pretends to believe that the idea of God is the property of philosophy, whereas it is borrowed from the religious life.'[3] The terms in which the religious relationships between man and God can be expressed vary greatly, as is obvious from the rich variety of historical religions and religious experience.[4] This situation creates the possibility of a comparative study of religions – a fascinating undertaking but not one for this work. What interests us primarily here, in this chapter at least, is to outline a particular philosophical understanding of the most basic feature of any religion, namely, that it distinctively concerns the close self-involving relationship alleged to obtain between human beings and God.

In religion, God is envisaged primarily, not detachedly as he is in himself, but rather in his relationship to humanity as its providential creator, sustainer and final goal. Through 'natural belief' or (as in the main monotheist religions) through 'supernatural faith', God is affirmed as God-for-man. This God, the object of religious worship, is attained and affirmed primarily as corresponding and providing resolution to deep specifically human experiences such as those of limitation, insufficiency, contingency, intransigence, fascination, dread, astonishment, hope and desire.

For many contemporary philosophers, the *philosophical* elucidation of this God of religious belief, this God-for-us, is best achieved by way of phenomenological enquiry and description rather than by way of metaphysical argument.

Phenomenology – introduction

Phenomenology, which traces its origin as a philosophical method to the primacy accorded by Descartes to the *cogito*, is a philosophical approach which interprets all beings, not metaphysically in terms of their self-possessed being, but rather in terms of and from the viewpoint of their manifestation as phenomena appearing to human consciousness. Any being, which is thus interpreted as relative, or co-relative, to human consciousness, must, for phenomenology, always be considered and appraised solely from this standpoint. It is a philosophy of cognitional immanence.

Phenomenology, which thus accords primary significance to phenomena as they present themselves to human consciousness, understands itself as the philosophical approach most attuned and adequate to a true understanding of all phenomena, including religious phenomena, as they manifests themselves to human consciousness. An object of religious consciousness is accessible phenomenologically only as an object for such consciousness; never as something of independent ontological significance (or insignificance). In the remainder of this chapter, I will indicate some general features of a phenomenological approach and its particular development as phenomenology of religion by some distinguished contemporary thinkers.

Pioneered in the twentieth century by philosophers such as Husserl, Heidegger, Sartre and Merleau-Ponty, phenomenology is, as I have just described, a philosophical approach which emphasizes the fundamental significance of conscious subjectivity in our appraisal of everything. This emphasis on subjectivity should not be construed as embracing a subjectivistic outlook or as necessarily espousing the idealist claims of an abstract transcendental subject. The phenomenological subject is affirmed as a being-in-the-world and in virtue of whom, as so existing, a world deploys and manifests itself. The subject is essentially a subject to whom a world becomes manifest, an intentional ex-static world-disclosing subject. The intending subject and the world it discloses, *noesis* and *noema*, are distinct but intrinsically connected. As Dan Zahavi remarks: 'We cannot look at our experience from sideways on to see do they match with reality, nor can we consider our experiences and structures of understanding as mere elements in the world we experience and understand. The relation between mind and the world is an internal one, a relation constitutive of its relata, and not an external one of causality.'[5]

Phenomenology is not interested so much in the supposedly independent and scientifically calculable properties of things, such as their atomic weight or chemical composition, as in the ways in which they show themselves immediately as they are – in their ways and modes of givenness. A loved one, a work of art, a social relation, a utensil or a number manifest themselves in effectively different ways. Moreover, the same object can appear in different modes, for example, as perceived, imagined, feared, desired, etc. Phenomenologists consider the investigation of these ways and modes of manifestation and givenness to be of central philosophical importance.[6]

To accomplish this investigation, phenomenology insists that we must suspend our naive natural inclination to take for granted the independent reality of the world. This suspension of the natural attitude, an attitude which overlooks or misconceives the irreducible relationship of the given phenomena of the world to consciousness, is called the *epoche* or, more comprehensively, the phenomenological reduction. It is a bracketing or suspension of the spontaneous and metaphysical presuppositions of the natural attitude such as the autonomous existence, independently of our consciousness, of beings of various kinds. It is a method which achieves a reduction, a leading back or return, to a presupposition-less world in which a strict co-relativity of knowing and known obtains and in which the being of things is methodologically identified with its manifestation to consciousness. Thus Heidegger remarks: 'For Husserl the phenomenological reduction . . . is the method of leading phenomenological vision from the natural attitude of the human being whose life is involved in the world of things and persons back to the transcendental life of consciousness and its noetic-noematic experiences, in which objects are constituted as correlates of consciousness.'[7]

This phenomenological reduction which suspends our naive commonsense presupposition of the independent reality of the world is not intended as an absolute denial of its reality but rather as a bracketing of the validity of this presupposition and of any attendant presumptions about its independent metaphysical status and structure. Therefore, rather than an outright denial of independently existing reality, what is achieved is a change of attitude towards it. One attains a first-person perspective which enables attention to be focused on an investigation of reality as it is given in its significance and manifestation for human consciousness, as the co-relative of this attentive consciousness.[8]

Phenomenology is critical of metaphysical realism which it views as a pre-critical naïve endeavour of the natural attitude to provide an account of the world and its modalities as though obtaining prior to our conscious engagement with it. For phenomenologists, the world that appears to us, and as it appears to us in various ways, is the only real world. There is no hidden world or reality behind or beyond that which is given experientially to our conscious incarnate subjectivity.[9] As Goethe, cited by Heidegger advised: 'look for nothing behind phenomena: they themselves are what have to be learned.'[10] The task is to investigate and determine phenomenologically the intrinsic character of this world's various modalities of manifestation and givenness to our consciousness.

Phenomenology of religion

Such phenomenological investigation, of what gives and manifests itself precisely as given and co-relative to consciousness, is very well adapted to undertake an exploration of religion conceived, as we have indicated, as an essentially first-person self-involving relationship with God – a God 'intended' and worshipped precisely as correlative and corresponding to the deepest conscious needs and desires of persons for meaning and value in their lives.

Hence, as might be surmised even from these brief remarks, it is not surprising that many contemporary philosophers, such as Emanuel Levinas, Richard Kearney, Jean-Luc Marion, Jacques Derrida, John Caputo and, to some extent, Paul Ricoeur, adopt a phenomenological approach in their philosophical consideration of religion. Let us consider how this approach has been developed.

Kearney develops his phenomenological – hermeneutical approach to religion chiefly in three books: *The God Who May Be* (2001), *Strangers, Gods and Monsters* (2003) and, more recently, *Anatheism* (2010). He introduces this approach with a robust dismissal of traditional metaphysical theodicy, or onto-theology as he calls it after Heidegger, which he sees as reifying God by reducing him to the status of a being, albeit the supreme or highest of all beings.[11] The onto-theological conception of God, developed in terms of Greek metaphysics is seen as a distorting reformulation of the dynamic biblical God into an immutable, self-sufficient pure act of being, existing as an eternal now with no past or future, without movement desire or possibility.[12] 'I subscribe to the new turn in philosophy of religion which strives to overcome the metaphysical God of pure act and asks the question: what kind of divinity comes after metaphysics?'[13]

This overcoming of the God of metaphysics is achieved through a phenomenologically inspired inquiry delivering an account of the biblical God of religious belief as an ethically enabling possibility rather than as pure act, first cause or highest being.[14] This God of religion, conceived as possibility, is not to be understood simply as an immanent possibility of the historically evolving world (such as the classless society) but rather as an ethically transfiguring possibility which transcends a subject's own intrinsic possibilities. Here we are in the domain of eschatology not teleology, of ethical invocation not latent purpose. 'From an eschatological perspective divinity is reconceived as that *posse* or *posset* which calls and invites us to actualise its proffered possibles by our poetical and ethical actions, contributing to the transformation of the world to the extent that we respond to this invitation.'[15]

Kearney elucidates this eschatological response to divine solicitation in terms of our response to the ethical appeal of the other person (the stranger, the widow, the heartbroken), calling us with an absolute claim to exercise goodness in her regard. 'The phenomenon of the persona calls for a new or quasi-phenomenology, mobilised by ethics rather than eidetics . . . Persona is the in-finite other in the finite person before me. In and through that person . . . we refer to this persona as the sign of God. Not the other person as divine, mind you – that would be idolatry – but the divine in and through that person. The divine as trace, icon, visage, passage.'[16]

The thrust of this elucidation is an attempt to respect the radical transcendence of the divine while still envisaging it from a phenomenological perspective of concrete human experience. It involves an eschatological appeal to 'a possible God', experienced not as a direct object of intentional consciousness, but as an enabling ethical invocation which enables us to respond to others in a manner beyond any self-regarding consideration.

This concern of Kearney to somehow contain the affirmation of divine transcendence within a phenomenological frame of reference is motivated in part as a defence against deconstructionist philosophers such as Jacques Derrida. Derrida, as Kearney interprets him, insists that since transcendent 'Otherness' can never be given phenomenologically, we can know nothing about its nature and therefore can say nothing about its ethical character. In response, Kearney maintains that we can be assured of the ethical character of the divine because it is experienced, not as a direct object of consciousness, but obliquely, indirectly and negatively as the phenomenologically accessible eschaton or absent goal who possibilizes our self-transcending conscious religious and ethical experience.[17]

The God thus considered, described enigmatically as 'presence-absence', 'possible-impossible' and 'eschatological Otherness', transcends our direct awareness but does not surpass all our phenomenal horizons of anticipatory experience.[18] Moreover, he is always envisaged in a religious optic in terms of God as he is for man. 'God does not reveal himself, therefore, as an essence *in se* but as an I-Self for us . . . The God of Mosaic manifestation cannot be God without relating to his other – humanity.'[19]

Further, and even more significantly, God thus envisaged is not only co-relative to man – but also in a way dependent upon man. 'God henceforth may be recognized as someone who has become with us, someone as dependent on us as we are on Him.'[20] More explicitly he tells us: 'God can be God only if we enable this to happen.'[21] And again, 'God will be God at the eschaton . . . But because God is posse (the possibility of being) rather than esse (the actuality of being as *fait accompli*) the promise remains powerless unless we respond to it . . . God depends on us to be.'[22]

Such talk about God as 'possible' and dependent upon us can be given a relatively anodyne phenomenological interpretation. It can be seen as envisaging God as the possible and possibilizing, but not yet achieved (by us), goal of our ethical and religious desire and commitment – a God who would be accomplished or 'realized' in our religious life, by us and for us, through sustained fidelity to the ethical invocation he represents. Whether this phenomenological perspective on God as he assumes significance for us, which is fair enough in so far as it goes, goes far enough is an issue to which we will return when we have considered further defence of this phenomenological approach to a religious affirmation of God.

Kearney's critique of 'onto-theology' and the development of an eschatological phenomenology of religion and ethics are also characteristic of the thought of Emanuel Levinas, one of his chief inspirations. For Levinas, the term 'metaphysics' can be translated, without loss, as 'ethics'. He sees the ethical relationship between persons as the primary irreducible structure which confers upon theological concepts the only significance they have. 'Ethics is the spiritual optics . . . There can be no "knowledge" of God separated from the relationship with men. The Other is the very locus of metaphysical truth, and is indispensable for my relation with God.'[23] The ethical appeal of the other person – the stranger, the widow, the orphan – is experienced as an acknowledgement of her asymmetrical ethical transcendence, requiring more of me than I can on that account require of her. It challenges the tendency to seek my foundation within myself envisaged as a *pour soi* or absolute freedom. It locates my centre of gravity outside myself at the service of the obligating encounter with the Other.[24]

For Levinas, as for Kearney, this ethical relationship with the transcendent other person is the locus of a phenomenologically accessible religious awareness of God. 'The dimension of the divine opens forth from the human face . . . God rises to his supreme and ultimate presence as correlative to the justice rendered unto men . . . The Other is not the incarnation of God, but precisely by his face, in which he is disincarnate, is the very manifestation of the height in which God is revealed . . . totality and the embrace of being, or ontology, do not contain the final secret of being. Religion, where relationships subsist between the same and the other despite the impossibility of the Whole – the idea of Infinity – is the ultimate structure.'[25]

However, as with Kearney, the question remains just how, or indeed whether, the transcendent God can be phenomenologically revealed in this ethico-religious experience.

Paul Ricoeur, another luminary in the domain of phenomenology of religion, helps to meet an objection about how a conscious subject might experience, without inventing it, an awareness of divine reality. The objection concerns the correlation of that which is known, as representation or objectivization, with the intentionality of the knowing subject – the correlation between *noema* and *noesis*. This typically involves the subject's claim to mastery over the meaning of its experience and its capacity to determine the scope of this meaning.[26] It would seem therefore that the significance of any alleged experience of the divine is a representation constituted and determined by the subject of the experience.

In response, Ricoeur points out that there are feelings and dispositions that can be called 'religious' which 'can transgress the sway of representation and, in this sense, mark the subject's being overthrown from its ascendancy in the realm of meaning.'[27] For example, there is the feeling of absolute dependence (Schleirmacher); the feeling of utter confidence, in spite of everything (Barth and Bultmann); the feeling of ultimate concern (Paul Tillich); the feeling of belonging to an economy of the gift, with its logic of overabundance, irreducible to the logic of equivalence, . . . the feeling of being preceded in the order of speech love and existence (Rosenzweig).[28]

For Ricoeur these feelings are absolute, in the sense of being detached from the relation by which the subject would retain mastery over the presumed religious object, over its meaning. These feelings, which are ways of being absolutely affected, bear witness to phenomenology's inability to open the intentionality of consciousness onto something wholly other. The fundamental dispositions which correspond to these feelings and affections can be seen as 'prayer' in its various forms such as complaints, supplications demands and praise. This religious response of prayerful obedience to a call must be distinguished from the problem-solving response to a question or problematic situation. We must distinguish clearly the epistemological relation between question and reply from the religious relation between call and obedient response where the superiority of the call is recognized and avowed.

Prayer turns to this Other by which conscious feeling is affected and this Other which affects it is apperceived as the source of the call to which prayer responds.[29] Hence, Ricoeur concludes: 'I therefore grant unreservedly that there can be a phenomenology of feelings and dispositions that can be qualified as religious by virtue of the disproportion within the relation between call and response. This phenomenology would not be merely descriptive but critical, as I just suggested.'[30]

Jean-Luc Marion

This endeavour to provide, by way of phenomenological elucidation, a philosophical validation of a religious acclamation of God is further developed in the thought of Jean-Luc Marion. He likewise challenges the unquestioned tradition of the 'subject' coming down from Descartes through Kant to Husserl which sees the subject as establishing rigorous preconditions for the emergence or self-giving of phenomena. In this tradition, what the subject intends or envisages establishes the context for what appears or is intuited. But what is given or intuited rarely fulfils what is intended and, indeed, usually falls far short thereof. Thus, for example, my intuition or experience of three colours arranged one on top of the other falls far short of all that I intend or envisage by a traffic signal. In such a phenomenon what is intuited is governed, comprehended, absorbed into what is conceptually intended or signified.[31] Again, sometimes an intention exceeds any possible intuitive fulfilment in virtue of a lack which precludes any objective knowledge. Such would be the case in intending the possibility of a square circle.

However, one can entertain a third possibility described by Marion as follows: 'The intention (the concept or the signification) can never reach adequation with the intuition (fulfilment), not because the latter is lacking but because it exceeds what the concept can receive, expose, and comprehend.'[32] This excess of intuition over intention he calls the saturated phenomenon. The giving intuition in such a possibility exceeds, submerges and saturates the measure of every concept.[33] This, he tells us is a possibility which Husserl, committed to the commanding role of the subject, did not exploit. However, for Marion, pursuing the force of this possibility is more faithful to Husserl's key principle that phenomena are to be accepted just as they give themselves out to be.[34] Moreover, the possibility opens the route to a new dimension of phenomenology – the phenomenology of our possible intuition of the divine. Pursuing this route we discover that 'access to the divine phenomenality is not forbidden to man; in contrast, it is when he becomes entirely open to it that man finds himself forbidden from it – frozen, submerged, he is by himself forbidden from advancing and likewise from resting. In the mode of interdiction terror attests to the insistent and unbearable excess in the intuition of God.'[35]

Let us consider what seems to be involved in Marion's discussion of the saturated phenomenon in this context of divine phenomenality.

For Marion, every phenomenon or manifestation that shows *itself* does so to the extent that it gives *itself* first. This has the noteworthy implication that the subject of experience is no longer seen as wholly or primarily determining the conditions of the possibility of experience, that is, of phenomenality.[36] What is given in experience does indeed require as its counterpart the 'given-to' pole of subjectivity, the *noesis* of the *noema*, to phenomenalize the given. But this given-to does not precede the phenomenon as though constituting the preconditions of its appearance. The impact of the 'given' upon the given-to is at least as great as the given-to upon the given. 'Each phenomenalizes the other as the revealed, which is characterized by this essential phenomenal reciprocity, where seeing implies the modification of the seer by the seen as much as of the seen by the seer. The given-to functions as the revelator of the given and the given as the revelator of the given-to.'[37]

In thus according an active, indeed primary, role to what is given in experience, the way is opened for Marion's characteristic claim that what is intuited can, exceed, overflow and utterly saturate the subject's capacity to envisage, intend or conceptualize it. In such instances of saturated intuition, the subject can exercise sufficient resistance to transmute the excess of intuitive givenness into that which shows itself, the phenomenon. Marion offers as an example of such decisive resistance 'the painter who makes visible as a phenomenon what no one has ever seen, because, in each case he is the first to succeed in resisting the given enough to make it show *itself* – and then in a phenomenon accessible to all.'[38]

Moreover, there remains, whether by way of Revelation or natural affection, the possibility of an intuitively experienced divine givenness or gift of such bedazzling, superabundant, unconditioned perfection and saturating impact that no intention or concept or signification can organize, contain or foresee it. In virtue of this bedazzling impact, the saturated phenomenon cannot be viewed or seen as an object of ordinary intending consciousness. It is perceived only in the negative mode of bedazzlement as the blur and overexposure that this phenomenon imposes on the ordinary conditions of experience.[39] 'In short, God remains incomprehensible, not imperceptible – without adequate concept, not without giving intuition.'[40] This excess of any comprehension accomplished in the intuition of God is marked by a kind of stupor, terror and fascination which the incomprehensibility resulting from the excess imposes upon us.

Phenomenological description and analysis enables us to conceive the formal possibility of an intuition of divine givenness by way of Revelation but not, of course, to affirm the actuality of such a phenomenon – an issue utterly beyond its scope. It simply indicates how such a phenomenon, *if* it is revealed, should be described in a way that does justice to its possibility.[41]

A principal aim of Marion's subtle account of saturated phenomena is to delineate the possibility of a phenomenologically given intuition of God (such, but not exclusively, as one finds in accounts of mystical experience), which nevertheless safeguards the divine transcendence.

But how, one might ask, can what is experienced be wholly transcendent if it is somehow calibrated with the perceptually intuitive capacity of the conscious subject? Marion's reply is that intuition of the divine is so dazzlingly saturating that it eliminates any constitutive activity of the subject. The subject is rendered wholly receptive, vis-à-vis any such saturating self-revelation of the divine, for example, the unique Judaeo-Christian Revelation. It is 'reduced' to the status of a secondary or derived subject, constituted rather than constituting. It becomes a *me* rather than an *I*, bereft of any limiting role of signification or containment and thereby denied any claim to be the ultimate foundation of the experience of phenomena.[42] Hence, the transcendence signalled in the intuition of the divine is in no way compromised by the limitations of the given-to subject. I do not lay hold of the transcendent. It lays hold of me.[43]

The preceding remarks illustrate, by reference to the thought of leading exponents, an outline of central features of a phenomenological approach to God. These include:

1. A rejection of the traditional metaphysical approach – dismissed as onto-theology or natural theology.
2. Fidelity to the non-negotiable ultimacy of the *epoche* or phenomenological reduction which brackets out the naïve natural attitude that nourishes acceptance of onto-theology and a world of

objects existing independently of human consciousness. Instead it reduces or 'leads back' the things of the world to their given revelation as phenomena to a subject who is likewise reduced to immanence through removal from the natural world by renouncement of the natural attitude.

3. Insisting that instead of talking about God in metaphysical terms, he must be envisaged as he is primarily encountered, namely, religiously in terms of his relationship to human experience. As Kearney puts it, God does not reveal himself as an essence *in se* but as an I-self for us essentially related to his other – humanity.

4. Attributing, in striking difference to traditional Husserlian phenomenology, a primary and active role to the phenomenon which gives itself from itself in intuition. This active role of what gives itself (*noema* rather than *noesis*) disputes the primacy of the role of the given-to or intending subject which, as so 'reduced', is henceforth characterized by receptivity and no longer viewed as what primarily constitutes phenomena.[44]

5. This opens up the possibility of a bedazzling, subject-bewildering intuition of the divine who utterly transcends human comprehension or constitution.

6. This also breaks down, philosophically, the chasm traditionally claimed to obtain between what may be disclosed rationally by philosophical reflection on the one hand and what is purported to be disclosed non-rationally by divine Revelation on the other. For the signifying subject or given-to is no longer empowered to legislate such a distinction but must respect every phenomenon which as a given is brought to manifestation by and for this given-to – however unexpected, unforeseen or even incomprehensible. 'For the same phenomenality applies to all givens from the most impoverished (formalisms and mathematics), to those of common law (physical sciences, technical objects), to saturated phenomena . . . including the possibility of . . . the phenomena of Revelation.'[45]

Remarks

What can we say about this phenomenological approach to God? It certainly provokes fundamental philosophical questions about its adequacy as an approach to an affirmation of God. However, before hazarding any critical observations, one should recognize its very considerable merits.

In the first place, it has the great merit of situating discussion about God in terms which are directly relevant to its primary pre-philosophical context, namely, the religious context where God is primarily envisaged, and experienced, in a self-involving way, in his corresponding salvific relationship to profound human exigencies. It is attentive to all the modalities and aspects of this personal experience and apprehension of the divine. Moreover, it emphasizes that, like every other given phenomenon, religious phenomena which are given in consciousness have every right to be taken as they give themselves to be. In this assertion it is simply applying Husserl's principle of all principles, that every originarily giving intuition is a source of right for cognition and must be accepted quite simply as it gives itself out to be within the measure and limits within which it gives itself to consciousness.[46]

Religious phenomena are thus to be treated as they present themselves to consciousness and not subjected any a priori criterion of what is rationally admissible. The possibility of what is impossible according to some a priori presupposition of rationality must be seriously entertained for what it is and not reduced to, or reinterpreted in, some more rationally acceptable version, for example, of anthropology, sociology, political ideology or psychiatry.

The phenomenological approach to God renders religious phenomena philosophically admissible as *facts,* justified de jure because given *in fact.* A religious viewpoint inasmuch as it embodies phenomena, which, as given, obtain with the same right as any other, is no less deserving of consideration of its claims than a scientific, moral or aesthetic viewpoint. As Marion puts it: 'the lived states of consciousness and the intentionalities of praise, of demand, of veneration, of repentance, of reconciliation, of confidence, etc., beliefs (from theological faith to various "holdings as true"), the volitions of charity, of fraternity, of peace, of sacrifice, etc., not scientific but experiential types of knowledge (vision, "presences", internal dialogues, words said in the heart, etc.) – all these lived experiences of consciousness would hence appear as phenomena by full right, at least to the extent to which they are given to consciousness.'[47]

Thus phenomenology endorses the rationality of the claim of religious phenomena to be considered specifically as such. In this it is unlike some other conceptions of philosophy which, in view of their conception of what is rationally admissible, dismiss such phenomena as *Schwarmerei* (religious enthusiasm or fanaticism). In particular, in the light of its conception of the saturated phenomenon, it opens philosophical space for revelation and indeed Revelation to enter into phenomenality, opens space to know something transcendent to ordinary experience that nevertheless is manifested experientially.[48]

In virtue of this openness to all religious phenomena, phenomenology can propose itself as an appropriate method in both philosophy of religion and theology – apt for the investigation of all given religious phenomena both those naturally given such as the experience of the holy, the mysterious, the sublime, and those given as Revelation such as the appearance of Yahweh to Moses in the burning bush.

Moreover, in its concentration on God as given to human consciousness, rather than as existing independently, phenomenology can find meaningful and illuminating some ways of describing God which are problematic to a more conventional metaphysical approach. Thus, for example, as mentioned above, observations by Kearney – such as 'the God of Mosaic manifestation cannot be God without relating to humanity'; 'God can be God only if we enable this to happen'; 'God is as dependent upon us as we are upon him' – can be construed phenomenologically in an uncontroversial and even enlightening sense. It can be seen as highlighting that aspect of our religious experience whereby through prayer, worship and moral endeavour we seek to enable God to become an effective reality in our consciousness. God, envisaged phenomenologically as God related intrinsically to human consciousness, assumes greater or lesser reality as God-for-us, to the extent to which we enable this to happen. The phenomenal reality of the religiously affirmed God, which is the only divine reality accessible to phenomenology, is dependent upon its experienced manifestation as a given phenomenon in human consciousness. Considered in this way, talk about God's dependence upon us etc. may be viewed as intelligible and unexceptional. It may be understood as emphasizing that God, given experientially as the supreme instance of the saturated phenomenon, can be more effectively manifested and progressively 'realized' in the interior life of prayerful attention than in the context of disinterested metaphysical speculation.

Further, the phenomenological approach to God can provide richer insight into the essential nature of religion than other approaches more suspicious of the claims of religious phenomena. Instead of seeking to explain, or explain away, religious phenomena in terms of their extrinsic causes, it seeks first to provide a faithful description of them as variously given in personal experience. It then offers an account, by way of free imaginative variation, of their intrinsic essential structure over a range of religions and religious experience. Thus phenomenology of religion, through careful attention and analysis can disclose a sui generis experiential structure in religion involving components such as (1) an ideal to be worshipped and aspired towards, (2) an existential experience of flawed separation or need for salvation and (3) a deliverer or power that overcomes the need or inherent flaw and attains the ideal. On this account, 'the three elements then that go to make up the structure of the religious dimension are the ideal, or religious object; the defect in existence, or need; and the saving power, or the deliverer.[49] Through the careful elucidation of such immanent structures of religious experience in its various manifestations, phenomenology can elaborate a more adequate and perceptive account of what religious phenomena involve than the 'hermeneutics of suspicion' which is typical of various reductive accounts of them in other human sciences such as sociology, politics and psychiatry. It provides a perspective on religious phenomena from which such reductive accounts can be effectively criticized.

However, notwithstanding these and other considerable merits of a phenomenological approach to God, we must consider some difficulties which it involves, particularly if it is viewed as an adequate, comprehensive and exclusive philosophical approach to God. Our aim is not to dispute these considerable merits but to enquire whether they provide all that might be required of a philosophy of religion or rather whether they need to be qualified, developed or complemented by further extra-phenomenological considerations.

A radical objection to a phenomenological approach to God is one which calls into question phenomenology itself. It does so by questioning the legitimacy of the phenomenological reduction which is the fundamental procedure of phenomenology dominating all its consequent procedures.[50]

The basic thrust of this objection is that rejecting as naïve the 'natural attitude', in which we allow ourselves to be carried along by the general evidence of independently existing reality, is itself extremely questionable. The alleged reason why phenomenology applies the bracketing reduction to the transcendent objects that present themselves as existing independently in a spatio-temporal 'fact world' to which I belong is that the naïve natural viewpoint which sustains this presentation involves a trap which the reduction puts out of play. For Husserl, we must extricate ourselves from this natural standpoint which finds this 'fact world' to be 'out there' and takes it just as it thus gives itself to me as 'something that exists out there'. *'Instead now of remaining at this standpoint, we propose to alter it radically . . . We put out of action the general thesis which belongs to the essence of the natural standpoint, we place in brackets whatever it includes respecting the nature of Being. I use the "phenomenological" epoche, which completely bars me from using any judgment that concerns spatio-temporal existence.'*[51]

The trap involved in the natural standpoint is the contradiction that consciousness, bemused by the material nature of the independently existing world regards itself as just another bit of this world, a thing in the material world which also somehow contains this world representationally in itself. It tends therefore to understand itself and everything else impersonally, on the post-Cartesian model of modern positive science, as an objective piece of an encompassing material world which excludes, in allegedly view-pointless objectivity, the claims of subjectivity.

The phenomenological reduction, it is claimed, enables consciousness to avoid this alienated mode of existence and to take itself out of the world and recover its intentional reality as the distinct but co-relative, co-constitutive, *noetic* counterpart of what is given, *noematically*, to consciousness.

But how, Roger Chambon asks, does the fact that the natural attitude takes account of the evident independent reality of things distort their manifestation and prevent them from appearing as what they are? It is understandable that one may wish to reduce, or 'lead back' from, 'the trap' involved in features of the materialism, or idealism, or the representationalism arising out of post-Cartesian philosophy – to recover the genuine significance of the original manifestation of things themselves. But on what grounds is the evident independent reality of things themselves subjected to the reduction? What entitles one to say that a trap is already at work in the way things originally present themselves? 'The being of the phenomenon is not its phenomenon-being but the setting it has in and from the trans-phenomenal being. There is no gap between the sensible profiles and the ontic (that is, really existing) attachments which withdraw it from the subject, thus preventing it from being a mere "appearance" . . . In fact reality never has to be "posited" because what is perceived appears directly as steeped in being.'[52] The phenomena are not the networks of things, but things are the source of phenomena. The phenomenological reduction may be correct in suspending the abstract 'reality' of the 'objective' world depicted by science but not the evident reality of things experienced in intuitive perception as independently existing.

Needless to say, committed phenomenologists would not accept this objection. They would insist that the bracketing (though not the outright denial) of the independent existence of things given in experience is essential to the entire phenomenological project. Moreover, they maintain that this phenomenological reduction with its attendant procedures is the only legitimate contemporary philosophical approach in the context of the modern preoccupation with human subjectivity, and certainly the most appropriate in a philosophical consideration of religion.

Fortunately, we do not need to enter into this debate here although in the next chapter we will be considering another philosophical approach, a metaphysical realist approach, which lends credence to the objection. However, all we want to leave open at this point, for fuller discussion in subsequent chapters, is whether or not phenomenology and its defining reduction is the only legitimate or adequate philosophical approach and how this consideration affects its legitimate application in philosophy of religion. For there it undoubtedly provides access to insights about religion and what it involves which are not otherwise available, for example, in the approach of metaphysical speculation and argument. It identifies and highlights the first-person, self-involving, human-consciousness-related significance of the primarily religious affirmation of God. It provides revealing description and immanent analysis of all that this God, as he is for human consciousness, involves cognitively, affectively and practically. It enables non-reductive interpretation of God as experienced in the devotional life of individuals and in their worship of this God invoked precisely as co-relative to religious exigencies.

Transcendence and experience

There is, however, a further difficulty which bears not on phenomenology in general but upon phenomenology of religion in particular. This is the difficulty in trying to make sense of the claim that the transcendent God can somehow be perceived in human intuition. This, for Kearney, occurs as the divine eschaton or *posse*, given experientially if obliquely, who enables our ethical endeavour. And for Marion: 'God remains incomprehensible, not imperceptible – without adequate concept, not without giving intuition.'[53]

The difficulty is how this can be the case without relativizing, and thereby undermining, the divine transcendence it affirms.[54] Is it really satisfactory to seek to legitimize, within a phenomenological frame of reference, an experiential affirmation of divine transcendence, even one envisaged so tentatively and modestly in terms of eschatological possibility and incomprehensibility? Can a God, accessible philosophically only as a phenomenon situated within human experience really be utterly transcendent? To maintain that God is integrally transcendent would seem to involve that he is unbounded by any human experience – yet it is precisely and only within human experience that he is located by phenomenology.

This difficulty can be addressed by considering the co-relative poles determining the conditions of ordinary experience, the objective pole and the subjective pole – the *noema* and the *noesis*.

The objective or given pole, the experienced divine reality, may be defended in its claim to manifest uncompromised transcendence by emphasizing that it is not given as the presence of an object or a being but rather as the absence of a presence, the absence of an object or being – a given no-thing. It is given, albeit to human consciousness, as an absolute, that is, non-relativized, experience of the radically Other – experienced as a bedazzling and even frightening given which utterly transcends the normally defining conditions of objective experience. The experienced divine transcendence is not compromised because, as unconditioned by the subject which receives it, it is given in a non-objectifying form of awareness.

However, from the perspective of the given-to or 'subjective' pole of experience, the situation is less amenable. The aim must be, in order to safeguard the absolute transcendence of the divine Other given in experience, to deny any active constitutive or constraining role for the conscious subject in its reception. The given transcendence if it is to be absolute cannot be relativized as necessarily conforming to the ordinary conditions of possibility of experience. Hence, for Marion, the conscious subject does not constitute what it receives and experiences but rather is constituted by it. 'The constituting subject is succeeded by the constituted witness. As constituted witness the subject remains the worker of truth, but is no longer its producer.'[55]

But this, Marlene Zarader argues, is impossible. There can be no phenomenon, absolute or otherwise, if a subject (however represented as affected rather than active) does not exercise its defining role and function of letting phenomena appear.

In response one may emphasize that what is involved here is a reversal, minimization and dispossession of the role of the subject vis-à-vis the experience of the divine. One may deny it any constitutive role, see it as passive resistance, affected rather than active, utterly powerless; a mute witness to an absolute experience rather than an actively effective subject. This indeed is the thrust of both Levinas's and Marion's approach to the matter, an approach which seeks to have done with the subject in order as Zarader puts it: 'to provide a clear space for a privileged givenness to shine forth from itself in its pure alterity.'[56]

However, for Zarader – whatever case might be made for the view that the transcendent Other, whose givenness exceeding the form of objects or even of beings, is therefore not prevented from being given within phenomenality – one cannot dispense with a positive role for the subject in the event. To do so is to undermine the very ground upon which phenomenology rests. 'To want the phenomenon to appear *absolutely*, without any reference to any instance that can guarantee its appearing, is to condemn oneself to losing it *as* phenomenon; and to deprive oneself, as a result, of all justification by phenomenality.'[57]

Marion is dismissive of this objection. He sees it as involving an unsophisticated univocal concept of subject (and also indeed of the concepts of experience and objectivity). 'How can one feign not to know that the entire question – the entire difficulty – consists in seeing whether "subject" cannot and should not be understood in many senses, or, in other words, if the critique of the transcendental subject does not free another sense of "subject," or more exactly of what comes after the subject.'[58] The subject to whom the phenomenon of divine transcendence is manifest is not the empirical ego, nor the transcendental *I* which determines the conditions of possibility of our ordinary experience of objects, but rather a subject secondary to and *derived from the phenomenon* that primarily gives itself in an excess of intuition, God the phenomenon par excellence. This secondary and derived *me* receives itself as a given-to from the phenomenon which gives *itself*. It is constituted as a given-to of witness, reception and response.[59]

This crucial step in Marion's phenomenology is subtle but not self-evident. The new derived *me*, this a posteriori given-to, which, by way of reduction, disqualifies and replaces the transcendental *I* nevertheless requires the characteristic a priori activity of this transcendental *I* to achieve the very reduction which replaces it.

Likewise, it would seem, this reductive activity of the transcendental *I* is required to achieve appreciation of the change in the conditions of possibility of phenomenality from the primacy of the constituting *I* to the primacy of what gives *itself* from itself.[60] Thus its active engagement and cooperation is required to transform itself from the ultimate foundation of the experience of phenomena to the derived recipient of what gives itself.

This self-denying ordinance of the subject in replacing its function as active operator with that of passive recipient may give the impression of a performative contradiction. But Marion does not think that it involves such a contradiction and believes rather that it disposes of Zarader's contention that one cannot, in phenomenology, dispense with the characteristically active role of the subject in achieving the appearance of phenomena.

For Marion, the subject as given-to does indeed play a role in the appearance of phenomena but not the active role Zarader seems to require of it because of her allegedly univocal conception of the subject. Because its role and function is now seen as passive and enabling, rather than active and determining, the subjective pole of the experience of divine transcendence can be acknowledged without compromising or relativizing this transcendence.

How does this passive enabling role of the subject function and does it genuinely ensure the alleged integrity of the divine transcendence? (One is reminded here of other less convincing accounts of intellectual passivity vis-à-vis an experience of God such as Averroes's denial of any individual active or even passive intellect, or Malebranche's assertion that in virtue of the pure passivity of the human intellect God is the object of human consciousness and the locus of all objective knowledge.)

Marion's treatment of this delicate issue of experiencing divine transcendence is careful and discriminating. There is no question of any knowledge of the transcendent God as an object of direct intellectual vision or awareness. As an intuition exceeding every conception, a saturated phenomenon is experienced as an invisible because utterly bedazzling, disorientating and even terrifying phenomenon which gives itself, and thereby legitimizes itself, from itself. It takes hold of and impacts our awareness rather than our awareness taking hold of and prefiguring its appearance.

But what role does the passive given-to subject play in the manifestation of this phenomenon? For Marion, it enables this manifestation to obtain through its receptive resistance to the impact or stimulus of the unseen given which must give itself before it can show itself. Its passive receptivity is also in a way an active capacity, a capacity of resistance which enable the given to phenomenalize itself.

Through this impact and resistance the 'visibility' of both the given and the given-to arise. Marion describes the operation as though the unseen given projects itself onto the given-to or consciousness as onto a screen – its impact upon the screen provoking this double visibility like the impact of the developing chemical on photographic paper makes the image visible. He evokes also the model of the prism which captures the invisible white light, and turning it into the spectrum of primary colours, renders light finally visible. And again, he adduces the suggestive model of electrical resistance where the restriction of the free movement of electrons in a cable transforms their invisible movement into phenomenalized light and heat.[61]

The point of these examples is to illustrate how only the given-to in its role of resistance to the impact of the given can bring that which gives itself to manifestation or to show itself as a phenomenon. The greater the impact, the greater the resistance required and the less scope for any constituting role for the given-to. The supreme instance of such non-objectifying resistance by a subject or given-to would be the transmutation of a givenness of divine transcendence into bedazzling phenomenality.

It is along lines such as these that Marion defends the claim that an authentic experience of divine transcendence as a saturated phenomenon is possible, since the subject enables the experience only by its resistance to the given and not at all determining it.

However, ingenious though this solution is it does not fully dispel the misgiving that a humanly experienced divine transcendence, even one enabled simply by passive resistance, cannot be an experience of a transcendent God. For the characteristic resistance itself of the subject cannot but characterize the phenomenon of divine transcendence which it enables. As Marion concedes, the nature of the resistance, in this case the resistance of a derived human subject, must influence the extent of the phenomenalization. 'For, if the given shows *itself* only by being blocked and spreading itself on the screen that the given-to has become for it, if the given-to must and can be the only one capable of transforming an impact into visibility, then the extent of phenomenalization depends upon the resistance of the given-to to the brute shock of the given – only the resistance of the given-to can transmute, up to a certain point, the excess of givenness into a fitting monstration.'[62]

Thus it would seem that whatever is primordially given prior to showing itself, including the transcendent God, attains phenomenality in virtue of a bifurcation into a given and a given-to or consciousness which accomplishes the manifestation. It is a truism that this phenomenal manifestation of divine transcendence can only obtain as enabled by a passively receptive human consciousness. (Here one thinks not only of Marion's account of divine givenness but of similar phenomenological claims such as Kearney's that God 'cannot be God without relating to his other – humanity'.) But is this the only way in which divine transcendence can obtain or be properly envisaged?

The answer would seem to be yes if one accepts as fundamental and indubitable the 'epoche' or phenomenological reduction which is a defining feature of phenomenology, one which suspends all transcendence in order to measure what is thus given in immanence.[63] If this is true then the given divine transcendence must be a structure immanent to human consciousness. Marion is explicit on this point: 'I made it my goal to establish that givenness remains an immanent structure of any kind of phenomenality, whether immanent or transcendent.'[64]

Givenness always remaining immanent does not preclude phenomena being actually given but only their objectivity beyond the limits of immanence.[65] Hence divine transcendence can only be given within the limits of immanence, in a bedazzling saturated phenomenon, to a subject which is not an actor or producer but a passive enabling receiver. But, however passive and reductively derived, this subject functions effectively as that to which divine transcendence is inevitably related as the required context for the only way in which it can be said to obtain, namely as a phenomenon immanent to human consciousness. If this is so there would appear to be some substance to Zarader's claim (dismissed by Marion): 'If in the framework of phenomenality, one cannot do without a pole that guarantees the meaning of the phenomenon ... then the transcendence of which the pole is a witness can only be relative: transcendence in immanence, an other for me. The phantasm of a pure or absolute alterity proves to be unachievable. Unachievable in phenomenology.'[66] Can a divine transcendence affirmed only as given within the context of phenomenological immanence be a credible affirmation of God?

One may be prompted to explore the hypothesis that the *givenness* of the divine transcendence, experienced as a phenomenon immanent to consciousness, can be viewed as a cipher or trace of a divine giver. On this hypothesis, the experience of the phenomenon of divine transcendence as being given can be seen unproblematically as an effect created by an ontologically transcendent giver or God. Divine transcendence on this hypothesis would no longer be said to be relative to human consciousness but, as indeed Marion himself wants to maintain, rather the reverse.

However, phenomenologists generally, and certainly Marion and Kearney, reject such an hypothesis. They see it as a lapse into the sort of *metaphysica specialis* or *theologia rationalis* characteristic of the onto-theology which the phenomenological reduction rigorously excludes. For phenomenology, as we have seen, everything that offers itself originarily in intuition is to be taken quite simply, as of right, as it gives itself out to be. The question 'why does it exist' is not to be answered by appeal to a cause but simply with the response 'there is what gives itself'. Every phenomenon is adequately and unquestionably in order quite simply as it gives itself without requiring a reference to any anterior authority of a sufficient condition such as a cause.

We can imagine and say that something is given and appears as given without referring it to another thing or being or object that would be the cause of its givenness.[67] For phenomenology, givenness does not require a metaphysical ground or efficient cause. It is not defined extrinsically in relation to a cause or giver. It is in no way equivalent to production.[68]

Marion sees givenness as a more fundamental and rationally more illuminating consideration than efficient causation which presupposes a metaphysical outlook foreign to phenomenology. In such a metaphysical system, he insists, the possibility of appearing never belongs to what appears. A phenomenon can appear only under the condition of some sufficient reason or cause. However, far from requiring such a reason, it is enough for a phenomenon to give itself through intuition. Intuition is justified de jure from itself by claiming to be the unconditioned origin. What is involved in phenomenology is the principle of sufficient intuition rather than the principle of sufficient reason.[69] Any onto-theological appeal to God as the giver or cause of givenness would be ruinous of the phenomenological project.[70]

Accordingly, in phenomenology God himself can be designated as the being given par excellence. 'That excellence indicates neither sufficiency, nor efficiency, nor principality, but attests to the fact that "God" is given and allows to be given more than any other being-given.'[71] God is found given without reserve, a loving diffusion of himself – who remains himself – to the other than himself; rather than a *causa sui* which can only fold efficiency back upon itself.[72]

Phenomenology and Revelation

Marion is careful to distinguish clearly between revelation and Revelation and the role which phenomenology can play in respect of each. 'By "revelation" I here intend a strictly phenomenological concept: an appearance that is purely of itself, that does not subject its possibility to any preliminary determination.'[73] In this sense revelation encompasses a range of those saturated phenomena in which the excess of intuition shields them from objective constitution. These include phenomena such as unpredictable pure historical events, the visual work of art such as a painting which can be looked at but not constituted, and the bedazzling face of a loved one – which becomes invisible as I seek to look at its invisible gaze weighing on mine. Finally, one can imagine a supreme instance of saturated phenomena, one of such excessive unconditioned intuitive excellence, a bedazzling, absolute transcendent givenness, which impacts lovingly upon a consciousness rendered passively receptive to the theophany which it phenomenalizes.

In this supreme instance of revelation one is envisaging the revealed divine transcendence accessible by way of Revelation. But Marion is careful to point out that this is not something that phenomenology can, as a philosophical tool, disclose from its own resources. In the case of the givens retrieved by Revelation (e.g. the Jewish and Christian Revelation), the transmutation of the given *itself* into what shows *itself* requires conversion and the exercise of theological virtues in a deepened resistance on the part of the given-to witness to the Revelation.[74] Although on the basis of its account of saturated phenomena, phenomenological analysis can admit formally the *possibility* of Revelation; revealed theology is required to confirm the *fact* of its phenomenality.[75] Beyond the phenomenological analysis which liberates the possibility of Revelation as a de jure phenomenon, the actual experience of its givenness is a matter for grace enabled faith and theological confirmation.

For Marion, phenomenology as philosophy of religion can play a crucial role in articulating and defending the possibility of Revelation against the various conceptions of rationality which dismiss it because of its unique and paradoxical character. He maintains that 'revelation' is the universal originary eventful mode of manifestation of every phenomenon insofar as it gives *itself* before showing *itself* and gives *itself* in what shows *itself.* This claim, he argues, abolishes, de jure if not de facto, the gap established by metaphysics between the exclusively rational world of supposedly constituted, producible and repeatable objects and the supposedly irrational world of revealed Revelation whose events are neither constitutable, nor repeatable nor immediately producible. The field of phenomenality is opened up to include as legitimate phenomena the whole range of saturated phenomena including the rational possibility of their supreme instance the given of Revelation.[76]

Moreover, although phenomenology cannot replace the particular protocols of revealed theology in confirming as legitimate, rather than illusory, the givens of an alleged Revelation, it can play an important role in adverting theology to appropriate and, more importantly, to inappropriate ways of considering the givens of Revelation. For the same phenomenality which applies to all other givens applies also to the givens of Revelation which should therefore be treated in a similar manner. Theology should respect this fundamental consideration and avoid, as is too often the case, the tendency to translate reductively the phenomenality of the givens of Revelation, such as creation, resurrection and divinization, into metaphysical objectifying categories of efficient causation, physical change and transformation, etc.

This point is emphasized by John Caputo for whom 'God' and 'experience' are intersecting notions that fit together hand in glove.[77] He explores their intersection phenomenologically because for him phenomenology, which is nothing but the cartography of experience, is what comes after 'onto-theology'.[78] Elucidating this remark he observes that a phenomenological account is characteristically concerned with describing the precise sense of appearing, with the structure of phenomenality, rather than with the objective reality of an appearance. 'Minimally, it would bracket a causal or realist account of experience and adhere closely to a descriptive account . . . In the case of Scriptures, it would concentrate on the "sense" of a faith that can move mountains rather than worrying about its objective physical or metaphysical possibility, on the sense of the angel Gabriel's Annunciation to the Virgin Mary rather than whether the evangelist records an actual historical episode.'[79]

Thus phenomenology can make common cause with theology in faithfully and appropriately elaborating the import of revealed phenomena and in helping it to avoid the phenomenologically inadmissible onto-theological reformulations of metaphysics. Phenomenology provides a new or a renewed, philosophical access to the possibility of revealed theology as a rationally legitimated domain of discourse. It does so by legitimising the possibility of the givens of Revelation as phenomena which give themselves from themselves to consciousness without any recourse to the agency of an extrinsic cause or giver. Phenomenology helps to legitimize revealed theology by excluding the illusory distraction of a metaphysical approach to God. In football terminology, it is a case of phenomenology and theology = 2, metaphysics and theology = nil!

The phenomenological approach to God which we have been considering in this chapter, and in particular Marion's brilliant and original elaboration of it, is a very valuable and irreplaceable contribution to philosophy of religion. It focuses attention on the fact that primarily God is found and acclaimed as corresponding, in a bedazzling unforeseeable excess of loving self-donation, to the existential openness of people to experience a meaning and value in their life which utterly transcends their own intrinsic capabilities. It articulates very perceptively the religious experience of people who in their interior life of prayer and worship are intentionally directed to God and assured that they are not just talking to themselves but are in the attentive presence of their God. It is a philosophy of religion which remains wholly focused on the intuitive experience of a personal relationship with God and with unfolding, from within, all that this religious experience may involve. It precludes, as mistaken and incompatible with its fundamental perspective, the impersonal extrinsic metaphysical speculation of onto-theology.

Nevertheless, however valuable and irreplaceable may be the phenomenological approach to God proposed by the philosophers discussed above, it does not commend itself universally as the only and indisputable philosophical approach. Even within the broad field of phenomenology itself it encounters serious objections. Thus for Husserl and Heidegger, given the philosophical primacy of the phenomenological reduction, a God transcendent in every way is beyond the range of phenomenality, beyond the scope of phenomenological enquiry. This is the point highlighted by Zarader's observation that a transcendent God accessible as a phenomenon can only be relative: transcendence in immanence, an other for me. The same point is made even more trenchantly by Dominique Janicaud who argues that to attempt to portray divine transcendence phenomenologically is like trying to square the circle, a theological attempt to hijack phenomenology. Phenomenology is essentially a philosophy of finitude and radical immanence whose self-imposed intrinsic limitation 'is, fundamentally, that of a critical and post critical philosophy of finitude: renouncing metaphysics as *metaphysica specialis* to explore experience in its phenomenal limits.'[80]

Likewise, and again from within a phenomenological perspective, there is Derrida's objection to the alleged phenomenality of divine transcendence. Whereas for Marion, divine transcendence is experienced as an excess of givenness which overwhelms every intention; for Derrida, on the contrary, it signifies an intention of infinite being which can never be intuitively given and is, therefore, forever beyond the possibility of phenomenology.[81] We will return, in chapters 5 and 6, to this crucial question of the significance attributed to divine transcendence in Marion's phenomenology.

The philosophers thus queried are well aware of and have indeed replied to such objections. However, the objections indicate that the phenomenology of religion which they propose, however valuable, involves certain difficulties which it may not be possible to resolve from within phenomenology. For example, Kearney's claim that God can be God 'only if we enable this to happen' or Levinas's that 'the dimension of the divine opens forth from the human face' can be given a perfectly sensible phenomenological interpretation. But if there is nothing further or different to be said by way of ontological qualification or repositioning of such claims, it would be difficult to reply to Merleau-Ponty's remark that one can never be sure whether it is God who sustains men in their human reality or vice versa, since his existence is affirmed only via their own.[82]

Perhaps phenomenology can indicate obliquely a requirement to go beyond itself. Levinas says somewhere that he wants to find within phenomenology the injunction to go beyond phenomenology. And Derrida tells us: 'That is what I am trying to do, also.'[83]

Maybe such an indication or injunction might be deciphered by revisiting the issue of the independent existence of beings given in the 'naive' pre-phenomenological natural attitude. Such existence of things is bracketed but not denied by the basic phenomenological reduction. The presumption is that phenomenology has ushered in a new way of thinking which renders the naivete of the natural attitude that affirms such existence, outdated and otiose.

But is it reasonable to ignore, simply because effectively bracketed, the issue of the independent ontological significance of what is given in the natural attitude? The independent existence of things seems too weighty a matter to ignore. Why should it not be raised one might ask? Answer: because it is excluded, by reduction, from phenomenology and cannot be raised within it. But why are questions which cannot be raised within phenomenology not to be raised at all? On what basis can phenomenology claim definitive authority over what questions may reasonably be raised? Even granting that some questions are bracketed out of court and even rendered suspect by its defining principles, alternative rational discussion of such questions cannot be precluded by these principles without simply assuming that this must be so. Therefore, while according to phenomenology all due respect as a distinctive and irreplaceable philosophical approach to God, one can reasonably consider whether there are not other approaches which may be equally valuable and perhaps complement in some measure the perspective of phenomenology. One such approach, bracketed out of play by phenomenology, is the approach to the existence of God based on the metaphysical analysis of the beings which we affirm in our natural pre-phenomenological outlook. In the next chapter, we will consider one significant version of this metaphysical approach.

2

Metaphysics

Introduction

Today, at least in the popular mind, metaphysics is not a subject that engenders great interest or enthusiasm. It is often viewed as an exercise in abstract, unverifiable and even fantastical speculation. Nor does it fare much better in the judgement of some prevailing philosophical viewpoints whether, positivistic, linguistic, relativistic or, as we have noticed in the previous chapter, in appraisal by phenomenology.

Nevertheless, it seems to me that metaphysical enquiry is, as phenomenology also rightly claims to be, a valuable and irreplaceable way of developing a philosophical view about everything including the existence and nature of God and our coexistence with him. How these two very different approaches stand in relation to each other is something which we can consider more fully in later chapters when we have outlined what is involved in a metaphysical enquiry.

The type of metaphysical enquiry that I propose to outline is the version of moderate rational realism developed effectively by Thomas Aquinas and which reaches back for its inspiration to Athens and Jerusalem, to Plato and Aristotle and Judeo-Christianity. Its contemporary revival is associated with names such as Gilson, Maritain, Geiger, Fabro, Marechal, Lonergan, Norris-Clarke, Geach, Kenny and, under the inspiration of Mercier, scholars of Louvain's 'Higher Institute of Philosophy'. Throughout the twentieth century it attracted considerable support from both continental European and Anglo-American philosophers interested in the philosophical justification of theism. However, metaphysical realism also has many effective contemporary defenders such as Searle, Armstrong, Nagel, Harre, Bhaskar, Hesse, Pettit and Papineau, who have no such objective.

There are, of course, various forms of metaphysics besides the metaphysical realism defended here. Indeed the philosophical idealism of Hegel outlined in Chapter 4 is an example of a very different metaphysics. As instances of alternative metaphysical approaches, one could cite the works of Plato, Descartes, Malebranche, Spinoza, Leibniz and, more recently, Peirce, Whitehead, Hartshorne, Bergson and various versions of

twentieth-century existentialism and linguistic philosophy. All of these
involve metaphysical claims under the broad description of metaphysics
as an account of the ultimate meaning of being in general and of human
existence in particular.

One way of introducing what moderate metaphysical realism involves
would be to say that it declines the phenomenological reduction referred
to in the previous chapter. This reduction, a defining characteristic of
phenomenology, reduces and brackets consideration of the independent
existence of things which we spontaneously accept in our natural,
pre-philosophical outlook. Metaphysical realism considers the natural
outlook to be basically in order as it is, and it seeks to give a fundamental
account of the independently existing order of things which it affirms. In
this account, the objects of human experience are affirmed to be more than
just objects of human experience and it tries to articulate what this 'more'
means. As Thomas Nagel remarks, it questions the presumption that 'the
first person singular or plural is hiding at the bottom of everything we say
or think'.[1]

Metaphysical realism, accepting that a real world exists independently of
our representation of it, seeks insofar as is humanly possible to provide an
objective impersonal account of it in judgements which strive more or less
successfully to conform to it.[2] The fact that the subjectivity of the person
making objective judgements about reality cannot be utterly overcome in an
absolute 'view from nowhere' does not affect the truth of realism. As Searle
remarks: 'The fact that alternative conceptual schemes allow for different
descriptions of the same reality, and that there are no descriptions of reality
outside all conceptual schemes, has no bearing whatever on the truth of
realism.'[3] The truism that 'nothing can be thought of as existing – apart
from a thinking subject', does not entail that 'nothing can be thought of – as
existing apart from a thinking subject'. The latter claim is in fact false.

In seeking to articulate the claim that things which are certainly objects
of our experience are more than this, metaphysical realism affirms that
what we are first aware of when we are conscious of something is that it
exists as a being independently of our awareness of it. We are conscious that
its self-possessed being, of which we are aware, is more fundamental than
the intentional or cognitive reality it has as an object of our consciousness.
Our primary awareness of anything is an intuition of its independent being,
an intuition expressed in the concept 'being' and affirmed in the judgement
'this exists'.

The whole thrust of subsequent metaphysical enquiry is to understand
the great variety of things given in experience from this fundamental
viewpoint of their 'being' or mind-independent existence. For our primary

pre-philosophical univocal apprehension of everything, simply as something which exists, is developed into the analogical metaphysical concept of being as comprising within its all-embracing unity the remarkable range of difference and diversity of beings which are given in our unfolding experience. Beings are found to differ in their being in various ways, for example, in number, in kind and in degree or level of being. For this individual being is diverse from that individual being, this dog differs in kind from that cat, and this person is a more comprehensive expression of being than that stone.

The analogical concept of being, developed to signify the being which is common to this manifold difference, is not formed as are univocal concepts by abstracting a nature common to many different individuals – as the universal specific concept 'dog' is formed by abstracting from the individuating differences of this spaniel Fido and this corgi Victor. For the real differences which characterize beings are themselves being and therefore must be included in and not abstracted from the all-embracing analogical concept being, the metaphysically developed concept of 'that which exists'. This difference is expressed by saying that whereas the intension and extension of univocal concepts vary inversely (i.e. the less specific the concept the wider its application), the concept 'being' has both the greatest intension and the greatest extension.[4] As Oliver Blanchette remarks: 'Only the concept of being is absolutely universal in that it includes whatever *is* in what we shall call its transcendental order . . . As a concrete universal, or as common to many, it is inclusive of the very differences in which it is diversified.'[5] Perhaps one might say that the metaphysical concept of being, as universal, abstracts, not *from* but *to* the inclusion, in the analogical unity of being, of the real differences which characterize beings. Or, perhaps better, one might speak of abstracting *from* the unreality and impossibility of any supposedly isolated and utterly unrelated particular individual and *to* its genuine reality as participating, in its own way, in the analogical unity of being. One might even speak of a 'metaphysical re-duction' or 'leading back to' the analogical unity of being – in contrast to the defining epoche or phenomenological reduction of phenomenology.

The development of such a realist metaphysics involves developing an extensive account not only of the unity of being but also more particularly of the diversity which characterizes it. This involves inter alia an account of the relationship between being and other transcendental properties such as truth, goodness and beauty; of the categories of finite being such as substance, quality, quantity, relation; of the intrinsic constitutive principles of individual beings such as matter and form, substance and accident, essence and existence; of the dynamic causal interactions and forms of dependency between beings; of the possibility of an explanation, foundation or origin of the analogical order of being itself.

These are metaphysical issues which have been and continue to be extensively discussed. Obviously this comprehensive programme is not something to be attempted here. However, what I do propose to do is to indicate what light aspects of such metaphysical enquiry can shed upon the question which interests us, the question of an appropriate philosophical approach to God. In particular I will indicate how such metaphysical enquiry, as perceptively explored by Aquinas, enables us to develop an account of the fundamental meaning of finite being and how from this one might proceed to a metaphysical affirmation and description of infinite being. Needless to say, this is a very different approach to that pursued by a phenomenological approach.

Finite and infinite – two doubtful approaches

At the outset, it will be useful to dispose of two related initiatives which provide illusory metaphysical shortcut solutions to the issue of our knowledge and affirmation of finite and infinite being. These are (1) St Anselm's famous, or if you prefer infamous, Ontological Argument, and (2) the claim that we can affirm the reality of finite being only because we are somehow already or concomitantly aware of the existence of infinite being. I will consider the first of these initiatives briefly, because it has been analysed, literally, ad infinitum, and the second in a little more detail because it will help to clarify the a posteriori character of what is involved in the approach of a realist metaphysics of finite and infinite being.

In chapter 2 of his work *Prosologion*, the eleventh-century theologian Anselm of Canterbury proposed a famous argument for the existence of God which has attracted the attention of a great number of philosophers, defenders and critics, ever since. The argument, briefly stated, is one which claims that God, rightly understood as that than which nothing greater can be conceived, must exist in reality as well as in the mind. For, since real existence is a perfection, to exist in reality is to be more perfect than to exist only in the mind. Therefore God, as that than which nothing more perfect can be conceived must exist really and not just as a mental concept. 'That than which a greater cannot be conceived cannot stand only in relation to the understanding. For if it stands at least in relation to the understanding, it can be conceived to be also in reality, and this is something greater. Therefore if "that than which a greater cannot be conceived" stood only in relation to the understanding then that than which a greater cannot be conceived would be something than which a greater can be conceived. But this is impossible. Therefore, something than which a greater cannot be conceived undoubtedly stands both in relation to the understanding and exists in reality.'[6]

In the following chapter, he adds the refinement: 'that than which nothing greater can be conceived' must be understood to exist, not only in reality as well as in the understanding, but also necessarily and not just as a matter of fact. For what has necessary existence has greater perfection than contingent things, such as islands and chairs and animals, which just happen to exist but might not have. Therefore, we may be sure of the necessary extra-mental existence of God for he must be conceived to be such that, unlike things whose existence is just a contingent fact, his non-existence is inconceivable.[7]

The most commonly accepted refutation of this famous argument is one first formulated by Kant. It denies that in saying that something exists one is predicating an additional property or perfection of a thing. Rather one is saying that whatever is involved in our conception of the thing has reference, is truly predicable of something or other of which we can have experience. Hence, to say that God exists is not to predicate existence of him but to say simply that 'God', however conceived, is truly predicable of something. And this we cannot know to be the case, since we have no experience of what we signify by our concept of him however exalted, eminent and appropriate the content of this concept may be.[8]

It might be argued, by a defender of the argument, that since 'existence' is an analogical concept, it need not always be taken as meaning only that some conception is truly predicable but might indeed, properly understood, signify the most distinctive characteristic of God. However, I think there is a more decisive objection which arises at an earlier stage of the argument.

At the outset of the argument, Anselm takes for granted that 'that than which a greater cannot be conceived . . . stands at least in relation to the understanding'. By this 'standing in relation to the understanding' he signifies that this conception of God is a coherent one, that is, that it signifies a positive possibility and not a contradiction. However, it seems to me that we cannot know a priori that the idea of God, as the necessarily existing greatest conceivable perfection, is in fact a coherent and positively possible idea rather than an incoherent contradictory one. For if we could know that our idea of God represents something positively possible, it seems to me that we would thereby know that God indeed exists and that Anselm is right in discovering the real existence of God in our idea of him. For if God did not exist he could not exist and the idea of him as necessarily existent would be a contradictory idea. To claim that the idea of God is a positively possible, non-contradictory idea is equivalent to affirming the existence of God. For his real existence is a condition of the positive possibility or coherence of the idea of him.

The problem is that we do not know a priori that the idea of God is a positively possible coherent idea. The most we can say is that the idea is a negatively possible one. In other words, we don't know whether the idea is positively possible, that is, coherent and non-contradictory or positively impossible, that is, incoherent and contradictory. We cannot know a priori whether what our idea of God signifies *could* be predicable of anything. We do not prove the existence of God a priori from the validity of our idea of him but rather, on the contrary and if at all, we prove the validity of the idea of God by proving his existence by a posteriori argument.

This conclusion to our remarks about the Ontological Argument is a helpful reminder that there is no metaphysical shortcut to a philosophical affirmation of God. It indicates that however useful Anselm's idea of God is in seeking to delineate what a worshipful God, as distinct from an idol, would be and have to be if he could exist, this envisaged possibility must, philosophically at least, await careful a posteriori legitimation and confirmation.

The second metaphysical shortcut which I wish to discuss is the claim that some awareness of God as infinite being is a concomitant condition of our affirmation of finite being. This is a recurrent idea with a long history in ancient, medieval, modern and contemporary philosophy.

It is anticipated in Plato's conviction that it is in virtue of our prior awareness of the divine world of ideas that we have standards which enable us to make comparative judgements about objects given in sense experience.[9] And Aristotle, in his account of 'measure', claims that it is in virtue of our knowledge of the most perfect member of a class that we can compare other members of the class in terms of more and less.[10]

According to St Augustine, we could not make comparative judgements concerning degrees of goodness were we not somehow aware of God the Supreme Good, in whose goodness all lesser things participate.[11] And St Bonaventure asks how could our intellect judge a being to be limited or defective if it did not have knowledge of a being without any limitation or defect?[12]

In this tradition in modern times there is, among others such as Spinoza and Malebranche, the striking example of Descartes. His own text speaks more eloquently and concisely than any summary: 'Nor should I imagine that I do not perceive the infinite by a true idea, but only by the negation of the finite, just as I perceive repose and darkness by the negation of motion and light; for on the contrary I perceive that there is manifestly more reality in infinite substance than in finite, and therefore that in some way I have in me the notion of the infinite earlier than the finite – the notion of God before that of myself.'[13]

From around the middle of the twentieth century, similar thinking was popular among a broad range of philosophers, many of them claiming inspiration from Aquinas. In an article in *Mind* 1957, T. McPherson claims that to really understand what you are saying when you affirm that 'the world is finite' is to affirm that 'there is an Infinite Being'. '"Finite" only has meaning in relation to "infinite". You cannot see something to be finite unless you are also somehow seeing something else to be infinite. We are invited to observe the finiteness of the world as if this were a first step in an argument for the existence of God. But to have seen the finiteness of the world is not to have taken the first step in such an argument, it is to have gone the whole way. This is not an argument for the existence of God but, in effect, a statement that God exists.'[14]

Here are some typical quotations from philosophers claiming inspiration from Aquinas. 'If we are convinced that in recognizing the (metaphysical) finitude of things we are also recognizing a real character, then we must equally be convinced that we have some intelligible notion of a being that is not finite.'[15] 'When we think of the finite we think of it against a background, so to speak, of the infinite; we are conscious in however obscure a way, of that which is free from all imperfection and it is only because of this consciousness that we can realize what is meant by limitation.'[16] 'Limitation in general is only conceivable by at least general knowledge of what surpasses all limit and a recognition of a relation of the limited to its infinite standard.'[17]

In a similar vein, there is the approach of a number of philosophers, broadly described as transcendental Thomists, who claim to discern – in the dynamic unrestricted openness of our intellect to being – the affirmation of infinite being as a condition of our awareness of beings as merely finite. They argue that because the beings of which we have direct experience do not exhaust the dynamism of our intellectual desire to know, they are affirmed as essentially finite. Reflecting on its affirmation of finite being as finite, the mind realizes that such an affirmation is, in a very real sense, a negation. It is the assertion that a particular being is nothing but mere finite being. Every negation, however, must be based ultimately on an affirmation. The only affirmation on which the assertion of finite being can be based is the affirmation of infinite being.[18] Joseph Marechal is typical of their approach: 'As long as any condition appears to us as "limiting" we can be sure that the ultimate goal of our intelligence is to be found beyond it, . . . The total objective capacity of our intelligence, pushing beyond every limitation other than non-being, extends in its scope as far as being pure and simple. To such a formal capacity there can correspond only one ultimate and saturating goal: *infinite* being.'[19]

Many other examples of this viewpoint spanning ancient to contemporary philosophy could be cited.[20] However, although its formulations differ its central intuition is clear. Stated simply, it is that awareness of the existence of infinite being, however obscure, implicit, or virtual, is directly involved in our affirmation of finite being as finite. The existence of God, far from being unattainable to the human intellect, is an a priori condition of any affirmation it makes of finite being as such.

I consider this an unsatisfactory metaphysical shortcut, even though it may seem to be more consonant with the phenomenological viewpoint outlined in the previous chapter. Indeed Marion goes so far as to say no important metaphysician has been able to avoid confirming the reality of saturated phenomena even at the price of a head-on contradiction with their own metaphysical presuppositions. Thus he considers that Descartes, in the passage quoted above, thinks of infinity as a saturated phenomenon.[21] And he suggests: 'Moreover, might it not be sufficient to translate "idea of infinity" word for word by "saturated phenomenon" to establish my conclusion.'[22] Levinas too finds Descartes discussion of the idea of infinite being highly significant as illustrating the priority of ethical Otherness over ontological sameness, of infinity over totality. Moreover, it is interesting to note that, long before Marion's innovative usage of the term 'saturated phenomenon', Marechal, in the passage quoted above, refers to infinite being, disclosed as the ultimate object of the human intellect's desire to know, as its *saturating* goal. Perhaps the bond which links the two viewpoints is a common interest in achieving an affirmation of God without resort to the more traditional, and much criticized, metaphysical principle efficient causation.

Nevertheless, there are good reasons to query the adequacy of this general point of view. Its central hypothesis is that finite being is defined in terms of infinite being and is unintelligible without this reference to such being. This hypothesis suggests the following questions. Can it be sustained apart from some sort of intuition of infinite being? Is it evidently true that finite being must be defined in terms of infinite being or does it merely appear evident from one particular theoretical point of view?

One might believe that this point of view involves a claim that we can somehow have an intuition of the reality of infinite being were its advocates not so emphatic in denying this. Thus Descartes would not say that he is aware of his own finitude in the light of his knowledge of infinite being but rather in the light of his positive *idea* of infinite being.

However, it is difficult to see how this idea can do the work required of it without some experiential basis for the assurance that it is not an incoherent idea.

Similarly, the philosophers who claim that knowledge of infinite being is involved as the objective final end of our unrestricted desire to know insist that such knowledge is only virtual. 'Obviously I do not experience its existence. But I do experience in myself the appeal of this being and perceive in my intelligence the desire to possess it. It is the disproportion between this desire and the good actually experienced that translates into the form of a negative judgement "this is only a finite expression of being".'[23] It might be objected that this seems equivalent to asserting that in knowing that finite being exists we are somehow aware that infinite being exists but yet unaware that we have this knowledge. But how could it be true that we know beings as finite because they do not correspond to the final goal of our intellect which is infinite being unless we are positively aware that infinite being is in fact the final end of our intellect? This objection suggests that the appeal to virtual knowledge does not adequately safeguard the view from the charge that it involves a vague but nevertheless direct intuition of infinite being or at least of its positive intelligibility.

Indeed, one wonders, is there not an internal contradiction in a position which although it seeks to establish the existence of infinite being as the utterly transcendent source of finite being, nevertheless makes infinite being an essential defining feature of an affirmation of finite being? Can such a position be maintained without compromising either the autonomy of the finite or the transcendence of the infinite? One is reminded of a similar difficulty, considered in our discussion of phenomenology, concerning whether a divine transcendence somehow available within experience is not inevitably a relative transcendence. To avoid such a problematic consequence must not this approach be so qualified that the infinite being which it adduces will be a mere reification of an abstract human ideal or limit idea.[24] Or, as Aquinas remarks: 'It is self-evident that there exists truth in general, but it is not self-evident to us that there exists a First Truth.'[25]

Moreover, it is not at all obvious that in coming to know the existence of finite beings as finite I discover that infinite being is the final end of my intellect. In knowing any finite beings as such I may discover that I desire to know whatever being there is. But it is not obviously contradictory to think that this apparently limitless desire to know signifies merely that one always thinks against a horizon – an imaginary limitless horizon or the horizon of an indefinitely expanding finite. I do not realize that the ultimate goal of my desire to know is infinite being, at least not until I have determined that such being exists. We have no way of knowing a priori that the perfection of being is intrinsically infinite and that we therefore apprehend and define finite being as less than the intrinsically infinite nature of being.

Nor is such a definition of finite being necessary. When we speak of finite being we need not mean being which is not infinite. We may indeed come to know that to affirm finite being and to deny the existence of infinite being is contradictory. But it is not necessary to know this in order to know and affirm that there are beings which are finite.

The metaphysical meaning of finite being

How to formulate what in ultimate analysis it means to be a finite being, that is, how one should understand the metaphysical meaning of finite being, is a rather difficult question. But it is one which we can begin to address by considering such beings as they give themselves from themselves to us in experience. It is through a careful analysis of the meaning and implications of such a posteriori experience that one may come to know both the fundamental intrinsic nature of finite being and its relationship to infinite being. The reverse procedure of understanding finite being in the light of an a priori idea of infinite being is not, as we have seen, a viable option.

Let us explore therefore what is involved in an a posteriori approach to the metaphysical meaning of finite being. The approach which we propose is broadly that indicated in the realist metaphysics developed by Aquinas in his innovative transformation of Aristotle's metaphysics in the light of the Judeo-Christian tradition.

Aquinas is quite explicit that our knowledge of the meaning of finite being is not obtained through some a priori knowledge of God as infinite being.[26] It is obtained rather through reflection on the typical achievement of our incarnate intelligence which is knowledge of the characteristics of material beings.[27]

What is it that constitutes a being as finite? If something is finite almost any aspect under which we consider it will manifest its finitude. The real problem lies in determining the defining feature of this finitude. Could, for example, temporal limitation be the defining feature of finitude? That things begin to be, endure for a certain period and then cease to be, clearly reveals a restricted and limited nature and all the objects of our experience seem, in principle, to be subject to this condition.

However, if to be finite means to be limited in time, it would appear that what is not limited in time must be, by definition, infinite. On this account, if the world is not limited in the sense of having a beginning and end (which according to Aquinas is philosophically possible but philosophically undecidable), must we say that it may be intrinsically infinite? However, for Aquinas, an analysis of the meaning of 'material world' suggests several features in virtue of which such a world should be called finite even on the hypothesis of its eternity. Even its temporality, whether of limited or eternal duration, as change extended in successive temporal expressions, bears the trace of intrinsic finitude.

He also discusses various ways in which the finitude of material beings can be appropriately described in terms of the quantitative limitation which affects them. He is inclined to deny the possibility of the existence of any actual quantitative infinite whether understood in terms of magnitude or multitude. At all events it would, in his view, be unknowable. The infinity associated with material being is a privative infinity, imagined only through the negation of finite determination. It signifies formlessness, indetermination and imperfection. In brief, a material infinite since it would exclude any determinate knowable quantity is in itself, as such, unknowable.[28]

His discussion of finite and infinite in terms of the quantitative aspects of material being is interesting because it mirrors the discussion of these terms by all Greek philosophers from Anaximander in the sixth-century BC up to and including Aristotle. For them the term infinite, *apeiron*, is identified exclusively with the indeterminate, the imperfect, the unfinished and the formless – characteristics of the chaotic material principle of things – whereas finitude is identified with determination, perfection and form.[29] From such a perspective to speak of an infinitely perfect being makes no sense. The possibility of such a being would simply not suggest itself. It would appear to be a contradiction in terms. This constituted a challenge for Aquinas who in the light of Christian belief will want to speak of God in terms of infinite perfection – an entirely paradoxical way of speaking for the Greek philosophers. Considerations such as these would have prompted the sophisticated analogical account of the terms 'finite' and 'infinite' which Aquinas developed.

Spatial and temporal limitations are certainly significant indications of the finitude of things. So too is the mutual opposition and relative perfection disclosed in the comparison of any two individuals, the possession by each of properties which the other does not have clearly manifesting the finitude of both. Nevertheless, for Aquinas, however valuable these may be as manifestations, they are not what fundamentally constitute the finitude of a being. The defining feature of a being's finitude is to be sought in its most fundamental internal composition and not in its external manifestations. To demonstrate this, he develops a strikingly original account of the metaphysical meaning of finite being. He argues that in any material being of which we have direct experience there is a twofold composition. The first of these compositions, that of matter and form, is more obviously indicative of a material being's finitude. The second one, that of essence and existence, is metaphysically more fundamental and indeed the defining characteristic of the finitude of any being – whether directly experienced by us or not. Let us consider each of these compositions briefly.

Reflection on our experience reveals that every material being is a unity composed of a material principle and a formal principle which, according to the traditional Aristotelian 'hylomorphic theory', are called potency and act or prime matter and substantial form. The theory is invoked as the most rational way of providing a philosophical account of evident features of material beings such as their existential instability, their capacity to change or be changed from one thing into another and their species-individual structure. All material being appears to be in principle corruptible and changeable – even if from a technical point of view it is more difficult to split an atom than to fell a tree. Likewise, all material beings manifest the property of being an individual instance of a formal structure which in principle can have many exemplifications.

To explain these basic features of material being, a fundamental composition is affirmed to obtain in every material substance between two co-relative and in themselves substantially incomplete principles. These are a principle of determinability, that is, potency or prime matter, and a principle of determination, that is, act or substantial form – in more everyday language, 'the stuff' and 'the organization' of a material being. Neither principle can be without the other, so that they are always a correlation of 'this form' and 'this matter' which in their concrete realization in a particular substance become quantified, are the subject of further accidental determination and are a source of dynamic interaction with other material beings in the spatio-temporal system.

For Aquinas, a material being, thus understood, must be called finite because it can have real existence, and real unity, as this individual being, only through the reciprocal completion and limitation of its constitutive principles, which considered separately and in themselves are incomplete and indeterminate. 'Now matter is in a way made finite by form and the form by matter. Matter indeed is made finite by form, inasmuch as matter, before it receives its form, is in potentiality to many forms; but on receiving a form, it is terminated by that one. Again, form is made finite by matter, inasmuch as form, considered in itself, is common to many; but when received in matter, the form is determined to this one particular thing.'[30] Considered in abstraction from the only real existence they can have as 'this finite form' and 'this finite matter' of a concrete individual, these constitutive principles of every material being can be ascribed a certain 'infinity'. For any form of a material being, considered abstractly in itself can be envisaged as realizable, in principle, in an indefinite or infinite number of subjects. Likewise, prime matter considered abstractly in itself, not as 'this matter' correlative to 'this form', but as the potential, utterly indeterminate subject of all possible material forms, and of none in particular, can in this sense be called infinite. 'Prime matter which as such is indifferent to all forms, and in this sense is said to be infinite, is rendered finite by form: and likewise form which as such can perfect different instances of matter, is rendered finite by the matter in which it is received.'[31]

However, form and matter, thus considered abstractly in themselves, correspond to no actual reality for material form and prime matter have real existence only together in a concrete, finite, material individual. The infinity ascribed to them as abstractly considered signifies the absence or privation of the only reality or perfection they can have which is as the mutually limiting correlation of 'this matter' and 'this form' of a particular being. Matter and form considered separately in abstraction from each other are unrealizable having only 'intentional reality' as abstract considerations.

Thus Aquinas, in his preliminary metaphysical consideration of the finitude of material beings, accepts a version of the traditional Greek view that to be finite connotes positive perfection and to be infinite connotes imperfection, privation and unreality. This obviously poses a problem for his wish to speak of God as supreme perfection yet not just another member, however eminent, of the system of finite beings. He will want, as we have noted, to find a way of speaking of God as infinite perfection – an incomprehensible idea for Aristotle, but implicit in the Judeo-Christian conception of God. His highly original way of addressing this issue is provided in his account of a more fundamental composition than that of matter and form in any finite being, namely, a composition of essence and existence.

As we have indicated, metaphysical realism seeks to provide a comprehensive account of everything in the light of, and in terms of, their actual existence. Aquinas, oriented no doubt by his Christian faith, saw the need for a more fundamental account of the existence of things than Aristotle and other philosophers imagined. The physical processes and transformations, in terms of which they spoke of the origin and dissolution of things, presuppose and cannot account for the existence of the beings which they affect. One must move beyond a formal consideration of what makes possible the mutation of one thing into another to an existential consideration of the contingent being which any such mutation presupposes. And this contingent existence of different beings calls for some understanding of how it can be that they in fact exist and exist thus.

Aquinas's way of seeking this understanding is to say that existence, *esse,* should not be seen as an indeterminate 'being there' which is found fashioned into various kinds much as prime matter is fashioned by various forms. If one can speak of *esse* as indeterminate, it is only in the sense that it is not a specific determination of anything but rather that towards which all specific determinations are oriented as towards that which constitutes them as actually existing. It is not the accidental property or essence or form of anything. Existence, *esse,* metaphysically understood, signifies act rather than form. It is the primary ontological act which accomplishes the reality of anything that exists. It is the ultimate and fundamental perfection of any object in virtue of which all that the object formally can be is called being.[32] '*Esse* is the most perfect reality of all, and this is clear from the consideration that act is always more perfect than potency. But any form whatsoever is not understood to be actual unless it is affirmed to exist. For "humanity" or "fireiness" can be considered as latent in the potentiality of matter, or in the capacity of an agent, or even just in the mind: but by having *esse* it actually exists. Hence, it is clear that what I call *esse* is the actuality of all acts and, therefore, the perfection of all perfections.'[33] The determining relationship in which form stands to *esse* is not that of act to potency but rather the reverse. Form is a determinate potentiality or capacity for being which is actualized by *esse* to exist as this being of this particular nature.

This conception of existence as the fundamental act and perfection, in respect of which everything else is relative and dependent for its being and perfection, raises metaphysical enquiry, beyond the level of ontic discussion of the matter, form and essence of beings, to a consideration of the significance and import of their actual existence.

However, although it is accurate to say that metaphysics is orientated to viewing everything there is from the perspective of existence (*esse*), considered as the ultimate act of being which originates all real perfection, it must also take into account that the reality thus envisaged manifests itself as intrinsically involving multiplicity and diversity. From our unifying foundational pre-philosophical intuition of any being simply as something existing, metaphysics advances to an analogical conception of being whose unity encompasses intrinsic diversity. The transcendental unity of being is at the same time an analogical unity of distinct beings each of whose act of existence is individually and incommunicably proper to it.[34] We apprehend that the absolute all-embracing perfection of actual existence is not realized as a simple undifferentiated unity but rather as diversified in a multitude of different individuals which differ from each other precisely by being, *each in its own way,* a particular expression of existence. 'And in this way this *esse* is distinguished from that *esse* inasmuch as it is of this or that nature.'[35]

Whatever existence is known directly is known as a particular determinate form of existence. We have no metaphysical concept, no positive comprehension, of unqualified existence simply as such. Any attempt to form such a concept, by abstracting from particular forms of existence will yield merely a logical construct which can claim no corresponding real foundation, for it abstracts from the only kind of existence of which we have experience.[36] Our positive knowledge of existence is co-relative to and coextensive with our positive knowledge of the particular forms or essences in which it becomes manifest to us. Our metaphysical concept of being always signifies a particular determinate form of existence.[37]

For Aquinas, to this complex character of our metaphysical concept of being, according to which it always signifies the absolute value of actual existence as realized in a particular way, there must be understood to correspond, in any reality thus signified, a real metaphysical composition of constitutive principles, namely the composition of essence and existence. And our understanding of being as thus composed is the basis for an account of the ultimate metaphysical meaning of finite being.

This composition of essence and existence in every being which we experience is a composition of two inseparable yet really distinct and mutually defining elements. They are not beings in their own right but rather principles of being which, as related to each other, constitute a concrete individual being. Of any individual being, thus understood, it is true to say that every aspect of it exists and that its existence is entirely of a particular determinate kind. Its constitutive principles though distinct are not independent. They are 'internally' or 'transcendentally' related to one another having meaning, definition and reality only in terms of each other.

They can be seen as standing in a relationship of potency and act. 'Existence is that which makes every form or nature actual; for goodness and humanity are spoken of as actual, only because they are spoken of as existing. Therefore existence must be compared to essence, if the latter is a distinct reality, as actuality to potentiality.'[38] For it is only in terms of such a relationship that one can account for an individual as composed of really distinct components yet possessing an indivisible unity.[39] However, in this case it is 'essence' or the formal determination which fulfils the role of potency as determining the particular form in which this act of existence finds expression. It is 'existence', conceived as ultimate act, which actualizes the manifold perfections which the order of being formally comprises; '*esse* is the actuality of all things including forms themselves.'[40]

According to Aquinas, 'being' thus understood is properly called finite being. Our metaphysical concept of being is a concept which intrinsically involves the idea of limitation or boundary. Hence, the metaphysical meaning of finite being is merely an elucidation of what we mean by being, namely, an individual being in which the act of existence is strictly limited and determined to a particular form by a co-constitutive principle, that is, its essential nature. 'Every creature is simply finite, inasmuch as its existence is not absolutely subsisting, but is limited to some nature to which it belongs.'[41] Needless to say, if our concept of being always signifies finite being, we will be precluded from speaking of God as a being. Aquinas, as we shall see (and *pace* Heidegger) accepted this consequence.[42]

It might be said that our concept of being is the concept of finite being because it always signifies a certain facticity, an act of existence, *esse*, which is always only this particular determinate act of existence. In our experience the act of existence, the all-embracing ultimate perfection, is always intrinsically limited by the essential natures of the individuals in which alone it finds expression.[43]

Therefore, although our metaphysical concept of being always signifies the absolute value of the act of existence, nevertheless, it signifies it, not as something unqualified but, on the contrary, as really limited in its expression by an essential principle which determines it to a particular individual form. Thus it might be called a relative absolute, meaning by this, not the inter-relativity of many beings in a given order, but rather the intrinsic relativity, or better, the co-relativity of constitutive principles in any given individual. And this is why Aquinas observes significantly that when we speak of a being as finite, we signify an intrinsic and absolute characteristic, rather than its relationship to other beings. In other words, the finitude of a being, strictly understood, signifies the intrinsic limitation of its act of existence by and to a co-relative essential nature rather than the limitation or boundary constituted, as it were externally, by the presence of other individuals. *'For "finite" is predicated absolutely, and not by reference to another, inasmuch as something is rendered finite in itself by its own intrinsic limitations.'*[44]

Consequently, although knowledge that there are many beings is indispensable to the reflection by which we come to know concrete being as that which is composed of essence and existence, nevertheless it is more accurate to state the metaphysical meaning of finite being in terms of this composition rather than negatively in terms of the mutual limitation through opposition of many individuals. For although there are many finite beings, in ultimate analysis they are not finite because they are many, but because individually their act of existence is limited to their determinate essential capacity.

It might be objected that in claiming that any metaphysical affirmation of being is always an affirmation of finite being because it is an affirmation of an act of existence, *esse,* as limited by a correlative formal principle or essence, we in fact imply a reference to infinite being as part of the meaning of finite being – a view which we roundly criticized earlier. For if we claim that the an act of existence is finite only in virtue of the limiting determination of a distinct formal principle do we not imply an awareness that the act of existence, considered as such and apart from its finite determinate expressions which we know directly, is in itself an infinite unqualified perfection?

However, this objection does not work and is based on a misunderstanding of our account of finite being. As Aquinas observes unequivocally, finitude is predicated of a being absolutely and not in virtue of any reference to another. 'Nor are things spoken of as beings by reference to God's existence but because of their own proper act of existence.'[45] Moreover, in this positive direct knowledge of being the act of existence is apprehended as an act that always obtains only as limited by a correlative capacity or essence.[46] Hence, at this stage of our metaphysical understanding, terms such as 'existence as such' or 'existence considered simply in itself' have no real significance. Such a hypothetical entity has no intrinsic intelligibility for us, and prior to a proof of God's existence even appears contradictory, since the act of existence is understood as one which obtains only in virtue of its correlation with a determining essence.

Admittedly, we can construct a logical notion of existence in general, which abstracts from all particular instances of the act of existence, and which is conceived as a most universal and indeterminate form rather than as the ultimate actualizing principle of each concrete reality. To existence considered thus in itself, as a mentally constructed universal, one can attribute a quasi-infinity since it is not limited to any particular instance.

However, existence considered thus as *esse commune* can signify nothing real inasmuch as it can be universal only by abstracting from the individualizing determinations which characterize actually existing beings.[47] In other words, to consider the act of existence as *esse commune* is to de-existentialize it and to relegate, or 'reduce', it to the purely ideal order so that the infinity thus attributed to it, far from connoting perfection, connotes rather imperfection. It connotes existence as lacking the finite determination through which alone it can obtain as actual reality. It signifies that whereby the ideal falls short of the real; that whereby the abstract falls short of concrete reality. It signifies a privative infinity of indetermination, lacking the various determining capacities or essences whereby individual acts of existence really obtain, and are known by us to so obtain, in contrast to the unreality of the abstract universal.[48] Clearly any such abstract universal idea of infinite or indeterminate being which we can form has no direct bearing on the issue of the existence of God envisaged as infinite being. If the existence of such being can be established at all, it will only be indirectly by some form of a posteriori demonstration and never through a direct or immediate inference from our concept of being.[49] Indeed, as we have seen, Aquinas goes so far as to say that since God is infinite existence, he must be said to be beyond being which, in our understanding of the term, always signifies something which exists in a finite way. Finite being is the proper object of our intellect whereas God's way of existing is beyond our understanding. If he can be appropriately spoken of as infinite being, it will have to be in some transferred analogical sense, quite different to our basic metaphysical understanding of being.

What is most significant in the realist account of finite being outlined above is the new intensive understanding of existence, *esse*, as the ultimate act in virtue of which all the formal or essential features of any being actually exist. Existence is not just that of which properties may be truly predicated. Not merely a given, a datum. Not just a product of change. Not just an accidental feature or state of essence, that is, a state of reality as opposed to a state of possibility. Indeed as ultimate act rather than form it is the ground rather than the consequence of all possibility, of all change, of all perfection.

This prioritization of existence, understood as act, over essence, which is now understood as correlative potency or formally limiting capacity of a concrete act of existence, has important metaphysical consequences. Unlike phenomenology, which is characterized by the bracketing or 'reduction' of, naturally given, mind-independent, existence, metaphysics makes this existence its central point of interest and ascribes it an ultimate and irreducible significance. It sets itself the task of attaining some insight into the how, why and wherefore of the analogical order of existence given to us in experience.

As with its Greek philosophical antecedent, it still identifies being with finite being and finite being with perfection, understood as a certain self-sufficiency and completeness in virtue of which something realizes all the relevant defining conditions whereby it can subsist in nature as a concrete individual.[50] It signifies the real order as transcending the incompleteness whereby the ideal order falls short of effective existence, the primacy of the concrete over the abstract. 'Things are seen to have a certain perfection which are self-subsistent in Nature which we signify by concrete terms such as "wise man" and the like. Those things however are imperfect which are not self-subsistent such as forms like humanity, wisdom, and so forth which we signify by abstract terms. There is this difference between these two that what is incomplete cannot perform any perfect operation. For it is not heat which warms but a hot substance, nor wisdom which understands but a wise person.'[51]

However, the context has shifted, from the Greek focus on material change and form as ultimate perfection, to the act of existence in its manifold expressions – no longer taken for granted as an unremarkable and unquestioned datum. It is in seeking some understanding of this diversified act of existence which we experience that the issue of the existence of a creator God can arise. Aristotle provided a metaphysics of matter, form and substantial change. Aquinas developed a deeper metaphysics of 'esse' realized in finite specific forms through the creative activity of God's *esse* which transcends all specific form.

The perfection of actual existence manifests an absolute quality. Granted this absolute character of actual existence, which gives itself directly and undeniably in our affirmation of being, the abstract consideration that it might not exist would seem to be excluded. The question which persists is not 'why is there being rather than nothing?' but rather 'why is existence instantiated thus and not otherwise?' Suppose, as indeed initially appears to be the case, that the act of existence can be realized only in a manifold of limiting formal determinations or essences. Is it also predetermined to those particular forms in which we know it to be realized? That being indeed exists involves the impossibility of its non-existence. But that anything in particular, for example a particular flower, must exist is not at all evident. Does the seemingly contingent facticity of any particular individual conceal a fundamental and inevitable necessity? Is what actually exists the measure of what can exist, and if so in what sense? Is the principle, in virtue of which the act of existence is deployed in various forms, immanent to the finite order or does it somehow transcend this order? Towards which conclusion does the philosophical interrogation of our concrete experience of the act of existence lead us? To a version of scientific naturalism, or pantheism, or possibly to a creator God? In the following section, we will indicate the lines along which a metaphysical affirmation of God as infinite creator of the finite order might be proposed.

Arguing to the existence of infinite being

We have already noted that we can have no a priori knowledge that the idea of God as infinite being is a positively possible coherent idea. The most we can claim is that it is negatively possible, that is, we do not know whether it is positively possible and coherent or positively impossible, and contradictory. We can only come to know that this idea of God is not contradictory by proving that he actually exists as infinite creator of all finite being. This idea of God as infinite creator of finite being is simply the nominal definition of him which precedes any proposed proof. Knowledge that this definition has any real reference depends on the success of the proof. Nor can we know a priori that such a proof is possible. Its possibility can be established only a posteriori by its actual achievement. As Aristotle said somewhere: 'We must mend the ship at sea'!

Any proposed proof for God's existence must be a posteriori and indirect, one which seeks to show that the finite beings of which we are directly aware transpire, on metaphysical analysis, to be unintelligible and even contradictory unless they are understood to be dependent for their existence upon an infinite creator. In other words, one proves the existence of God through the principle of causation applied to finite being as metaphysically conceived. This principle cannot be assumed to be a universally true self-evident principle. To assume a priori that it is universally true would be to assume, not prove, that there is a first cause of finite being. Nor is it a self-evident principle – as Hume and others have indicated. Nor can one argue inductively to its universal application from its de facto applications in the physical sciences. This would imply that causation is univocal whereas if it is to apply to divine creation it must be understood analogically since the dependence of creatures on the causality of God is an absolutely unique relation. In brief, the proof for the existence of God involves *proving* that the principle of causation is applicable, analogically, and beyond its empirical instances, to the entire order of finite being metaphysically conceived.

It is not the aim of this outline of a metaphysical approach to God to examine in detail, with a view to evaluating their validity, various a posteriori proofs which have been proposed. I have addressed this topic elsewhere giving an affirmative exposition of various arguments for the existence of God.[52] What is of interest here is the basic structure of such proofs and, if successful, what information they indicate about God.

The basic structure of the a posteriori arguments is a demonstration that various features of the domain of finite beings, whose actual existence we affirm, turn out, on metaphysical analysis, to be incoherent, impossible and contradictory unless they are understood to exist, and in the manner in which they do, because wholly dependent upon a cause beyond the domain of finite being. Thus, for example, it is argued that the contingent, existentially unnecessary, perishable character of every finite being is impossible if everything that exists is contingent in this way. And since this contingent character of finite beings is obviously not impossible, because it actually obtains, therefore not everything that exists is contingent in this way. Such contingent finite being, it is argued, must be understood to be dependent upon a non-contingent and non-finite necessary being. Similarly, it is argued that the different measures and degrees in which existence finds actual expression in the manifold finite beings of our experience, can be shown, on metaphysical analysis, to be unintelligible and even contradictory unless understood as dependent upon the existence of an originating cause not belonging to that diversified domain of finite being. Likewise with other arguments, based upon other distinctive features of the domain of finite beings, which show that these features are impossible or contradictory (which they obviously are not since they actually obtain), unless understood as originated by a cause which transcends this finite order.

Metaphysical arguments for the existence of God are sometimes contemptuously dismissed as leading only to a 'God of the gaps' invoked simply to fill a gap which has not yet been filled, but will be filled, by science. One can concede that the God established by such proofs is indeed a 'God of the gaps'. But not, however, a God of contingent gaps which science might one day fill – but rather, in Anthony Kenny's felicitous observation, 'a God of the necessary gaps, that is to say, gaps in explanation which can be demonstrated not to be capable of being filled by a particular type of explanation.'[53]

In such arguments, it is worth noting that the principle which plays the most important role in establishing the transcendental validity of causation, and thereby the existence of God, is not, as is often claimed, the dubious Principle of Sufficient Reason. According to a version of this principle, attributed to Leibniz, there is a sufficient reason why everything is as it is and cannot be otherwise. This, it seems to me, is certainly not evident and indeed if asserted would negate God's freedom in respect of creation. The principle which is in fact involved is rather the more modest, but also more evident, 'Principle of Non-Contradiction' according to which nothing can at once both be and not be, both exist and not be possible. This is the principle which enables one to move from a seemingly contradictory situation of finite being, considered simply in itself, to a resolution of the apparent contradiction by an affirmation of the existence of an explanatory cause beyond the domain of finite being.

Having affirmed the existence of God as the not finite, or infinite, cause of finite being as such, a realist metaphysics must give an account of what it means by this affirmation and what further knowledge about God it implies. Here again, I confine comment to providing an outline of what such an approach to the meaning and nature of an affirmation of God as infinite being involves and to indicating some of its distinctive features.

The metaphysical meaning of infinite being

The first point to be clarified is the status of knowledge claims such as 'God exists' or 'infinite being exists'. Such affirmations should not be understood, as in a way Malebranche understood them, to mean that although we have no direct knowledge of the divine essence or nature, we do have some direct knowledge of the divine existence. Such an interpretation of these statements is misleading and false. They should be understood rather as signifying the truth of assertions claiming that there is a subject of which terms such as 'God' and 'infinite being' are affirmatively predicable.

In other words, what such statements signify directly is not God or his existence but the truth of propositions about God. Furthermore, the meaning and truth of such propositions about God are not founded on any direct knowledge of infinite being but on the indirect metaphysical implications of our knowledge of finite being. As Aquinas puts it succinctly: 'existence, *esse*, is understood in two senses: in one sense it signifies the act of existence: in the other sense it signifies the composition of a proposition whereby the mind attributes a predicate to a subject. We cannot know the existence or nature of God in the first understanding of existence, *esse*: but only in the second. For we know that this proposition which we form about God when we say "God exists" is true and we know this from his effects.'[54]

However, having indicated that the statement 'infinite being exists' affirms the truth of a proposition about God, we still need to consider what it means.

In proving the existence of God as the cause of all finite beings, we establish that he is not a member of the class of finite beings and therefore may be described as not finite or infinite. However, a description which enables us to identify an object is not necessarily a statement about the nature of that object. For example, to describe humans as capable of making fire, or of playing the piano, is not a definition of human nature. Likewise, to refer to God as infinite being because he is the transcendent cause of finite beings is not evidently equivalent to making a statement about the divine nature, particularly if God does not create through necessity of nature. Can it be an intrinsic character of the divine being not to be like finite creatures if in fact there need never have been any creatures? Since any idea we may form of infinite being can acquire metaphysical meaning only through the mediation of our knowledge of finite being, the question arises can such an idea ever signify a positive perfection of the divine nature. Obviously when we call God infinite being, we want to say at least that as the transcendent cause of finite being he cannot be called finite in his being or in his causality. But is this negative description any more informative than the description of a lump of coal as not amusing? Aquinas realized that for some, such as the great Jewish-theologian Maimonides, it was not more informative.[55]

However, he maintained that when we predicate infinite being of God, we not merely deny that he is like finite beings but also affirm an intrinsic attribute of the divine nature itself. In order to indicate in what sense God can thus be spoken of positively as infinite being, we must describe how the term 'being' can come to signify real being without thereby meaning finite being – which as we have seen is its primary meaning for us.

The key to understanding this development is his innovative insistence that *esse*, the act of existence, is the ultimate principle of all perfection. 'That which I call *esse* is the actualisation of all acts and therefore the perfection of all perfections.'[56] Indeed in metaphysics we call something being only and insofar as *esse* is truly predicable of it.[57] It is the attribute of actually exercised *esse* which constitutes real being as real and radically marks it off from non-being, or intentional being or merely possible being.

It is this firm grasp of the truth that actually exercised *esse*, that is, existence understood as ultimate actualizing perfection, the fundamental characteristic of real being, which provides Aquinas with a sure norm for distinguishing real being metaphysically from merely apparent or imaginary beings such as blindness, bank overdrafts, dragons, triangles, etc. He likes to point out that although one can say there is blindness, blindness cannot be called being since it has no *esse*. In the same way he analyzes an old muddle which baffled Parmenides and Plato and which even still confuses certain conceptions of finite being. It is the confused opinion that because we can predicate terms such as 'not-being-John' of Peter, therefore 'non-being' must somehow be. Aquinas can reply that to say a predicate, for example, 'non-being' is truly predicable is not at all equivalent to affirming that non-being exists or is a being.[58] Metaphysically, only what actually exercises *esse* is being.

What emerges from these considerations is that *esse* is so intimately constitutive of metaphysical being that it is impossible that there be any real being which does not possess the act of existence – 'impossibile est quod sit aliquod ens quod non habet esse'.[59] Consequently, if we are to speak of God as real and not imaginary, as indeed the proofs of his transcendent causality require, he must be understood to somehow realize the perfection of *esse*, the act of existence. However, he cannot do so in the manner of finite beings, to the domain of which, as their creator, he does not belong. And since such beings are defined as that in which the perfection of *esse* is really limited by a distinct essence, he must be such that, in him, the perfection of *esse* is not limited by the formal determining limitation of a distinct essence, but realized rather as subsistent unrestricted plenitude of the act of existence. And this fundamentally is what we mean when we speak metaphysically of God's infinite being. Moreover, from this description of God's infinite being as that in which *esse* is not limited by a distinct essence but realized rather as absolutely comprehensive, simple and self-sufficient act of existence, it follows that he also realizes in the same manner all the transcendental perfections such as truth and goodness which are intimately associated with and characterize being. For since *esse* is the ultimate source of all perfection of being, God, who as *Esse Subsistens* (self-subsistent unlimited act of existence) possesses the perfection of being in an unlimited manner, likewise possesses in an unlimited or infinite manner all aspects of perfection which characterize being intrinsically.[60]

However, although we thus have reason to affirm that the term 'infinite being' signifies objectively a positive and intrinsic perfection of God, we do not have any positive conceptual understanding of the perfection thus signified. In our understanding, the term 'infinite being' is wholly relative to our knowledge of finite being and acquires meaning for us only as the negation of what we understand by finite being. Although we know it to be true, we have no positive understanding of what is signified when we say that God's infinite being is that in which the perfection of *esse* obtains as not limited by the specifying causality of a distinct essence but rather as essentially unrestricted act of subsistent existence.[61] We know that this account of 'infinite being' is an appropriate way to speak of God and that it signifies perfection which he possesses intrinsically and uniquely. But we have no positive insight into the perfection thus signified. Though we know we use an appropriate identifying reference when we speak of the divine perfection as infinite being, we do not thereby attain an intelligible definition of it which we can positively understand. It is utterly beyond our comprehension.

Brief discussion of objections

There are various objections to the account of infinite being outlined above, some of which we should briefly consider.

A serious objection to the account is one which argues that in view of what we have said earlier about finite being, it appears contradictory to describe any reality as infinite being. For have we not stressed, in our account of the meaning of finite being, that being as metaphysically conceived always means finite being? Further, have we not also said that according to our metaphysical understanding *esse*, the act of existence, always signifies a principle of being which is realized only as transcendentally related to a distinct and formally limiting correlative essence, so that to envisage *esse* as not thus limited is to conceive being as falling short of fulfilling the conditions through which alone it can actually exist? Consequently, when we affirm being as not limited in this way, as 'infinite being', do we not ipso facto move into the purely abstract order of logical fabrication? In other words, does not such a conception connote precisely that whereby the ideal falls short of the real, the chasm that divides the abstract from the order of real existence. If we give the term 'being' its appropriately articulated metaphysical meaning, would it not be more metaphysically accurate not to call God infinite being or even being at all? Would it not be more correct to say, with Maimonides, that he is utterly beyond description and that any metaphysical terms we predicate of him are predicated in a totally equivocal sense?

In reply, Aquinas first of all admits that in our understanding the positive metaphysical meaning of the term, 'being' always connotes 'finite being' and that therefore, strictly speaking, God as infinite must be said to be beyond the order of any such existing beings – *extra ordinem omnium entium existens*.[62] Nevertheless, although he can thus be said to be beyond being (*ens*), it would not be true to say that he is beyond existence (*esse*). For, as we have seen, *esse* signifies the ultimate and absolute act of all-real perfection, the principle through which whatever really exists is affirmed metaphysically as really existing. Consequently, although one can conceivably attribute meaning to the statement 'God is not being', it would be meaningless to affirm that 'God', meaning thereby the creative source of all finite being', is truly predicable and yet deny that God really exists. Rather God can be said to be beyond being because his *esse* infinitely transcends the kind of *esse* in virtue of which *we call* something a being, namely, *esse* which is correlative to a distinct and limiting essence. In other words, in our articulated metaphysical understanding, God can be said to be beyond being precisely because his *esse* is not finite but rather, *Esse Subsistens*, an infinite self-sufficient act of existence.[63]

What is fundamentally involved here is a dramatic reorientation and transformation of our initial metaphysical conception of being. The original and highly innovative claim that being is to be understood primarily and fundamentally in terms of *esse*, the act of existence, rather than essence or form, has more far-reaching implications for our understanding of being than we can initially apprehend. These only become apparent in the light of the indirect metaphysical arguments through which we establish that all finite beings, whether mutable or not, are dependent for their existence upon a transcendent creator.[64]

By establishing the existence of a transcendent cause of finite being, we are compelled to accept what we might not otherwise have suspected, namely, that our manner of signifying the perfection of being is not the ultimate or completely adequate criterion of how the perfection of being is actually realized. Our discussion of the meaning of finite and infinite being is, one might figuratively say, rotated through a 90 degree shift from a horizontal to a vertical plane with dramatic consequences.

Prior to the affirmation of a transcendent cause of finite being our metaphysical concept of being always signifies finite being. It is understood as being in which the act of existence always and only finds expression as limited to the formally determining capacity of a distinct essence. We can indeed form an abstract concept of *esse*, absolutely considered, as the ultimate act of every being that exists. But this idea of existence, as not limited to any particular expression, is the abstract idea of *esse commune*. It connotes a certain notional infinity in that it is conceived as realizable in an unlimited number of instances.[65] It obtains only as a logical construction in our mind and as such signifies nothing which actually exists, just as the abstract concept 'animal' signifies nothing which exists apart from Aristotle, Plato, this cat, this dog, etc. The abstract concept of *esse commune* certainly does not signify the transcendent existence of God which has yet to be established. 'What is common to many has no reality as such except in the mind . . . Much less, therefore, is *esse commune* itself anything apart from all existing things except in the mind alone.'[66]

All of this confirms how, at this initial stage of our metaphysical understanding, our conceptions of being and existence, insofar as they are ascribed any real significance, refer only to finite being. It is this situation which changes radically with the affirmation of a transcendent cause of finite being. Thereafter, *esse* understood as not limited to the finite capacity of a particular finite essence no longer means simply the abstract idea of *esse commune* which we understand adequately, but rather the *Esse Subsistens* that is God – which we do not understand at all.[67]

With this affirmation that the transcendent cause of finite being is *Esse Subsistens*, the metaphysical meaning of being is deepened and transformed, and we can see why it is not contradictory to speak of God as infinite being. The difficulty arose from the fact that according to our primary metaphysical understanding of being, the act of existence obtains only in finite modes so that 'infinite being' could only connote the abstract non-reality of *esse commune*. However, in the light of the affirmation of God as cause of finite being, we achieve a more profound understanding of the meaning of both finite being and infinite being. We come to appreciate that our primary metaphysical understanding of being as simply finite being is a consequence not only of the objective nature of finite being but also of the finite character of our positive understanding of being. We can now say that although something is certainly called being in virtue of *esse*, our primary identification of being with *esse* as limited by a determining essence is a consequence, albeit an inevitable one, of our limited intellectual perspective. And we understand that in reality, and more properly, 'being' is primarily predicated of the unlimited plenitude of *Esse Subsistens* upon whom, as their transcendent cause, all finite beings depend absolutely for their entire being. 'Our intellect understands *esse* in the mode in which it is found in lesser things from which it gets its knowledge. In these *esse* is not subsistent but inherent. However, reason discovers that there is self-subsistent *esse:* therefore, although what is signified by us as *esse* is signified in a concrete mode of signification, our intellect nevertheless, in ascribing *esse* to God, goes beyond this mode of signification attributing to him that which is signified but not the mode of signification.'[68]

We are led to recognize that being primarily and properly signifies infinite being and that finite beings should now be understood in terms of their dependent participation in being, that is, as beings which possess the act of existence in a limited manner and in total dependence upon infinite being who possesses it in an unlimited manner.

However, this new understanding that infinite being is primarily and properly predicable of God does not eliminate the inadequacy of our manner of signifying the divine perfection. Neither before nor after the proof for the existence of God can we have any knowledge of infinite being which is either direct or independent of our knowledge of finite being. In our human way of understanding, there is always a connotation of limitation in our way of signifying the infinite being of God, a limitation not at all present in God himself.[69] When discussing the divine perfection, we must distinguish the perfection signified from our limited way of signifying it.

This inadequacy of our thought and language to represent what is objectively meant by 'infinite being' has several cautionary implications. For example, though we may predicate 'substance' of God to signify that he exists per se, we deny that he is a substance in the manner in which we conceive this term according to which it is a generic term connoting a finite composite being.[70] Again, when we speak of infinite being as one or as individual, we must exclude the usual connotations of quantitative materiality associated with terms such as those that suggest that God can be spoken of in numerical terms, or as all of one piece when what is intended in fact is simply to indicate that his infinite perfection is indivisible and incommunicable.[71] Likewise, when we predicate 'infinite being' of God, we should say 'God is infinite being' rather than 'God is *an* infinite being'. For infinite being is not *a* being among other beings, that is, is not comparable with other beings as one particular kind of being among other particular kinds of being.[72] Nor can one speak of *an* infinite being as though there might be several such beings. For a multiplicity of absolutely infinite beings is obviously contradictory.[73]

In the light of his account of God as infinite being, Aquinas develops a detailed metaphysics of various attributes of God which are likewise identical with his infinite act of existence, the source of every perfection. These perfections or attributes possessed by God include his goodness, truth, beauty, his knowledge, freedom, and omnipotence, his simplicity, immutability and eternity. These are all elucidated as a consequence of the underived, self-possessed infinite act of existence which God is. 'The measure of a being's perfection is its degree of *esse*: a being is said to be more or less perfect in proportion to the contraction of its *esse* to a greater or lesser mode of excellence. Hence, if there were a being to which the whole perfection of *esse* belonged, no excellence possessed by anything would be lacking to it.'[74]

Coexistence of finite and infinite being

A particularly significant feature of this philosophically realist approach to God is its treatment of the coexistence of God with his creation. There are three great issues in a philosophical discussion of God: an issue of meaning; an issue of existence; and an issue of coexistence. It is this third issue, the issue of coexistence, which today often exercises people more than the other two. It is seen as an issue of how to reconcile the claims of human autonomy, creativity, scientific enquiry and technological capacity with the affirmation of an omniscient and omnipotent creator of the existence, conservation and activity of everything.

Obviously there are distinctively contemporary features of the way in which this issue presents itself today which would not have been addressed by Aquinas in his treatment of the issue. Nevertheless, his general approach to the issue is still interesting and illuminating whether considered in its bearing upon the meaning of either infinite being or finite being.

First of all, he is quite explicit that the coexistence of finite and infinite involved in the idea of creation in no way compromises or diminishes God's infinite being. God's creation of the world is absolutely free, without any possible intrinsic or extrinsic ground of obligation.[75] Moreover, granted the free decision to create, there can be no requirement to create any particular world, for example, the best possible world – which Aquinas considered no more meaningful than the biggest possible number.

Nor does it make sense to think of God's infinite being as somehow limited or undermined by the creation of finite being as though finite could be added to infinite to create a contradictory more-than-infinite-being. This pseudo-difficulty arises from a mistaken view that finite and infinite being can be metaphysically compared as instances of a common genus. It implies a universal or quantitative conception of being according to which the amount of being possessed by one individual necessarily constitutes a limitation of all other beings by excluding from them its own self-possessed content of being.

However, such a conception of the coexistence of distinct perfections does not hold good even on the level of the coexistence and communication of finite perfections. In order to realize the fundamental inadequacy of such a conception, we have only to reflect, for example, how the interpersonal sharing of knowledge or love in no way diminishes these perfections in the donor.

The point to be emphasized is the radically different manner in which finite and infinite being possess the perfection of being and hence the impossibility of opposing them as though they were comparable members of a common genus. The perfection of infinite being is not limited by the reality of creatures whose perfection he adequately pre-contains as their total cause. It is not a defining condition of infinite being that it is the only being which exists.

We call a being infinite if it is *Esse Subsistens*, that is, being whose *esse* is not limited by a distinct essence. If there is being which is infinite in this sense, its infinite perfection is in no way affected either by the presence or the absence of beings whose *esse* is limited. Finite and infinite are ways of being which are strictly incommensurate: 'For God is not a proportionate measure of anything.'[76] Creatures possess the perfection of existence in a proper though limited manner and in total dependence upon a cause whose essence is to possess it in an unqualified and infinite manner. Once finite beings are thus understood to be by limited participation what infinite being is essentially, it is manifest that the existence of beings distinct from and other than God has no negative implication for his infinite perfection.[77]

When we turn to consider the impact of the coexistence of finite and infinite being upon our understanding of finite being, Aquinas has equally interesting things to say. The general thrust of his account is one which views this coexistence as providing us with an enhanced appreciation of the intrinsic meaning and value of the finite beings of our experience.

Our realization that finite being must be ultimately understood as created highlights not merely its radical dependence, but also its positive participation in the perfection which characterizes the infinite being of God.[78] Any Manichean worry about the evil or absurdity of things is dispelled, and their existence is apprehended as intrinsically good and meaningful and valuable.[79]

The important feature of creation, as distinct from any other kind of causality, is that it is an absolute supra-temporal origination of finite existence, *esse*, and not a temporal process or transition from some imaginary 'non-being-stuff' into being. 'God makes things out of nothing as will be shown later on (q.45, a.1), not as if this nothing were a part of the substance of the thing made, but because the whole substance of a thing is produced by Him without anything else whatever presupposed.'[80] Creation includes time, matter, space and all motion and process. Recognizing it involves a mental quantum leap beyond the formal order of processes and transformations to the totally originating order of existence. As Herve Thibault aptly remarked: 'Creation is not a transition or coming-to-be. It does not belong to the order of time and duration, but to the order of *esse*. And the basic reason why *esse*, cannot originate through process or transformation, is that this act is absolutely first in the order of being: it presupposes nothing, whereas all other actuations depend on it.'[81]

Here again we see the innovative importance of Aquinas's account of the ultimacy of the act of existence, *esse*, with regard to every other perfection.[82] It is an innovation which dramatically distinguishes his metaphysics from that of his personally admired Aristotle in which God and matter are two coeternal principles, and God is only the attracting goal, which acts by way of finality – rather than efficient causation – to account ultimately for motion in an already existing world. It indicates how wide of the mark some phenomenologists are in suggesting that Aquinas's philosophy of God is essentially a reproduction of Aristotelian metaphysics with God featuring as just another, albeit supreme, being in a system of comparable beings.

For Aquinas it is unprovable, and a matter of metaphysical indifference, whether the finite world is of limited or eternal duration. In either case it exists only and totally because of the act of existence by which it has been originated into being by the transcendent causality of *Esse Subsistens*. However, this emphasis upon creation as primarily a matter of receiving the foundational perfection of the act of existence, from which all other perfections derive, opens the way for his robust confirmation of the self-possessed order, activity and excellence of the finite world.

He was well aware of the tendency of some Islamic scholars (a tendency revived by seventeenth-century Occasionalists such as Malebranche) to emphasize the perfection and omnipotence of God by depreciating the perfection and causal efficacy of created beings. However, for Aquinas, to deny the efficacious secondary causality of creatures in deference to divine perfection is a self-defeating exercise. For how could such a world, devoid of any proper activity, possibly manifest the divine goodness? 'To detract from the self-possessed activity of things is to detract from the divine goodness.'[83] An inert world in which no creature could produce any effect and in which every effect is produced immediately and only by God is incompatible with the conception of God as infinitely wise and good.[84]

Creation is a dependence which enables all beings to exist, to continue to exist, to act and interact as the sort of beings that they are. As the various sciences make abundantly clear, we can think about the existence, nature and activity of things without any reference to their being created. Being a created dog does not make it bark in a different way to just being a dog. As Aquinas put it: 'The relation to its cause is not part of the definition of a thing caused.'[85]

Indeed he would have considered it crucial that the affirmation of infinite being should not contradict our initial metaphysical understanding of the nature and activity of finite beings. Because, for us, this understanding is the only guarantee of the validity of our philosophical affirmation of infinite being. We argue to the existence of infinite being as the required transcendent cause of features of the existence and activity of finite beings, which appear inexplicable and even contradictory when considered simply in themselves. If finite being appears unintelligible and ineffectual in a new sense as a consequence of our affirmation of infinite being, then the affirmation destroys itself. It is crucial to the metaphysical understanding of both finite and infinite that created agents, acting according to their proper nature and participating in the framework of existence created by God, should through their transforming actions contribute instrumentally to the attainment of the existence of new beings of which God, *Esse Subsistens*, is creator and principal cause.[86]

This intrinsic and efficacious activity of secondary causes generally applies with special significance to the particular sphere of human autonomy and activity. God's transcendent causality with regard to my nature and activity does not interact with them to make them *become* dependent upon him. It gives them existence which, as his gift, is thereby dependent upon him. The fact that my existence and nature as an autonomous agent thus exist dependently upon God's free act of creation does not thereby change me into a robot. God's causal action does not act, as an excessive consumption of alcohol might, as a countervailing force on my free action. Because the free activity of each agent, one human the other divine, pertain to radically different orders of efficacy, it can be said without contradiction that they each bring about properly and freely the same effect.[87]

Likewise, for Aquinas, the primacy of conscience is not compromised by knowledge that our free decisions are dependent upon the concomitant creative causality of God. Any action contrary to what we judge to be reasonable is always wrong whether or not our judgement is correct. Hence, he remarks, a person would act wrongly if having judged it evil to abstain from fornication she in fact abstained, or having judged it evil to accept the Christian faith she in fact accepted it.[88] Knowing that God is the transcendent cause of our own free decisions does not dispense us from acting conscientiously. Nor does it guarantee that our free conscientious decisions are always correct or reasonable.

Summary and conclusion

The preceding pages have provided an outline of a realist metaphysical approach to God, and principally of how Aquinas developed such an approach. It has concentrated on a central theme in any such account, namely, the metaphysical meaning of finite and infinite being and the manner of their coexistence. Starting from an initial pre-philosophical awareness of the finitude of things, disclosed by their quantitative limitation, their temporal limitation and their mutual limitation through opposition of many distinct beings, the enquiry proceeded upon a progressively deepening path of metaphysical disclosure.

It began with an account of the finitude of material beings in terms of the Aristotelian theory of the mutually limiting composition of act and potency in such beings, according to which the indeterminate capacity of prime matter achieves particular determination through a correlative principle of substantial form. This hylomorphic account of the finitude of material beings can explain the transformations but not the existence of such beings. The discussion proceeded to a more metaphysically fundamental account of the intrinsic limitation of any finite being in terms of its limiting composition of essence and existence. Here one finds Aquinas's dramatically innovative application of the classical Aristotelian theory of potency and act, which originally cast matter in the role of indeterminate potency or capacity for perfection, and form in the role of fundamental, defining and perfecting act. In Aquinas's account, it is *esse*, the act of existence, which is understood as the fundamental originating act of every being, from which every other perfection derives, and in relation to which they stand as a formally determining capacity or potentiality. Finite being, as metaphysically conceived, is the realization of a particular instance of *esse*, the act of existence, in correlation with the formally limiting capacity of a distinct essence.

In this account it is important to note, as Aquinas remarked, that finitude is thus attributed to something intrinsically and absolutely and not, as has so often been proclaimed in the history of philosophy, in virtue of some reference to an objectively valid idea of infinite being. At this level of metaphysical understanding, the only notion we have of *esse* as not limited by a distinct formally determining essence is the abstract idea that we may form of *esse commune* which, like any other abstract idea, signifies incompleteness rather than perfection, the incompleteness whereby abstract thought falls short of the finite perfection of a concretely realized act of existence.

It is only in the light of an argument for the existence of God as transcendent cause or creator of the domain of finite being that the affirmation of infinite being as actual unrestricted plenitude of existence, *Esse Subsistens,* is finally achieved. Moreover, the argument for the existence of God is an indirect one involving the principle of non-contradiction. It is not, as is sometimes suggested, an immediate inference from our metaphysical understanding of finite being. If we say that knowledge of the existence of infinite being is implicit in our experience and understanding of finite being, we must be careful not to conclude that we therefore have some vague, indistinct awareness of the existence of God. We may indeed implicitly know and desire God, the supreme truth and goodness, in our seemingly limitless desire for knowledge and happiness. However, as Aquinas remarked, what is implicit is known to be implicit only by being made explicit and this cannot be achieved by immediate inference but only, if at all, indirectly by causal argument.[89]

Nor, having developed the affirmation of God as transcendent cause of finite being into the affirmation of him as infinite being, *Esse Subsistens,* have we any direct understanding of what is signified positively by 'infinite being'. We know that the term is truly and intrinsically predicable of God. We show indirectly and negatively that it signifies his perfection as pure act of existence, which as identical with his essence is not, as are finite beings, limited in existential perfection by the specifying causality of a distinct essence. But we have no comprehension of the perfection thus signified which utterly transcends everything we can understand.

However, as we have seen, in the light of this affirmation of infinite being as *Esse Subsistens,* a more fundamental understanding can be provided of the metaphysical meaning of finite being and of its coexistence with infinite being. Finite being can now be metaphysically described in terms of the real but limited and totally dependent participation of creatures in the infinite perfection of God to whom the ultimate act of existence pertains absolutely, primarily and essentially.

Moreover we have seen how this participation through creation in the infinite being of God confirms the initial metaphysical appreciation of the intrinsic perfection and proper activity of finite beings.

The account illustrates how the terms 'finite' and 'infinite' take on ever-richer analogical levels of significance as we progress in our metaphysical understanding of being. Thus the metaphysical significance of 'finite being' is progressively enriched as it passes, through various interdependent levels of ontological analysis, from an initial pre-philosophical consideration to an ultimate account in terms of its limited and dependent participation in the perfection of infinite being. Similarly with the elaboration of the metaphysical meaning of 'infinite being' which, for us, is contextually dependent upon our understanding of 'finite being'. We have seen how, in the light of Aquinas's elucidation of the meaning of being in terms of *esse* or act of existence (understood as the ultimate foundation of all perfection), the conception of infinite being is transformed, by argument, from the 'horizontal' level of abstract incomplete *esse commune* to the awe-inspiring 'vertical' level of *Esse Subsistens*.

As an attempt to provide a metaphysical account of everything in the light of the implications of a realist affirmation of extra-mental being, the account of finite and infinite being, developed by Aquinas, is an intellectual tour de force. It represents a very different 'approach to God' to that represented by phenomenology of religion.

However, it has, with some justification, been represented as a detached impersonal account of God, a God evoking little sentiment and enthusiasm. In reply it can be pointed out that it is not the purpose of metaphysical enquiry to generate religious fervour. It portrays a transcendent and omnipotent God in whose presence one might indeed be circumspect rather than sing and dance – a God upon whom we are totally dependent in every aspect of our existence and vis-à-vis whom it might be wise indeed to adopt the maxim that 'the fear of the Lord is the beginning of wisdom'!

Moreover, from this metaphysical perspective on God, religion, in so far as it is implied, is not seen as an exercise of the theological virtues of faith, hope and charity, but rather as a specific exercise of the moral virtue of justice. Aquinas speaks of it as the virtue by which we render unto God the worship which is his due as creator and sustainer of all things.[90] Religion, in this context, is more a self-involving exercise of appropriately acknowledging our relationship of dependence upon God than one of entering into a loving relationship of friendship with him which strictly theological considerations might indicate. This independently existing God of metaphysics, to whom creation is asymmetrically related, is not envisaged, as he is envisaged in phenomenology, as accessible only and always as God in intimate relationship to human consciousness. If from a metaphysical perspective finite being can be said to participate, in a limited way, in the infinite being of God, it must at once be affirmed that this infinite being is incomparable with such finite being. As *Esse Subsistens*, pure act of existence, it utterly exceeds our comprehension which is always a comprehension of finite being. The metaphysical approach to God terminates in acknowledgement of a state of unknowing, an acknowledgement of what one writer has called 'the darkness of God'.[91]

Aquinas commends the metaphysical enterprise of exploring the mystery of infinite being but warns against expecting to comprehend it.[92] His final word is that in order to refer appropriately to God's existence we must even deny that he is being as we understand it and acknowledge our ignorance of his surpassing existential perfection. 'When therefore we proceed towards God by way of remotion, we first deny of him anything corporeal; and then we even deny of him anything intellectual, according as these are found in creatures, such as "goodness" and "wisdom"; and then there remains in our mind only the notion that he is, and nothing more: wherefore he exists in a certain confusion for us. Lastly, however, we remove from him even "being" itself as it is found in creatures: and then he remains in a kind of shadow of ignorance, by which ignorance, in so far as it pertains to this life, we are best united to God.'[93] No trace here of the alleged onto-theology proclaiming God simply as the highest or supreme being in the system of beings!

From these considerations, it is abundantly clear that the phenomenological and metaphysical approaches to God are very different. One crucial difference is the very different significance which they attribute to the extra-mental existence of things which we unproblematically acknowledge in our natural pre-philosophical attitude.

In phenomenology such existence is always to be bracketed and transcendentally reduced to enable a pure philosophical elucidation of essential structures of phenomena, including religious phenomena, precisely and only as given to human consciousness.

In metaphysics the extra-mental existence of things is ascribed an absolutely irreducible objective significance and is explored in terms of *esse*, understood as act of existence. It is considered and analysed, through its various levels of manifestation, to its ultimate foundation in God affirmed as *Esse Subsistens*.

One is confronted with the alternatives of a phenomenological 'God without Being', as proclaimed in the challenging title of one of Marion's books, or 'God, *Esse Subsistens*, and existential source of all being', as argued metaphysically by Aquinas.

This difference, and others, between a phenomenological and a metaphysical approach to God will have to be considered further to explore the possibility of their compatibility or complementarity. But before doing so a third approach to God must be considered, one in terms of another allegedly comprehensively explanatory first principle. It is the approach of theology, developed in the light of faith in divine revelation – an account of God and the world derived from truths about them professed to be revealed by God himself.

3

Theology

Introduction

Any outline of a theological approach to God should always be offered with due diffidence. For it is somewhat presumptuous of anybody to claim to be sufficiently informed, detached and self-effacing to be qualified to comment with assurance about what God wants us to know about himself and our relationship with him. As Marion remarks: 'One must obtain forgiveness for every essay in theology.'[1] This is particularly true in my case as I am not a professional theologian.

However, throughout the course of history, there has been no shortage of such essays; each elaborating its own account of divine matters in terms of its author's own particular religious affiliation, theological tradition and personal insight. In this chapter, I try for my part to outline with some comparative indications what, from the perspective of Christian belief, a theological account of God and our relationship with him involves, and how it differs from the philosophical approaches we have already considered. The discussion is oriented more towards the general nature of such a theological account and the basis on which it claims to be true, rather than towards the more substantial theological task of elaborating the range of specific truths involved in an account of Christian belief.

In very general terms, theology is the systematic ordering and exposition of truths revealed by God. More simply, it is trying to understand what God has told us about himself and ourselves. These revealed truths are known by us, and known as revealed, through a divine gift of faith which dramatically extends the range of our access to truth beyond what we can ascertain by using only our own power of rational enquiry. Within this broad definition there is of course room for a wide range of interpretation of these divinely revealed truths – interpretations which reflect, inter alia, the cultural background, denominational affiliation and philosophical presuppositions of different theologians.

The important point to bear in mind is that all theology is an attempt to get beyond intrinsically human systems of truth, for example those available to phenomenology, to metaphysics or to positive science, and to elaborate systematically, in however mediated a manner, what God himself has disclosed about himself and our relationship with him. Such a systematic representation of divine truths provides, one might well believe, the most fundamental and comprehensive knowledge of all reality, deriving as it does from a first principle, God's own revelation, which is in every way the most fundamental and dependable source of truth. Needless to say, this is an evaluation which will commend itself only to those who already profess faith in an alleged divine revelation and judge it to be an entirely dependable access to truth rather than a source of mystification or delusion.

Christian theology, as a systematic account of revealed truth, is based upon a religious history of salvation telling the story of the creation of the world and of mankind's fall from grace and subsequent redemption. This history of salvation, the divinely inspired narrative of a divine initiative, apprehended and expressed in human terms, is vividly recounted throughout the Bible. It culminates in an account of the life, death and resurrection of Jesus, the incarnate Son of God the Father, and of the subsequent outpouring of the Spirit of God as guide and inspiration of the redeemed people of God who are the church established by Jesus.

Among the many remarkable disclosures revealed in this story of salvation, one in particular stands out as the central truth which theology is always and, one might say, in its every statement trying to comprehend and articulate. It is the astonishing assertion that we are loved by God – are no longer merely created beings but have become part of God's own life. The theological approach to God and our relationship to him, as distinct from what might be known philosophically, is one which proclaims that the life of God is a life of love and that we have been divinized, have become, through grace, part of this life. In the remarkable words of St John: 'And we have come to know, and have believed, the love that God has in our behalf' (1 Jn, IV, 16).

Needless to say, this astonishing claim that through his love for us we have become part of God's own life is one which, even if it doesn't quite fly in the face of reason, certainly exceeds anything which we might have been able to find out for ourselves about our relationship with God. It constitutes a radically new way of looking at everything, a particular account of everything provided by God himself, which it is the task of theology to unfold as coherently, completely and as systematically as possible. Theology is the, culturally conditioned, engagement of human reason in the effort to achieve a faithful developed understanding of the true account of everything as disclosed by Revelation.

The question naturally arises: on what basis can one claim that such a theological account of everything is indeed true rather than fictitious?

The short answer, which theology seeks to elaborate, is that the account is known to be true because it is guaranteed by the faith of the believer.

'The faith of the believer' can be understood in an objective or a subjective (but not simply subjectivistic) sense. Understood in an objective sense, 'the faith of the believer' signifies that which is believed, the content of revelation as formulated in summary form in the Creed and elaborated systematically in theology. Understood in a subjective sense, 'the faith of the believer' refers to the personal engagement of the believer – as a concrete, historically situated and culturally conditioned subject – assenting and being committed to the faith in its objective sense. In its objective sense, the faith unfolded by theology is declared to be true because it is truth revealed by God himself. In its subjective sense, the assent and commitment of faith is declared to be reliable and justified because it can be shown to be a well-founded commitment. This confirmation of the subjective faith of the believer as a well-founded commitment is itself an important dimension of a theological approach to God. Let us consider a little more closely what it involves.

The believing subject

Traditionally, the act of faith is understood to involve three main features: an intellectual judgement, a commitment of the will and a divine gift of grace. Although the act of faith is voluntary and not unavoidable or inevitable, nevertheless, it is not arbitrary or gratuitous. It involves rational comprehension and intellectual conviction. However, since it is a commitment to the truth of a divine revelation which is beyond the range of human reason, its attainment implies the enabling support of divine grace. Because of this requirement of a divine enabling grace, faith is traditionally referred to as an 'infused' theological virtue. But this does not mean that it should be thought of as though it were a supplementary brain implant generating brainwashed assent and robot-like activity. In virtue of the other components involved, that is, the human intellect and will, the faith of the believer is affirmed as an intellectually justifiable, reliably motivated and freely sustained commitment to God's revelation accepted as such.

This intellectual justification and reliable motivation of faith can involve various moments, differently evaluated, as we shall see, in alternative theological traditions. It can involve purely intellectual argument, interpretation and judgement concerning the existence and nature of God. But it also involves attending to the historical evidence of God's revelation provided by the objective experience and teaching of examples of great holiness and prophetic witness to God – holiness and witness most evidently and perfectly manifested and exemplified in the life of Jesus. Further, and more intimately, there are the interior, existential experiences of each individual believer which illuminate and sustain their personal conviction and enduring fidelity, and which confirm their sense that their faith embodies a true communion with God. When these three constitutive moments are mutually interactive, faith in God will not be confused with simple belief, with a naïve or superstitious credulity, an arbitrary commitment or an absurd gamble, an ephemeral sentiment or a fleeting impression; nor will it come down to a scientific hypothesis or an historical observation. As one commentator observed: 'In an original and fruitful synthesis, it unites reason and heart, objectivity and subjectivity. For the upright soul, the faith is justified; the Good News deserves to be welcomed with joy. "Blessed are the pure of heart, for they shall see God." (Matt.5.8).'[2]

Although most theologians would agree that the faith of the believer involves a combination of intellect, will and divine grace, and that it is reliably justified and motivated, nevertheless there is considerable difference in various accounts of how all of this is so. This is particularly evident in the difference in relative value usually attributed by Protestant and Catholic theologians respectively to the role of natural human reason vis-à-vis grace in their account of faith. As a general rule, Catholic theologians emphasize the positive role to be ascribed to human reason in an account of the nature of faith whereas Protestant theologians de-emphasize its significance and indeed often tend to see it as constituting an obstacle rather than a help. The contrasting positions are perspicuously illustrated by Karl Barth in the Protestant tradition and Thomas Aquinas in the Catholic. It will be helpful to illustrate, in broad outline, the difference in approach of these two representative theologians.

Karl Barth

According to Barth, we know God not through natural reason but through faith in his self-revelation to us.[3] The attainment of this faith has nothing to do with natural human knowledge. It is the work of God's grace alone, an act of God operating in man and enabling him to recognize his sinful nature and to acknowledge Jesus Christ as his Saviour and Redeemer. Being essentially a sinner, he is cut off from attaining the knowledge of God of which he is capable. It is only by the grace of God, and the faith in Christ which it alone enables, that he can fulfil his capacity to know God and attain a true notion of him and of our relationship with him, which he has enabled. 'What could be more irrational and laughable, ridiculous and impossible, than God's words to Abraham? . . . Moreover, all the articles of our Christian belief are, when considered rationally, just as impossible, mendacious and preposterous. Faith, however, is completely abreast of the situation. It grips reason by the throat and strangles the beast.'[4]

The idea that natural knowledge, in the guise of natural theology, has any role to play in the attainment of faith is an illusion, and a dangerous one at that. Alleged natural knowledge of God is not part of the solution to the challenge to provide a reliable account of faith. It is part of the problem. For all reliance simply upon our natural intelligence to enlighten us, even in a preliminary way, about the nature and existence of God can result only in idolatry. Barth drives home this conviction with the trenchant observation: 'And with Paul, as with all the prophets and apostles, idolatry is not a preparatory form of the service of the true God, but its perversion into the very opposite . . . On the contrary, we have to begin with the admission that of ourselves we do *not* know what we say when we say "God", i.e. that all that we think we know when we say "God" does not reach and comprehend him who is called "God" in the symbol, but always one of our self-conceived and self-made idols, whether it is "spirit" or "nature" or "fate" or "idea" that we really have in view . . . Only God's revelation, not our reason despairing of itself, can carry us over from God's incomprehensibility.'[5]

Further he remarks: 'If God had not become man, as is recognized and confessed in the second article (of the Creed), then everything we could conceive and say to ourselves about God *over* man and about God *with* man, would hang in the air as arbitrarily, as mistakenly and as misleadingly, as the corresponding ideas which in the long run have been fashioned about God and man in all religions and cosmic speculations.'[6] The only reliable use of reason in divine matters is that, when enlightened by the grace of faith, it operates consciously and exclusively to unfold theologically the truths of divine revelation recognized as such.

Thus Barth remains implacably opposed to all 'natural theology', to all claims to knowledge about God by way of human reason alone. Because only God can reveal himself as he truly is, for Barth; as one commentator remarks: 'a natural knowledge of the true God is impossible, because man, being essentially a sinner, is incapable of co-operating in his own justification, and because his relationship with God is the work of God and God alone.'[7]

Since whatever can be known truly about God is known only by divine revelation, any alleged natural knowledge of him, for example, by way of the analogy of being, is inevitably idolatrous. The vitality of natural theology, the claim to knowledge of God by natural reason alone, derives from a disposition to resist grace and a powerful impulse of sinful human nature to explain and justify its existence in terms of an ultimate principle or '*God*' of its own creation. Natural theology is the idolatrous product of the free self-affirming act of sinful man.

For Barth, the only acceptable 'proof' of the existence of God is that which he gives of himself in our faith. He has no intention of arguing against the claims of alleged 'proofs' for God which he suggests are rather comical contrivances. They might serve some purpose in a discussion of pagan so-called gods. The five so-called proofs of God might be relevant to a discussion of these idolatrous 'Supreme Beings'. 'The Bible never uses the kind of argument we find there; it simply speaks of God as of him who has no need of proof. It speaks of a God who *proves himself* at every step; here I am, God says, and because I am, live and act, what need is there to prove me? This proof that God gives of himself is the proof referred to by the prophets and apostles. How can we speak otherwise of God in the Church? God has no need of our proofs.'[8]

Clearly, in Barth's theology of faith, there is no room for the traditional arguments of natural theology, such as the 'Five Ways' of Aquinas. And he denounces the alleged natural knowledge of God affirmed by the First Vatican Council. The only argument to which he is sympathetic is Anselm's so-called Ontological Argument. But he denies that this is proposed as a philosophical proof of God's existence. On the contrary, at the outset the argument accepts on faith the truth of his existence. It simply seeks to give an intelligible account of how this known, because revealed, truth of his existence is evident from reflection upon the similarly revealed truth that God is indeed that than which a greater cannot be conceived. It is a work of faith-seeking understanding. '"That than which a greater cannot be conceived" only appears to be a concept that he forms for himself; it is in fact as far as he is concerned a revealed Name of God . . . It goes without saying that for him the Existence of God is given as an article of faith. This Existence of God which is accepted in faith is now to be recognized and proved on the presupposition of the Name of God, likewise accepted in faith, and is to be understood as necessary for thought.'[9]

Barth's rejection of any natural knowledge of God is not based primarily on philosophical considerations, for example, such as those adduced by Hume or Kant. It is based upon theological considerations which argue that, according to the Bible, any knowledge of the true God is inaccessible to sinful man through his own resources. It becomes accessible only, under the guidance of the Holy Spirit, through the faith-enabling grace of God's revelation of himself in Jesus Christ. Left to himself in his sinful state, he is capable only of idolatry, of worshipping only false gods of his own fabrication.[10]

This rejection of natural theology remains a constant throughout Barth's career. However, in his later years he is less vehement in his condemnations and is even disposed to see in the writings of philosophers such as Schleirmacher and Jaspers an acceptable philosophical *envisaging* of access to God – but only an *envisaging* and not access itself. In all knowledge of the true God, the initiative always remains with God alone and the grace of his faith-enabling revelation.[11]

Anticipating later discussion, one can speculate about the relationships which might be explored between Barth's theological approach to the knowledge of God and the two philosophical approaches we have already considered, namely, the phenomenological and the metaphysical. It seems clear that there is little sympathy from Barth for the metaphysical approach which culminates in a highly developed natural theology. The picture is not so clear in the case of phenomenology. True, it doesn't involve the knowledge claims about the existence and nature of God advanced in the metaphysical approach. However, inasmuch as its starting point for the exploration of knowledge of God is what can be described and understood only as given co-relatively to human consciousness it might appear to contravene, or at least qualify, Barth's theological requirement that the initiative for all such knowledge must be centred only on God's unpredictable and eventful self-revelation. However, as we shall illustrate later, there may be a closer affinity of Barthian theology with phenomenology, at least with that of Jean-Luc Marion which, as we have seen, makes the philosophical case for envisaging the possibility of divine revelation but leaves exclusively to theology the knowledge of the eventful realization of this possibility.

Let us consider now a very different approach to the role of natural reason in an account of the believer's faith in God, namely, that provided in the theological approach to God developed by Thomas Aquinas.

Thomas Aquinas

When one considers the relationship which obtains between the components of grace, intellect and will in his account of a believer's faith, it seems very obvious that Aquinas, by contrast with Barth, attributes considerable importance to the role of natural reason in developing his account. This, as we shall see, is undoubtedly true but, for several reasons, needs to be understood in a rather qualified sense.

In the first place, we should recall, as I indicated in Chapter 2, that according to Aquinas, we have no natural knowledge of the self-evident nature of God's existence or no direct awareness of his existence however vague or indistinct. Certainly he agreed that in virtue of our seemingly limitless desire for truth and happiness we can be said to have implicit knowledge of and desire for God the supreme truth and goodness. But what is implicit is known to be implicit only a posteriori when it has been made explicit by way of indirect causal argument. 'For man naturally knows God in the same way as he naturally desires God. Now, man naturally desires God in so far as he naturally desires beatitude, which is a certain likeness of the divine goodness. On this basis, it is not necessary that God considered in Himself be naturally known to man, but only a likeness of God. It remains, therefore, that man is to reach the knowledge of God through reasoning by way of the likeness of God found in His effects.'[12]

Secondly, Aquinas is as insistent as Barth in maintaining that theology, unlike the natural knowledge of God attained in philosophy, originates and proceeds, as from a first principle, from faith in God and what he has revealed to us about himself and our relationship to him. 'In the teaching of philosophy . . . the first consideration is about creatures, the last of God. But in the teaching of faith, which considers creatures only in their relation to God, the consideration of God comes first, that of creatures afterwards.'[13]

Thirdly, for Aquinas, the 'light of faith' does not enhance the natural ability of the human intellect, for example, by raising it to a higher level of intelligence enabling it to comprehend and affirm new 'supernatural' truths.[14]

The *lumen fide* does not make the divine object of faith supernaturally more evident or meaningful to the human intellect or enable it to perceive new *truths* about it which exceed the intellect's natural capacity. From the viewpoint of human intelligence the act of faith is very imperfect. It is not an intuitive insight. It adheres to non-evident assertions under the influence of the will (*ex imperio voluntatis*), a will which in turn is moved by grace.[15] For Aquinas, human intelligence, as such, is not enhanced by an additional 'light' which enables it to achieve a greater intellectual grasp of either the meaning or truth of the assertions of faith. It is not a cognitive 'sixth sense'! Inasmuch as it relates to human intelligence, faith does not yet truly unite us to God. For faith is about what is absent, not about what is present. However, God is made affectively present to the believer when by her will she assents to God.[16]

This 'affective presence' of God engendered by the loving movement of the graced will to embrace what is proposed to faith is not a matter of attaining new or additional knowledge of or about the divine object of faith. It is a matter of us being enabled to relate *ourselves* more intimately, personally and lovingly to what is already known as proposed to faith – and to make it more present to the affective fibre of our subjectivity. 'The benefit of this new light, not being to reveal to us something unknown but to enable us to see what is already known in a new affective hue, pertains properly to the realm of our subjectivity.'[17]

The foregoing considerations indicate that, contrary to what is sometimes suggested, Aquinas had a rather measured and qualified view of the role of the human intellect in an appropriate account of the faith of the believer. It is not that through which, aided by grace, new meaning and truths about God, inaccessible to the unbeliever, are attained. If it plays a role in assenting firmly to propositions which for it are non-evident, it does so under the loving impetus of the graced will. In the domain of faith, the human intellect is not operating comfortably in its natural milieu of intuition, understanding, reasoning and judgement concerning objects of its experience. It does not grasp intuitively what it affirms by faith.[18]

Nevertheless, it remains true that Aquinas places great confidence in the role of natural reason in the development of his theology. He can do so partly because of his carefully measured account, mentioned above, of the part it plays in the attainment and maintenance of the faith of the believer. Let us consider further this significant role of the natural human intellect in his theological approach to God.

A powerful motivation of Aquinas's insistence upon the competence and importance of natural reason within theology is his conviction that the light of faith cannot be at odds with human reason. Faith and reason, he insists, are necessarily compatible with each other. Faith, considered as a light which enables us to adhere to divine revelation, can be such a light only because we are able to see, to understand, what it proposes. Even though it is God who by grace determines and enables the faith of the believer, he does so through a determination and enabling of our natural ability. Undoubtedly, Revelation signifies something radically new vis-à-vis the scope of natural reason. It is an event in the deep sense of a manifestation of divine truth to human reality. But it can be such only by insertion in a human history which includes the possibility of its arising. There are truths about God attainable only through faith in his gracious revelation and there are truths about God available through rational reflection on his creation. They cannot contradict one another for they each derive ultimately from God the unique source of all truth. 'The existence of God and other like truths about God, which can be known by natural reason, are not articles of faith, but are preambles to such articles; for faith presupposes natural knowledge, even as grace presupposes nature.'[19]

And so, for Aquinas, there are truths, such as the existence of God, which strictly speaking are not articles of faith, since they are accessible to natural reason. Such truths however are for the most part held on faith since their attainment by reason is precarious and usually accessible only to the few with leisure to devote time to such specialized enquiry which presupposes almost the whole of what can be known by philosophy. 'As regards those truths about which human reason could have discovered, it was necessary that man should be taught by a divine revelation, because the truth about God such as reason could discover, would only be known by a few, and that after a long time, and with the admixture of many errors. Whereas man's whole salvation, which is in God, depends upon the knowledge of this truth.'[20]

The feature of this theological account of the relationship between faith and reason which contrasts most obviously with that of Barth is his claim that some of the truths revealed about God are accessible to natural reason. These are the truths featuring in natural theology (so abhorrent to Barth), which claim to provide dependable knowledge, by way of our natural intelligence alone, about the existence and attributes of God such as his goodness, unity and omniscience. However, even though naturally knowable, it is appropriate that they be revealed in view of their importance for salvation. Even for the philosopher the revelation to faith of these naturally knowable truths about God is a powerful psychological pointer and encouragement to engage in the philosophical enquiry which, with much effort, may attain them. But once successfully attained, these naturally knowable truths are known and therefore no longer simply believed as is the case with the indemonstrable truths of faith such as the Trinity and the Incarnation which are utterly beyond the range of our natural intelligence.

Underlying this nuanced defence of natural reason's ability to attain, in principle, dependable truth about God and about the credibility of faith in divine revelation, is Aquinas's conviction that original sin did not entail the corruption of human nature, including natural reason.[21] It simply deprived it of the added grace through which it was enabled to attain a supernatural goal beyond its own resources, namely, the vision of God.[22] This is a far cry from the insistence of Martin Luther (Barth's forerunner and inspiration): 'Sin has not merely deformed nature most shamefully, but has perverted it in the worst possible manner.'[23]

Aquinas's conviction that the effect of original sin was the loss of an added grace and not the perversion of human nature itself is reflected in his confidence, which we have noted, that natural reason is capable of attaining some, admittedly limited, valid knowledge about God.[24]

One significant illustration of this confidence is his conviction that the meaning, though not the truth, of the articles of faith and of their theological interpretation and development is fully accessible to natural reason – to that of the unbeliever as well as that of the believer. The light of faith, as we have said, does not disclose a new level of supernatural meaning to the intellect. It is a gracious gift promoting a loving adherence of the will to the divine reality, enabling it to sense or grasp affectively that it is God who reveals himself in the statements of faith. In virtue of this affective orientation of the will, we are enabled to adhere intellectually, with divinely assured certitude, to the *truth* of these non-evident statements.[25]

This insight that faith does not affect the meaning of the articles of faith and their theological development, a meaning which is unproblematically accessible to natural reason, has as a consequence that these Christian beliefs and their theological development is accessible not just to believers but to unbelievers also. In other words, an unbeliever can be an excellent exponent of Christian theology.

Of course for the believing theologian her theological reflection is a work of faith seeking understanding and as such is for her an elaboration not just of the meaning of Christian beliefs but also of their truth. The unbelieving theologian provides a theological account of the beliefs which Christians believe to be true. His theological account is one prefixed by 'according to Christian believers . . .' The believing theologian provides a theological account of the Christian beliefs which she believes to be true. However, her 'I believe that . . .' which implicitly prefixes her theological claims can be rephrased by the prefix 'according to the Christian believer which I am . . .' The phrase 'which I am' can be put in parenthesis without any loss of meaning concerning what is affirmed.[26]

Perhaps the difference between the two accounts might be better described by reserving the term 'theology' for the account provided by the believer, which affirms both the meaning and truth of the theological statements, and using the term 'philosophy of religion' for the account which concentrates only on the meaning of theological statements and is prefixed by 'according to Christian believers . . .' However, in both cases the meaning of the theological statements enunciated is identical. The only difference is that in one case their truth is steadfastly affirmed in faith, whereas in the other this affirmation of their truth is abstracted from – the assertion that this is how things really are, the assertion that '*et ita est in re*' is suspended.

Considered in this way it would seem that, because of its robust confidence in natural reason, the theology of Aquinas lends itself to constructive dialogue with the more contemporary interest in philosophy of religion. This latter seeks to attain a non-reductive understanding of the essence or specific meaning of religion in general and of Christianity in particular. The thesis inherent in the thought of Aquinas that the meaning of what Christians believe and its theological development is available to natural reason, which cannot however pronounce on the truth of the statements involved, must resonate with any philosophy such as phenomenology which proceeds, initially at least, by way of bracketing the question of what exists independently of our awareness of it and limits itself to a description and analysis of what gives itself in experience.

It would be an absurd anachronism to claim that Aquinas can be considered as a phenomenologist. This is precluded by the intervening epistemological turn of modern philosophy, since Descartes, which accords fundamental primacy to human self-consciousness. This epistemological turn which underpins and characterizes phenomenology is very different from the basically metaphysical orientation of Aquinas's philosophy – and of his theology also to the extent that it involves philosophical reflection. Nevertheless, one can articulate, on the basis of his explicit teaching, what today would be called his philosophy (as distinct from his theology) of the Christian religion. It would be the systematic presentation of everything signified by his theological statements but understood in abstraction from their claim to be the truth about how things really are. Such a thought experiment provides us with a useful perspective from which to evaluate a philosophy of religion such as phenomenology which is based precisely upon this bracketing, by phenomenological reduction, of truth claims about how things exist independently of our awareness of them.

For Aquinas, we can know by *natural reason* what is meant in Christian belief by statements such as, 'The Word became flesh and dwelt amongst us'. However, he was equally certain that knowing by *faith* that this is truly how things are is a much bigger claim than the simple claim to know the meaning of the statement. Highlighting this distinction emphasizes a dimension crucial to Christian faith which must pose a problem for any phenomenology of Christian belief which methodologically abstracts from the issue of how things really are otherwise than as the noematic correlates of our noetic consciousness. Phenomenology abstracts methodologically from the existential adhesion and assent which the effective act of faith involves. Can any narrative represented simply as a correlate of human consciousness – however compelling in its impact and desirability and even if apprehended as representing a given which exceeds the power of human inventiveness or constitution – ever be an adequate expression of what Christian belief involves? It is perhaps by pursuing this issue that the value and relevance of a metaphysical approach to God can be confirmed as an indispensable intermediary between a phenomenological and a theological approach – between an approach governed by the fundamental primacy of human consciousness and an approach governed by the fundamental primacy of God's revelation. And perhaps, in turn, each of these two approaches may be seen as indispensable in mediating the gaps between the other two!

These remarks about demonstrable and indemonstrable truths of faith, and about the competence of natural reason in grasping the meaning if not the truth of articles of faith and their theological elaboration, all relate to 'the faith of the believer' considered subjectively as the personal assent, engagement and commitment of the believer to the revealed word of God. But they also have a bearing on the theological elaboration of 'the faith of the believer' in the objective sense of that which is believed, the content of the divine revelation made accessible to the believer. Let us look a little further into the significance of the faith of the believer and its theological elaboration in this objective sense.

The object of faith

Earlier in this chapter, we emphasized that a central truth of Christianity, which theology seeks to elucidate, is the remarkable claim that the life of God is a life of love and that we humans are loved by God with a love which elevates and transforms our existence in a way which enables us to become partakers in this divine life. As Herbert McCabe observes: 'Jesus announces . . . that he is loved by the Father and simultaneously announces that we are taken up into this love. (There is no gap between God in himself and God-for-me.)'[27] Involved in this central tenet of Christian belief is the assurance, which is quite inaccessible to natural reason, that we have a meaning and value which far exceeds the understanding of ourselves as finite beings created into existence by the free decision of a benevolent creator. The understanding of ourselves as created finite beings, in principle accessible to metaphysical reflection, is an understanding of ourselves as standing in an asymmetrical, non-mutual, relationship of total dependence upon the creative act of God, conceived negatively and affirmed indirectly as infinitely perfect being.

This creator God, corresponding to our understanding of ourselves as created finite beings, is *Esse Subsistens,* the pure act of unlimited existence in which the metaphysical approach to God culminates. This God, envisaged as benevolent creator might be described as having a benign providential interest in our well-being analogous to our biblically based requirement to be solicitous for the world which is placed in our care. In such an account there is no reference to a loving relationship between mankind and God. Any such suggestion would be literally incongruous, one out of joint with the metaphysical condition of total dependence of the finite creature on the one hand and the transcendent unrelatedness of God to anything finite on the other. Circumspect obedience on the one hand and omnipotent authority on the other hand would appear to be a more appropriate description of the relationship.

A relationship of love implies a context of equality and mutual appreciation which is foreign to the master-servant imagery of creation, an imagery which is a powerful factor in the contemporary rejection of God in the name of human freedom.

In view of this consideration, one can appreciate the rejection by many contemporary philosophers and theologians such as John Caputo, Richard Kearney and Jean-Luc Marion of the traditional metaphysical approach to God with its emphasis on the primary and irreducible significance of the analogy of 'being' in any discussion of the relationship between man and God. For such philosophers, the concentration upon an account of the relationship between man and God in terms of a distinction between finite and infinite being, and the dependent being of the former on that of the latter, misses the point that the really fundamental relationship between man and God is not one of creaturely dependence in being but one of love – a gracious initiation into the life of God's love.

It is such considerations about the distracting and even potentially misleading character of metaphysical discussion about God and our human relationship to him primarily in terms of 'being' that provokes Marion to title one of his books *God without Being*. By this contention, he does not intend to insinuate that God does not exist but rather the relative unimportance of this attribution to God particularly with reference to his significance for us. Is it obvious, he wonders, that the first question to ask about God is whether he exists? Is being the highest and primary name of God? 'Under the title God Without Being, I am attempting to bring out the absolute freedom of God with regard to all determinations, including first of all, the basic condition that renders all the other conditions possible and even necessary – for us, humans – the fact of Being . . . But for God, if at least we resist the temptation to reduce him immediately to our own measure, does the same still apply? Or, on the contrary, are not all the determinations that are necessary for the finite reversed for Him, and for Him alone? If, to begin with, "God is love," then God loves before being, He only is as he embodies Himself – in order to love more closely that which and those who, themselves first have to be.'[28]

For Marion, this reversal of the order between being and loving, between the Old Testament name 'I am who I am' (Exod. 3.14) and the more profound, though consistent, New Testament name 'God is love' (1 Jn 4.8), involves both a philosophical and a theological initiative. Philosophically, it calls for a rejection not only of any, metaphysically motivated, onto-theological determination of God as the supreme being who grounds other beings, but also for a rejection of any other allegedly more critical view which still accords primacy to a determination of 'God according to Being.' Instead, 'I shoot for God according to his most theological name – charity.'[29] Phenomenology, not metaphysics, provides the appropriate method for theological reflection. 'In short, phenomenology would be the method par excellence for the manifestation of the invisible through the phenomena that indicate it – hence also the method for theology.'[30]

Theologically, Marion argues that God gives himself to be known according to a more radical horizon than the horizon of being – the horizon of the gift itself. In this horizon what appears as a pure given, with neither deduction nor legitimation, is agape, charity – the utterly gracious and unforeseeable gift of God's love.[31] This love, inaccessible to rational metaphysical enquiry, and intimated phenomenologically negatively in the melancholic experience of the vanity of life, comes to us in and as pure gift, one not derived in any way from within the horizon of being. The world and we ourselves are not beings initially which subsequently become loved. It is because we are loved that we are beings. Being is secondary to love. Without love our being is engulfed in a prevailing sentiment of emptiness and nothingness, which Marion seeks to illustrate through his perceptive phenomenological description of the effects of melancholy.[32]

This remarkable theological claim, inaccessible to philosophy, that God is love and that we are initiated into this divine life, at first sight certainly seems to pose a serious difficulty to the whole metaphysical approach to God, which I have outlined in Chapter 2. Is such an approach really, as Barth and many other contemporary thinkers maintain, a distraction, an irrelevance and even a form of idolatry? Is it an attempt to contain God within the confines of our own rational capacity to reflect in wonder on the mystery of being? Does not the theological approach to God, which discloses what God himself has revealed to human experience about himself as love and our loving relationship to him, cohere admirably and without requiring any metaphysical mediation, with the phenomenological project of providing a faithful description of any phenomenon manifesting itself in human experience, including any 'saturated' phenomenon manifesting itself as divine revelation? Is not this contention that the believer can accept as trustworthy what is given, not metaphysically, but in a faith experience as divine revelation, simply an application of the fundamental phenomenological claim that 'every originary presentive intuition is a legitimizing source of knowledge; everything offered to us in "intuition" in an originary way (that is in its personal [leibbaft] reality) must be received simply as what is presented, but also only within the limits in which it is thus presented'.[33]

This line of thought, which questions the appropriateness of a metaphysical approach to God, would appear to be reinforced by the contention that, at best, such an approach can culminate only in the claim that the most fundamental relationship between finite beings, such as ourselves, and God is the relationship of creation, the relation of creature to creator. This contention it would seem is rejected by a theological approach to God which argues that our most fundamental relationship to him is not that we are creatures of a creator but that we are loved by a God who is love and that the raison d'être of our existence is to be partakers in the love which is his divine life. As Herbert McCabe puts it: 'So the gospel announces that our fundamental relationship to God is not that of creature to creator – a relationship which cannot but be one of servant to master. For the gospel, our fundamental relationship is that of lovers, of lovers in equality. We have this equality to the Father because we are given a share in the life of Christ.'[34] This account of the nature of God and of our relationship to him is developed theologically by elaborating the good news of the gospel, the truths of faith expressed in the Creed, the traditional teaching and sacramental life of the church, the Christian way of life and its ultimate goal, that is, direct knowledge and love of God.

Undoubtedly this theological approach to God and our relationship to him surpasses immeasurably any metaphysical account based upon an analysis of the nature of being, even one which attains an affirmation of God as infinitely perfect being and of ourselves as finite beings dependent upon him as our provident creator.

But does this theological approach to God thereby refute, undermine and render irrelevant or even idolatrous such a metaphysical approach as is often maintained particularly by convinced phenomenologists? Let us take note of some considerations, to be more fully considered in later chapters, which suggest that this may be too hasty a conclusion to draw.

Remarks

First of all, it is necessary to recall that however sublime and wonderfully inspiring the theological account of our loving incorporation into God's own life is, it nevertheless remains true, and indeed an article of faith, that we and the universe we inhabit are created finite beings and that God exists independently of this order of finite being. We believe in God 'the creator of heaven and earth' who has made us 'a little lower than the angels' (Heb. 2,7), and we acknowledge with the Psalmist that 'Before the mountains were brought forth, or ever thou hadst formed the earth and the world, even from everlasting to everlasting, thou art God' (Ps. 90). Thus the theological account of God and our relationship with him in terms of charity certainly does not disqualify an account of this relationship in terms of creation and the respective modes of being signified by the terms of the relationship. Indeed it presupposes and implies such an account.

We might indeed want to emphasize that the consideration of God in terms of love is a more fundamental consideration than the consideration of him as creator of an order of finite beings. For we know through revelation that he is in himself a life of love, but is only properly called 'creator' because we have been freely initiated into existence by him. Moreover, the act of creation itself can be seen as an expression of God's love, the full extent of which in our regard becomes apparent to us only through faith in his revelation that we are incorporated into his own life. But serious difficulties emerge if we try to confine our attention to this revealed account of the depth of God's love for us and do not relate it to the context of our situation as created finite beings. These difficulties have a bearing both on our understanding of God and on our understanding of our own autonomy.

The theological claim that we are divinized and partake of the divine life because given a share in the life of Christ does not mean that to be human is part of the meaning of God's life as such. God's Trinitarian life does not as such involve human finitude. The Son of God is begotten not, as we are, created; is divine not, as we are, divinized. Unless our status as created finite beings is kept clearly in mind, we are likely to end up with a very anthropomorphic view of God when we speak, however correctly, of becoming divinized through partaking in a life of love which is essentially divine. We are in danger of transforming the theological truth that 'God is love' into Feuerbach's reductive aphorism 'Love is God'.[35]

Likewise the theological claim that we are divinized by grace to share in the divine life does not mean that we cease to be creatures and become as it were an emanation of the divine life which replaces our created human nature. The divine life into which we are initiated by grace is an astonishing enhancement, not abolition, of our human nature. We retain our own created human nature with its distinctive autonomy, freedom and responsibility, which enables us to act as free agents both in response to our 'supernatural' vocation and in our personal engagement in a natural world with other people. Herbert McCabe again: 'we must not lose sight of the creative side of God, for on this hangs the autonomy of our own nature

. . . To acknowledge the Trinitarian Godhead then is not to deny God as creator, it is simply to refuse to settle for God as creator, it is to refuse to be content with a creature/creator, master/slave relationship with God. This sets us the task of accommodating the creator God within the context of the Trinitarian God of love.'[36]

However, it might be argued, in response, that this task can be satisfactorily addressed without involving, what is in the eyes of many theologians and phenomenologists, a discredited metaphysical exercise in 'natural theology'. We have already seen how Karl Barth is a representative theological critic of such natural theology. Heidegger is its iconic philosophical critic whose views have been endorsed by so many contemporary philosophers. His famous critique of the onto-theological character of western metaphysics is proposed not simply as a destruction of a philosophical error but also as a demolition of an ungodly God. This ungodly God, conceived by traditional metaphysics as the supreme being and cause, not only of all other beings, but also of itself, *causa sui*, is a God who cannot fulfil a genuinely godly role namely as an object of religious devotion. For Heidegger, a truly godly God is one to whom we can pray and offer sacrifice, a God we can worship, a God before whom we can sing and dance. The metaphysically envisaged creator, the supreme being and *causa sui*, is not an object of religious veneration which a truly godly God must be.[37]

Moreover, even if faith-inspired Christian belief in God as 'creator of heaven and earth' must, in some way, correspond to or confirm a natural and independently accessible understanding about our contingent creaturely human condition, why need this take the form of a metaphysical analysis of the nature of finite beings? Might not such apprehension of our existentially dependent condition be more effectively confirmed by a phenomenological account of features of religious experience such as those elaborated in Schleirmacher's account of the sense of absolute dependence or Otto's elucidation of our numinous intimation of the holy? Is not this enriching congruity of faith with the contours of natural religious consciousness more effectively disclosed by careful phenomenological description of how it is realized in the concrete self-involving experience of the Christian believer than by impersonal onto-theological analysis of the metaphysical structure and origin of the realm of finite being?

Such reflections are at one level certainly very persuasive. They suggest that the phenomenologically elucidated dialogue between faith and first-person-singular lived experience will provide a more reliable approach to the great issues of the existence, nature and coexistence of God than the supposedly more objective impersonal disclosures of natural theology.

Nevertheless, on closer examination, the matter is not so evidently straightforward. One is reminded of Gilson's warning that metaphysics has a tendency to bury its undertakers! For it is arguable that a serious problem arises from the methodological exclusion of any appeal to the findings of natural theology in what proposes to be an adequate approach to the existence of God and our relationship to him.

I mentioned this problem earlier when discussing the distinction between Aquinas's theology and what might be proposed today, on the basis of his confidence in the scope of natural reason, as his philosophy of the Christian religion. This philosophy of the Christian religion would involve more than his own explicit account of the competence, in principle, of philosophy to establish through metaphysical reasoning those demonstrable truths about the existence and nature of God, the *preambula fidei*, which are logically, although not necessarily de facto, presupposed by faith. It involves the further claim that the religious meaning (though not the truth) of all assertions expressing or theologically developing Christian Revelation is available to natural reason – the natural reason of the unbeliever as well as that of the believer. This opens up the possibility of providing an intelligible account of the meaning and value of the Christian faith as it appears to the Christian believer but abstracting from any judgement about whether it is a true account of how things actually are. Knowledge of the truth of the assertions would be accessible only through faith, to theology rather than philosophy.

Such an approach would be similar to a phenomenological description of the essential structure of Christian belief as it reveals itself concretely in the religious experience of the believer. Such phenomenological description will respect the specificity and irreducibility of the Christian religion as it gives itself in experience – for example, its irreducibility to psychological or sociological translation. It would do so by way of the 'phenomenological reduction' which enables a sympathetic re-enactment of the noematic-noetic structure of Christian belief but from a neutral perspective which abstracts from any judgement about the truthfulness of its claim to reveal how things really are independently of this belief.

However, and here is the difficulty, Christian faith does declare how things are, and indeed how they are independently of any believer claiming them to be so. The Christian faith 'as it appears to the believer' is not the measure of what this faith objectively proclaims. No narrative recounting the Christian faith as it appears or gives itself to believing consciousness is an adequate account of it if it leaves in abeyance, or suspension, or abstraction, or brackets, the objectively dependable truth value of what it narrates.

To this it might be replied that the Christian faith and its theological development 'as it appears to the believer' is not apprehended as a philosophical or scientific report about the nature of reality which might be objectively true but rather as a revelation of God's salvific plan for mankind disclosing to a religious, not a scientific or metaphysical, intentionality an eschatological goal or final end of human life. As somebody remarked about the controversy over Galileo's heliocentrism, 'It is not the purpose of the Bible to tell us how the heavens go but how to go to Heaven.'

This of course is true. But the question still remains whether the narrative recounted by way of 'disinterested', 'neutral', 'detached' and 'phenomenologically reduced' description of God's loving salvific plan for mankind, which appears as veridical to a Christian believer's religious consciousness, might depict an illusion rather than a truthful portrayal of how things really are? However compelling and desirable this phenomenologically inspired religious account of mankind's ultimate meaning and value appears to the eye of faith, the question remains can its objective validity be confirmed from within a phenomenological viewpoint? For such a viewpoint obtains only by way of a methodological bracketing of any subject-independent truth claim. Such bracketing suspends any metaphysical judgement or claim about the independent reality of the God of Christian religious experience – even though this God is portrayed in the sympathetic but neutral phenomenological description of the object of religious consciousness as objectively real and true for this religious experience of the believer. The phenomenological description of the religious experience of the believer is, as Ricoeur observes, an ontologically neutralized imaginative and sympathetic re-enactment of it – one conducted from the abstract perspective of 'as if'.[38] One might say, it suspends operationally the assent which is accorded axiomatically in the religious experience it describes. It seems therefore, as I have said, that the problem for phenomenological description of religious experience is how to effect a transition from within its 'as if' perspective to an unbracketed affirmation of the object of this experience.

One way in which this transition can be attempted is, as I indicated in the discussion of the phenomenological approach to God in Chapter 1, to claim that the object of religious experience is given in this experience in a way which exceeds the intrinsic intentional capacity of the subject of the experience. The constitutive intentional capacity of the conscious subject is, it is claimed, no longer to be taken as the measure of what is available phenomenologically. This claim involves a profound modification of the Husserlian immanentist view of phenomenology. For Husserl, as Jeffrey Kosky remarks: 'Phenomenality could be defined broadly as the appearing that remains in and for consciousness when all ecstatic openness to transcendence has been shut down or closed by the reduction. It is, in short, the field of immanence.'[39] Indeed Husserl explicitly extends the reduction to the transcendence of God.[40]

Since an unbracketed affirmation of God is not accessible phenomenologically by way of the Husserlian emphasis on the active constitutive role of the conscious ego, it must be sought rather by emphasizing the way in which phenomena of religious experience are given as irreducible to the activity of the conscious subject. In respect of this givenness of such phenomena, the conscious subject experiences itself as the passive recipient rather than constitutive agent of what it experiences.

Indeed it is precisely by such emphasis, such a reversal of perspective, that philosophers such as Levinas and Marion achieve an effective affirmation of God. They do so, one might say, by a more radical reduction of Husserl's transcendental reduction, a reduction which enables the assured affirmation of the experiential givenness of God. Thus Marion can adopt the slogan: 'So much reduction so much givenness.' We have seen how in his account of the saturated phenomenon a veridical if bedazzling and iconic experience of God is achieved – an experience in which the conscious subject is utterly passive, refashioned as a graced recipient rather than a constitutive agent.

Likewise for Levinas, the ambition of the conscious subject to actively and adequately encompass everything within a totalizing concept of being is disclosed, from within phenomenology, to fail because any such concept cannot encompass the experience of the cognitively irreducible Other. Levinas's affirmation of the transcendence of the Other is proposed not as an overcoming of phenomenology but rather a radicalization of it. 'The presentation and development of the notions employed owe everything to the phenomenological method.'[41] The ethically demanding givenness of the face of the Other, felicitously referred to by Levinas as 'the curvature of inter-subjective space' defies the conventional noema-noesis correlation and discloses the Other as overflowing, transcending and 'in-adequate to' the constituting capacity of intentional consciousness. In this experienced asymmetry, this 'relation-without-relation' which is the ethically invoking transcendence of the Other, Levinas finds the religious presence of God manifested and revealed. 'The dimension of the divine opens forth from the human face ... God rises to his supreme and ultimate presence as correlative to the justice rendered unto men . . . The Other is not the incarnation of God, but precisely by his face, in which he is disincarnate, is the very manifestation of the height in which God is revealed.'[42]

For Levinas, this manifestation of the presence of God in the ethical acknowledgement of the asymmetrical transcendence of the other person is aptly illustrated by the traditional doctrine of creation. 'The absolute gap of separation which transcendence implies could not be better expressed than by the term creation.'[43]

It seems to me that to spell out how this valuable suggestion might be confirmed requires the elaboration of the sort of indirect metaphysical argument about the radical existential dependence of finite being on the creative initiative of God characteristic of natural theology. It would be essentially an argument which makes metaphysical sense of the ethically engaging asymmetry of the Other by demonstrating it to be a dependent cipher of the asymmetrical relationship between God and his creation.[44]

Similar argumentation suggests itself in the case of making sense of the iconic presence of God intimated in the saturated phenomena of divine revelation so powerfully described by Marion. The 'presence' of God given in religious experience, and more particularly in the faith experience of the Christian, however perceptively described phenomenologically, is not the immediate vision of God anticipated in our hoped for eventual beatific vision in heaven. This presence of the 'God whom no man hath seen' can only be a presence which is a dependable and dependent icon or cipher of the divine reality. It is a presence given as prior to and as refashioning the passive subject to whom it is given, not in vision, but in a transforming awareness and sentiment of transcendence. This phenomenologically described drama of gift, givenness and given-to, which transmutes the excess of givenness into saturated phenomena in which the bedazzling invisible presence of God is somehow iconically experienced, naturally invokes an enquiry into its implicit ontological structure – just as similar inquiry was invoked in the case of Levinas's asymmetrical Other. The icon or cipher invokes a metaphysical deciphering.

The suggestion in both cases, and for phenomenology of religion generally, is that the phenomenological description of the given of religious experience whether natural or revealed invokes a corresponding level of metaphysical enquiry and argument about the implicit order of reality which subtends the description. The phenomenologically described rich tapestry of religious experience portraying an experienced drama of transcendence and immanence evokes a more impersonal metaphysical account of the ontological threads or principles which underlie it, sustain it and provide its objective philosophical foundation. Undoubtedly this impersonal objective metaphysical account is greatly enriched by the faith-inspired theological account of the divine origin and goal of creation in general and of the divinized character of human existence in particular. But it is not negated or contradicted by it. These considerations claim a distinctive and irreplaceable role for a metaphysical approach to God even in the context of a discussion of the congruity of a theological approach with a strictly phenomenological one. It is a contention which I will have to consider and develop further in subsequent chapters. But before doing so, I must consider a radical attempt to combine the various approaches to God which we have been discussing into a larger, unified and entirely comprehensive speculative system. This is the great systematic synthesis developed early in the nineteenth century by Hegel – the reaction to which still profoundly influences much contemporary philosophy of religion.

4

Spirit

Introduction

The approaches to God considered in the previous three chapters, the phenomenological, the metaphysical and the theological, are distinct and often portrayed as mutually exclusive. They are each animated, as has been mentioned, by a distinct first principle. 'Human consciousness' in the case of phenomenology; 'being' in the case of metaphysics; 'God' in the case of theology. In view of their supposed mutually exclusive character, one or other is sometimes championed as the only correct approach to God and the others dismissed or relativized as defective. In this chapter, I want to outline a rather different approach. It is an approach which seeks to overcome the differences in various approaches to God and unify them in a higher synthesis. Here it is no longer a case of different, exclusive or even complementary approaches to God but rather one in which this seeming opposition is overcome in a profoundly unified system. This approach can be illustrated by considering its development in the thought of its greatest nineteenth-century exponent G. W. Hegel.

Hegel's philosophy, like those we have considered, is also animated by what may be called a unifying first principle, namely, 'Spirit'. The way in which he develops this philosophy of spirit involves the most ambitious attempt to include and explain everything, including all dimensions of human existence and experience, within a unified system of thought. It is an enormously detailed and complex undertaking, and here I must confine the account to (1) a broad indication of how the various approaches to God are integrated into, and indeed integrate, the entire system; (2) its description of the relationship between religion and its theological elaboration on the one hand and philosophy on the other.

A central problem for Hegel was one which had been progressively articulating itself since its modern formulation in the thought of Descartes, namely, the problem of the coexistence of finite and infinite, of man and God.[1]

Stated simply, the philosophical revolution inaugurated by Descartes (1596–1650) consisted in provisionally calling in question the independent reality of the external world, including his body, and directing the quest for a dependable foundation for meaning, certitude and value inwards to the intrinsic resources of his own subjectivity rather than outwards to a created world given directly in sense experience.

It is no longer the self-revelation or epiphany of being which grounds thought as consciousness of being. Rather the new principle of immanentism inaugurated by Descartes, which has dominated the evolution of modern philosophy, inverts the direction of thought and prescribes that it take as its absolute starting point the luminous presence of the thinking subject to himself – a subject defined as identical with his own thought. Husserl acknowledging the significance of this Cartesian innovation observes 'that in philosophy the Meditations were epoch-making in a quite unique sense, and precisely because of their going back to the pure ego cogito. Descartes, in fact, inaugurates an entirely new kind of philosophy. Changing its total style, philosophy takes a radical turn: from naïve objectivism to transcendental subjectivism – which, with its ever new but always inadequate attempts, seems to be striving towards some necessary final form, wherein its true sense and that of its radical transmutation itself might become disclosed.'[2]

However the realities, provisionally excluded by Descartes's methodical doubt, are retrieved by him through an appeal to his clear and distinct idea of God. From this clear idea of God as infinite, eternal, independent, omniscient, supremely perfect and omnipotent being, he judges himself enabled to pass directly to the certainty that God exists and that he cannot be deceptive. 'Nor should I imagine that I do not perceive the infinite by a true idea, but only by the negation of the finite, just as I perceive repose and darkness by the negation of movement and light; for, on the contrary, I see that there is manifestly more reality in infinite substance than in finite, and therefore that in some way I have in me the notion of the infinite earlier than the finite – the notion of God before that of myself.'[3] It is significant that both Levinas and Marion attribute positive value to Descartes idea of God as a valid way of transcending the claims of subjectivity. For Levinas, the affirmation of the irreducible primacy of the idea of God, an idea beyond my capacity to produce, is evidence of the obligating transcendence of the Other. And for Marion this Cartesian idea of God is an instance of 'saturated phenomenon' which exceeds and overwhelms the ambitions of the constituting ego.[4] Aquinas would not have been as impressed since he believed that we cannot philosophically judge the idea of God to be positively possible, that is, non-contradictory, until we knew in some other way that he actually exists.

The upshot of Descartes's affirmation of God is that human subjectivity, far from being the absolute or creative source of meaning and value, merely assents to an order which it discerns in itself as deriving from a more fundamental principle, namely, the 'divine will'. The problematic relationship of coexistence between finite subject and infinite creator is thereby highlighted for subsequent philosophical reflection.

The issue is intensified in the thought of Immanuel Kant (1724–1804) for whom human subjectivity does not discover meaning and value as something divinely pre-established but actually constitutes them in virtue of its own intrinsic resources. In his *Critique of Pure Reason*, the universality and necessity of science and the imperative absoluteness of moral values are grounded not in the mind and will of God but in the a priori forms of human understanding and the autonomy of pure practical reason.

The only role accorded to God in this account is as an object, not of knowledge, but of a rational faith which assures us that the summum bonum, which man must morally require of himself to pursue, is an attainable goal. In other words, since we recognize that it is a duty to promote the summum bonum, we must therefore presuppose its possibility, and since it is possible only on the condition of the existence of God, it is therefore morally necessary to affirm the existence of God.[5]

Kant's rigorous restriction of any discussion of God to the context of the requirements of practical reason has far-reaching consequences. It not only excludes the claims of traditional natural theology to provide us with rational knowledge of the existence of God. It also leads him to reject the idea of supernatural revelation and the possibility of any theology based on such revelation. It subordinates the interpretation of Christian faith to the requirements of the moral philosophy which we have derived autonomously from our practical reason. 'Though it does indeed sound dangerous, it is in no way reprehensible to say that every man creates a God for himself, nay, must make himself such a God according to moral concepts . . . in order to honour in Him the One who created him.'[6]

Clearly, in the light of Kant's account, the issue of the coexistence of finite and infinite, of man and God, had become a crucial one for modern philosophy. Could this coexistence really be maintained in any meaningful sense in the light of Kant's penetrating critique of traditional natural theology and his affirmation of the irreducible claims of autonomous human subjectivity? This issue sets the scene for an account of the sweep of Hegel's philosophy of spirit which, as I have mentioned, seeks to reconcile this tension between finite and infinite into a higher synthesis.

Hegel – early work

For Hegel this was not simply an impersonal philosophical problem. From the time of his youthful theological studies, it was a serious existential issue as he sought to comprehend the object of his reverence, namely, the Christian religion. His early essay 'The Positivity of the Christian Religion' (1795–6), inspired by his admiration for the beauty and naturalness of Greek folk religion and his respect for the austere rationalism of Kant's ethical teaching, led him to reject what appeared to be the imposed and dogmatic character of the Christianity he had been taught. He accepted Kant's view of religion as essentially only the affirmation of respect for morality and obedience to the moral law. In his view, at this stage of his development, the religious thinking of Jesus 'undertook to raise religion and virtue to morality . . . Jesus, on this view, was the teacher of a purely moral religion not a positive one.'[7] For him; religion is positive when it is understood as an authoritarian imposition of a system of dogmas and commands by a radically transcendent God.

It is significant that even at this early stage of his career, Hegel links the question of positivity to the issue of the relation between divine and human nature, between the infinite and the finite. Indeed he observes that 'an examination of this question cannot be thoughtfully and thoroughly pursued without becoming in the end a metaphysical treatment of the relation between the finite and the infinite'.[8]

However, before he comes to elaborate this metaphysical treatment, his early theological view underwent a significant development which would influence the later course of his purely philosophical reflection.

In an essay entitled 'The Spirit of Christianity and Its Fate' (1798–9), he no longer identifies the essence of Christianity with Kantian moral philosophy. Enlightenment rationalism cedes ground to Romantic sentiment, and Christianity is interpreted more as a pantheism of love than a system of moral imperatives. Here Judaism is seen as the religion of positivity par excellence, the worship of an authoritarian God who imposes an oppressive legalism on an alienated and isolated people.

Jesus, according to Hegel, seeks to overcome this alienation by teaching that a morality of laws and rules should give way to a morality of love. If we respond to an exhortation to accept the unifying power of love as the key to a truly human way of life, the content of the moral law will continue to be affirmed as a consequence of the logic of love, but its specifically legal form, its quality of legality, will have been overcome. His gospel of love 'exhibits that which fulfils the law but annuls it as law and so is something higher than law and makes law superfluous'.[9] Consequently, it is wholly inadequate to interpret Christianity in terms of a Kantian respect for moral law which involves a sharp distinction between duty and inclination. Kantian moral philosophy is itself a form of legalism in which the master-slave relationship is interiorized and man as affective individual is dominated by man as universal legislating reason. Jesus showed that love, understood as an inner harmony of inclination and reason, is a fundamental disposition of life, transcending the order of duties and commands. What Jesus wished to draw to our attention was that morality must be raised from the 'thou shalt' of law to the 'is' of love.

This moral insight has a theological counterpart revealed in the religious teaching of Jesus, namely, that the unifying power of love rather than the objectifying and analytical quality of thought is the key to the truth about reality. Through love we can come to a concrete awareness of the unity of our life with infinite life and through it with all life. 'To love God is to feel one's self in the "all" of life, with no restrictions, in the infinite.'[10]

During this early 'theological' period of Hegel's career, he held that philosophy, envisaged as a reflective and analytic discipline, is incapable of attaining a rational comprehension of that loving union with infinite life which religion accomplishes. Thus in his 'Fragment of a System' (1804), he affirms that philosophy is necessarily subordinate to religion. 'This partial character of the living being is transcended in religion; finite life rises to infinite life. Philosophy therefore has to stop short of religion because it is a process of thinking and as such a process, implies an opposition with non-thinking [processes] as well as the opposition between the thinking mind and the object of thought.'[11]

The subsequent course of Hegel's career can be seen as an attempt to work out at an all-inclusive philosophical level of reflection the unified conception of reality inherent in his early theological interpretation of Christianity as a pantheism of love. It will be a form of philosophical reflection in which philosophy no longer 'has to stop short of religion'.[12]

Spirit

The philosophy of spirit, which characterizes his philosophical maturity, is animated by his assurance that the manifold oppositions which our understanding (*Verstand*) establishes, for example, between subject and object, mind and nature, being and thought, appearance and reality, can be reconciled dialectically by a superior philosophical exercise of reason (*Vernunft*). This exercise of reason is the disclosure of spirit as the active unification of all oppositions, and all oppositions are grasped as ultimately reconciled self-differentiations of spirit. God, being and human consciousness are comprehended together in an integrated unity – an onto-theo-logical synthesis – which is not simply the truth about reality but rather the inner living truth of reality.

For Hegel, only such a unified animated totality, embracing all differentiation, is adequate to the exigency of radical philosophical enquiry for unity, comprehensiveness, unconditionality and autonomy.

Spirit, as comprehensive rationality, is abstract self-conscious being opposing itself to itself in a form of extreme otherness, namely matter, which it recognizes as its alienated self and restores to itself in a higher synthesis of concrete self-awareness. Spirit has precedence over matter both logically and ontologically. The corollary of this animating first principle of Spirit is Hegel's guiding maxim: 'the real is the rational and the rational is the real.'[13] As Quentin Lauer puts it, for Hegel: 'The structures of thought are the structures of reality, because subjective rational thinking and objective rational reality are products of the thought which transcends and embraces both . . . Concepts (plural), are then the moments of the Concept, each deriving its determinateness from identification with the whole, "absolute Spirit," the all-unifying concrete concept.'[14]

Most significant in Hegel's repudiation of any ultimate irreducible distinctions is his rejection of any ultimate distinction between finite and infinite. The existence of infinite spiritual reality is not, for him, a problem. It is spontaneously attained through the religious elevation of the soul to its true principle. For religion is essentially a natural elevation of finite life to infinite life. Further, this awareness of the existence of the infinite, of which the religious impulse affords us such a lively assurance, is readily confirmed by reflective appraisal. Reflection discloses that thought, in the very act of assenting to the various dimensions of finitude as such, has already transcended the barriers of finitude and attained an affirmation of the infinite as the animating *source* of its consciousness of finitude. As Hegel himself puts it: 'The limitation of finiteness exists for us insofar as we are above and beyond it . . . Thus the infinite is what is above and beyond the limits; it is something other than the limited; it is the unlimited, the infinite. Thus we have finite and infinite.'[15]

If we accept the identity of the real and the rational it follows that there is no insurmountable problem about a transition from the infinite as an exigency of thought to the real existence of the infinite. Similarly there is no chasm to be bridged between finite and infinite by way of causal argument. For the existence of the infinite is confirmed in the very dialectic of thought itself which discloses the rational, and therefore the real co-relativity of finite and infinite. Kant's objections to the metaphysical affirmation of the existence of the infinite are swept away as resting upon a false opposition between the real and the rational. Even the traditional 'proofs' for the existence of God of natural theology can be rehabilitated, admittedly in a modified sense, when this illusory opposition is abandoned and the true relationship of finite and infinite is appreciated. They can be accorded a modest role and value, not as detached impersonal demonstrations of a previously unknown infinite, but rather as descriptive elucidations of the more basic religious movement of the spirit whereby it elevates itself from finite life to infinite life. In other words, 'they ought to comprise the elevation of the human spirit to God and express it for thought'.[16]

We must not, Hegel insists, rest complacently in a bare assertion of the infinite or be deterred by pious platitudes about the total otherness and unknowability of the infinite. 'We must rid ourselves completely of this opposition of finite and infinite, and do it by getting an insight into the real state of the case.'[17] His whole philosophy of spirit can be seen as an unrelenting effort to attain this 'insight into the real state of the case'.

In accordance with the exigency for unification which animates his philosophy, Hegel repudiates any ultimate opposition of finite and infinite such as understanding, rather than dialectical reason, might postulate. In contrast to the traditional causal understanding of the finite-infinite relationship, according to which the finite is totally dependent upon a self-sufficient transcendent infinite which is intrinsically and eternally independent of the freely created order of finite being, Hegel describes the order of finite being as a necessary aspect of the process whereby the infinite accomplishes its full and true reality as infinite. It accomplishes it through a process of self-differentiation and mediation whereby in finite being it negates the merely abstract affirmation of itself as sheer self-identity and thence returns to a concrete affirmation of itself as absolute spirit through a negation of this negation. 'The finite is therefore an essential moment of the infinite in the nature of God, and thus it may be said it is God Himself who renders Himself finite, who produces determinations within Himself.'[18]

For Hegel, who certainly considered himself an orthodox Christian, it is important to affirm both the genuine though relative reality of the finite and the absolute and irreducible reality of the infinite. What must be overcome is the tendency of pictorial religious thought and the mere abstractions of the understanding to petrify this distinction into a hard and fast and final opposition. What is required is the dialectical thinking of the philosophy of absolute spirit which discloses the identity in distinction between the finite and the infinite. This philosophy portrays the fundamental identity in distinction of finite and infinite as the necessary self-finitizing process of absolute spirit through which it accomplishes its concrete universality as absolute spirit.

Understood as an objectification of the divine life, the whole finite order, culminating in the religious and, above all, the philosophical activity of the human spirit, is seen to be required if God is to achieve that concrete knowledge of his limitless virtuality which constitutes his true infinite actuality. All the vicissitudes and alienations inherent in the finite world, which are characteristic of this stage of 'God in his otherness', must be comprehended as necessary moments of the process whereby the absolute spirit returns to a realization (in the dual sense of becoming aware and becoming real) of itself through the religious and philosophical liberating movement of a self-transcending finite consciousness. In short, both finite and infinite require each other and their unity in distinction for the accomplishment of their true reality and full intelligibility. The following quotation from his *Lectures on the Philosophy of Religion* gives apt expression to this conviction:

> For the logically developed and rational consideration of the finite, the simple forms of a proposition have no longer any value. God is infinite, I am finite; these are false bad expressions, forms which do not adequately correspond to that which the Idea, the nature of the real object, is. It is equally true that God exists as finite and the Ego as infinite. The 'is' or exists, which is regarded in such propositions as something firmly fixed, has, when understood in its true sense, no other meaning than that of activity, vitality, and spirituality . . . God is movement towards the finite, and owing to this He is, as it were, the lifting up of the finite to Himself. In the Ego, as in that which is annulling itself as finite, God returns to Himself, and only as this return is He God. Without the world God is not God.[19]

Hegel and theism

If one were to designate a philosophy as theistic by reference to the ubiquity and centrality of its affirmative reference to God then, on this criterion, Hegel's philosophy would be classified as decisively and even extravagantly theistic. Such a description would, however, be an oversimplification and potentially misleading and has been, one suspects, at the root of much philosophical talking at cross purposes. For it fails to take account of the profound transformation of meaning which the term 'God' has undergone in the context of Hegelian philosophy.

Among the features involved within the traditional connotation of 'God' (at least the connotation of God within the theological and philosophical mainstream of the Judeo-Christian, and indeed Muslim, monotheism) are: (1) the absolute freedom of God in respect of creation; (2) God's unqualified transcendence vis-à-vis the order of finite being; (3) the eternal immutability of God's infinite perfection.[20] Admittedly these notes reappear in Hegel's conception of God. But they do so in a highly accommodated sense.

Hegel speaks of 'the free creative activity, which can realize itself without the help of a matter that exists outside it'. Similarly, he tells us: 'God creates a world, God determines; outside of Him there is nothing to determine. He determines Himself when He thinks Himself, places an Other over against Himself, when He and the world are two. God creates the world out of nothing.'[21] Thus Hegel confirms the traditional conception of divine freedom in respect of creation to the extent that he insists that in creating God cannot be constrained to create by anything extrinsic to his nature, for other than through creation there is no being extrinsic to God. Creation is ex nihilo and not a 'creative' transformation of some pre-existing intransigent formlessness.

However, the traditional conception of divine freedom in respect of creation goes further and insists that God cannot be said to create through any intrinsic necessity of nature which urges him towards greater self-expression. For as infinite perfection, he actually and eternally enjoys all possible perfection of being. Nor, in the traditional conception, can we attribute any necessity of creation to the divine intellect or will. For example, just as one's knowing certainly and infallibly that Socrates is sitting does not negate the contingency of his sitting, so likewise, as Aquinas remarks, although 'it follows that God knows all things that take place in time most certainly and infallibly, yet the things that happen in time neither are nor take place necessarily, but contingently'.[22] Likewise, the divine will cannot be said to ordain necessarily the creation of finite being in order to realize a desirable goal. On the contrary, the divine love of infinite perfection finds complete fulfilment in his own actually infinite being. Any decision to create obtains, not in order to achieve an unrealized perfection, but to communicate perfection already fully possessed.[23] Indeed for Aquinas it is inappropriate to speak of the divine will in terms of either necessity or contingency as these terms are used to describe conditions which obtain in creation. 'There is likewise a difference to be noted on the part of the divine will, for the divine will must be understood as existing outside the order of beings, as a cause producing the whole of being and all its differences ... And according to the condition of these causes, effects are called either necessary or contingent, although all depend on the divine will as on a first cause, which transcends the order of necessity and contingency.'[24]

Hegel cannot subscribe to this stricter conception of divine freedom. For, in his view, the 'creation' of the finite order is an intrinsic necessity of the divine nature. It is only in virtue of the itinerary of spirit in and through the processes of finite reality that the infinite can accomplish its true and full reality. Only through an exteriorization of itself in the order of finite being can the divine nature achieve the complete expression and total fulfilment of its intrinsic finality. 'Without the world God is not God.'

Likewise, the meaning of divine transcendence is transformed in the Hegelian account of God. Traditionally, the notion of divine transcendence has signified that God, in virtue of his infinite perfection, utterly exceeds and is really independent of and distinct from the whole created order of finite being. It implies that the divine perfection is neither intrinsically modified nor extrinsically limited by the reality of finite beings. It emphasizes that finite and infinite are distinct levels of being which are strictly incommensurable. If the divine nature can be said to pre-contain *eminenter* the perfection of created finite realities, it does so only in virtue of, and in the manner of, its own actual infinite perfection. It is in no way affected in its being by the finitude which characterizes the mode of reality of created things.[25]

Hegel also affirms the transcendence of God. There is he argues a real distinction between the infinite and the finite. The infinite perfection of the divine reality is irreducible to any set of finite realities. However, in contrast with the traditional view, this distinction is not envisaged as though the reality of the infinite is independent of that of the finite. Hegel's conception of the identity in distinction of the finite and the infinite is one which requires that transcendence be understood as a characteristic of the divine life as dynamically operative throughout the finite order rather than as characteristic of God as radically independent of the finite order. Correlatively, the realm of the finite is seen as an essential feature of the auto-constitution of the life of God. 'The human, the finite, frailty, weakness, the negative, is not outside of God, and in its character as otherness it does not hinder unity with God; otherness, the negation is consciously known to be a moment of the Divine nature. The highest knowledge of the nature of the Idea of Spirit is contained in this thought.'[26]

This is a conception which, in traditional terms, would be seen as attempting the impossible task of doing justice to divine transcendence in terms of the immanence of God in the finite and the participation of the finite in God but avoiding the conception of the self-sufficiency of God's infinite perfection vis-à-vis the finite. In effect, Hegel's view of transcendence signifies the dynamic 'going beyond' itself of spirit into its own otherness in the various dimensions of finitude, and the corresponding 'going beyond itself' of the finite which finally achieves the full accomplishment of absolute spirit. Thus transcendence, for Hegel, signifies, not an immutable ontological characteristic of God with respect to the finite order, but rather a dynamic activity animating the identity in difference of finite and infinite.

Also involved in his treatment of creative freedom and divine transcendence is an equivalent modification of the traditional conception of God's eternally immutable perfection. Traditionally this signified his 'simultaneous, whole and perfect possession of interminable life'. It expressed God's transcendence of time in his being and in his activity. It excluded from the divine perfection any suggestion of temporal succession or process of change.[27]

Hegel too speaks of God's eternal immutable perfection. 'The absolute, eternal Idea is, in its essential existence, in and for itself, God in His eternity before the creation of the world, and outside of the world.'[28] He is even quite lyrical on this topic telling us that 'God exists in His eternal truth, and this is thought of as the state of things which existed before time was, as the state in which God was when the blessed spirits and the morning stars, the angels, His children, sang his praises.'[29]

This for him, however, is only an approximate and abstractive way of considering the divine perfection. It represents only an exclusively theoretical contemplation by our understanding of a universal blueprint of the divine reality. 'This Universal contains the entire Idea, but it only contains it, it is the Idea potentially only.'[30] The concrete realization of this potentiality implies a whole historical process of manifestation. Only through the self-finitizing process of exteriorization and historical reflective re-appropriation does the potentiality of spirit enter into adequate conscious possession of itself. 'Spirit is just this act of advance into reality by means of Nature, i.e., Spirit finds its antithesis, or opposite, in Nature, and it is by the annulling of this opposition that it exists for itself and is Spirit.'[31] Thus notwithstanding the obvious and acute metaphysical tension between the notions of infinite eternal perfection and finite historical process, the whole context of Hegel's viewpoint obliges him to bind them together in his conception of God.

These considerations indicate what a profound transformation the traditional conception of 'God' has undergone in the framework of Hegel's philosophy. From a theistic viewpoint, the benign interpretation of his achievement would be that, through a brilliant refinement of our philosophical conception of the divine nature, he has vindicated for modern man an authentic affirmation of the God of Christianity.[32] In particular, it would be argued that he has reconciled the affirmation that God is the absolute source of all meaning and value with the emergent claims of human subjectivity and creativity by disclosing the fundamental identity which underlies and sustains the distinction of man and God. He shows that man and God could both be said to be the source of the meaning and value disclosed in the world because their distinction is comprehended as expressing only different dimensions of the same absolute reality. 'The possibility of reconciliation rests only on the conscious recognition of the implicit unity of divine and human nature; this is the necessary basis. Thus Man can know that he has been received into unity with God in so far as God is not for him something foreign to his nature, in so far as he does not stand related to God as an external accident, but when he has been taken up into God in his essential character in a way which is in accordance with his freedom and subjectivity; this, however, is possible only in so far as this subjectivity which belongs to human nature exists in God Himself.'[33]

However, although such an interpretation of his philosophy of God appears to be faithful to Hegel's own intention and expressed conviction, it is not the only or, perhaps, the most plausible one. A more circumspect appraisal of his achievement might argue that its cumulative effect is the elimination of the affirmation of God and the substitution of an essentially non-theistic doctrine of absolute spirit. Thus James Collins remarks that the upshot of the new conception is to establish the truth about the God of theism by establishing its inadequacy and insensitivity to the true nature of the absolute. Hence, instead of the provisional and somewhat loose designation of his philosophy as onto-theo-logical, 'the ruling framework of Hegel's philosophy is more precisely called an onto-pneuma-logic, to emphasise the centrality of his unique conception of self-developing spirit'.[34]

A deeper insight into which of these interpretations is more convincing requires some discussion of the relationship in his thought between religion and its theological elaboration on the one hand and his fully elaborated philosophy of spirit on the other. We have seen how this philosophy of spirit which is driven, as he says, by 'the resolve which wills pure thought' unfolds in accordance with the affirmation of the identity of the real and the rational. As philosophy of spirit it combines in a single philosophical system the two incomplete philosophical approaches governed by the principles of 'being' and 'human consciousness' which we considered in our opening chapters. It remains to be seen whether or to what extent this philosophy of spirit also embraces within its ambit the system of truths, animated by the affirmation of God's revelation as its first principle, which religion and its theological elaboration proclaims. Is this theological 'truth' contained within or irreducible to the philosophy of spirit?

Religion and philosophy

The relationship between religion and philosophy is at the heart of Hegel's philosophy of spirit. For him, religion and philosophy are undoubtedly the two most sublime activities of man and, more fundamentally, the two most decisive activities in the accomplishment of the full self-realization of absolute spirit. 'The relationship which grounds all religion and all philosophy is first of all the relationship of spirit as such to nature, and then that of absolute Spirit to finite spirit.'[35]

In both religion and philosophy, spirit becomes consciously manifest to itself. Both of them are necessary to this process of self-manifestation which embraces the articulation of the whole of nature and human history. But only in philosophy does this auto-constitution of spirit achieve consciousness of itself adequately and in an appropriately pure form.

For Hegel, as we have already noted, religion arises in human consciousness as a spontaneous self-transcending elevation of finite life to infinite life. This spontaneous wellspring of religion is not, however, as he tended to suppose in his early writing, a sheer romantic immediacy involving only, sentiment, intuition and imagination. Precisely as an activity of spirit, it is a mediated immediacy involving the element of thought. It involves not just the mere feeling of dependence, which even animals who cannot transcend their limitations experience, but also a genuine cognitive transcendence of the realm of finitude mediated through concepts derived from a variety of sources, for example, lived experience, education and revelation.[36] The true appraisal of the spontaneous pre-reflective aspect of religion and the responsive chord it strikes in human sensibility and affectivity is not that it is intransigent to rational articulation but rather that in its origin and deepest signification it is the work of God rather than simply of man, the activity of absolute spirit mediated through the finite channels of human subjectivity. 'Thus religion is the Divine Spirit's knowledge of itself through the mediation of finite spirit.'[37]

Religion represents a decisive yet ambiguous phase in the life of absolute spirit. It is decisive in that it signalizes the conscious self-repossession of spirit from its necessary dispersion and exteriorization in nature and finite cultural institutions. It is ambiguous in that, although it is a true and necessary expression of spirit's conscious appropriation of itself, it is not the definitive expression of this appropriation which occurs in a pure form only with the transformation or elevation of religion into philosophy. Religion, even the 'perfect religion', is inadequate to the appropriate formulation which the philosophy of spirit alone provides.

Religion announces the conscious reconciliation of spirit with itself but the form of this announcement is coloured by overtones of the long process of alienation which has been overcome. For religion, although its object is the absolute, thinks this content in the manner characteristic of its state as intermediary between the finite realm of feeling and perception on the one hand and the liberated speculation of philosophy on the other hand. It thinks its content in the form of representational thought (*Vorstellung*).[38] This is a form of thought suspended between the particularity of imagery and the universality of rational thought. It seeks to attain to the pure universal significance intimated in a limited individual image of the absolute but fails to extricate itself effectively from the image's sensuous and 'natural' acceptation. It arrives merely at a circumscribed anticipatory representation of the absolute. According to Hegel, in considering the teaching of the various religions, we must bear in mind that they express themselves in the form of representational thought. Thus, for example, the theme of the Father begetting the Son, the creation story, the account of Christ's birth, death and resurrection, all belong to the realm of representational thought whose truth in a pure form is accessible only to philosophy.

Although religion 'intends' the living conscious reconciliation of finite and infinite, its roots in sensibility and the concomitant limitation of its own representational form of thought expose it to the danger of misrepresenting in various ways the true relation of finite and infinite. It is prone, for example, to represent the poles of the relationship in such exaggerated opposition that the only conscious bond that can be claimed between them is the 'unhappy consciousness' of a master-slave relationship.[39] Moreover, even when the fundamental unity in distinction of finite and infinite life finds true religious expression in the doctrines of Christianity, this truth remains inadequately disclosed. For it is represented in the form of external relationships and contingent events; not in the strictly rational form of 'inner connection and absolute necessity' in which the complete liberation of spirit is finally attained. 'The witness of the Spirit in its highest form takes the form of philosophy, according to which the Notion, purely as such, and without the presence of any presupposition, develops the truth out of itself, and we recognise it as developing, and perceive the necessity of the development in and through the development itself.'[40]

Thus by reference to his own philosophy, animated by the guiding first principle of spirit taken as the absolute standard of integral and liberated consciousness, Hegel appears to establish a critical relativization of all religion and a criterion which enables him to discern evidence of human alienation in different historical forms of positive religion. Hence, the intimation in his early theological writings that the theme of religious positivity 'cannot be thoughtfully and thoroughly pursued without becoming in the end a metaphysical treatment of the relation between the finite and the infinite' is more than fully borne out. Not merely positivity, but also in contrast to some of his earlier views, religion as such appears to be subordinated to and assimilated within the superior rationality of philosophical system.

As might be surmised, he detects a very profound level of alienation in the forms of religion which, unlike his own conception of absolute spirit, attach particular importance to attributing an unqualified transcendence of God vis-à-vis the finite order. This is particularly evident in his account of the Jewish religion.

As described by Hegel, Judaism is the religion par excellence of divine transcendence.[41] It avers that God is the unique almighty Lord and that the world is totally dependent upon his incomprehensible divine majesty. The fundamental relationship between man and God is that of created slave to absolute master. God created all people for his own honour and glory. In practice, however, it is only through a divinely chosen and therefore isolated people, the Jews, that this goal is to be achieved. Effectively, he is the God of Abraham, of Isaac and of Jacob.

According to this view of Jewish belief, the prerequisite of man's control over nature, of his empirical happiness and of his attainment of the Promised Land, is acknowledgement of God's absolute creative sovereignty over nature and human life; an acknowledgement which must be endorsed by unquestioning submission and obedience to the divine law precisely as such. The entire sphere of a true believer's actions must be regulated, in the most minute detail in accordance with laws which are accepted and obeyed, not as arising from human reason, but as handed down by God. The people of God is accordingly a people adopted by covenant and contract on the conditions of fear and service.[42]

Thus, for Hegel, the Jew is a slave who has alienated, handed over to God, his freedom, his autonomy, his authentic creativity and subjectivity. He has not yet achieved a conscious realization and self-assurance of his kinship and unity as spirit with the absolute; nor of the exigencies of this spirituality in an authentic religious relationship.[43] Because of his impoverished conception of human life, he submits to an absolute dichotomy between man and God and locates the source of any meaning and value which might adorn human existence in the inscrutable providence of an utterly transcendent Lord.

The anguish and alienation inherent in the Jewish religion prepare the way for Christianity which is, in principle, the authentic religious expression of the unity of finite and infinite. The enslaving irreducible transcendence of God is overcome in its doctrines of the Son of God's incarnation, death and resurrection and the indwelling of the spirit in the church. The truth herein expressed is, of course, obscured by the limitations of its religious representation in the form of contingent historical events and must be elucidated in terms of its properly philosophical formulation. Nevertheless, what it does express, however imperfectly, is the necessary truth that 'the unity of the divine and human natures has been brought into human consciousness and has become a certainty for it, implying that the otherness, or as it is also expressed the finitude, the weakness, the frailty of human nature is not incompatible with this unity, just as in the eternal Idea otherness in no way detracts from the unity which God is'.[44]

Further, the consciousness of God as finitized in human nature, depicted in the doctrine of the Incarnation, is developed in the doctrine of Christ's passion and death into a consciousness of this self-effacing God. But consciousness is rescued from this 'the most frightful of all thoughts' that God has died, by the doctrine of the Resurrection which signalizes the most perfect accomplishment of the absolute as totally reconciling infinite spirit. We are brought to the liberating realization that if we wish to speak of God, we must understand him not as the abstract transcendent God of theism but as the absolute who endures self-estrangement, finitude and even death itself in order to attain his true spiritual reality as universal self-consciousness.[45]

With our appreciation that the new conception of the divine life as active encompassing resolution of all oppositions concerns not Christ alone but all humanity, we enter fully into the Kingdom of Spirit. We overcome our particularity and, notwithstanding our frailty and finitude, comprehend ourselves as part of a divine movement of reconciliation in which we are united with God and with our fellow humans. This new awareness finds expression in a spiritual community which in religious representation we call the 'church'. In this community, animated by the consciousness of our identity with the divine spiritual totality, we are, in principle, united through universal love with all people and ultimately with every dimension of our worldly existence – for example, economic, scientific, aesthetic and political. Above all it is in its political life that the spiritual community gives most effective external witness to the liberating consciousness which animates it. 'The true reconciliation whereby the Divine realizes itself in the region of reality is found in moral and legal life in the State.'[46]

Hegel attaches great importance to this close relation between the spiritual liberation attained through true religion and the attainment of genuine socio-political emancipation. 'There is but one conception of freedom in religion and the State. This one conception is man's highest possession, and it is realized by man. A nation which has a false or bad conception of God, has also a bad State, bad government, bad laws.'[47]

Let us return to the topic of the relationship between religion and philosophy and to the issue of whether, for Hegel, philosophy merely perfects or radically transforms religion. We have seen how, for him, although Christianity is the liberating definitive religious embodiment of the true relation of finite and infinite, nevertheless this relationship finds fully adequate expression only in its appropriate philosophical formulation. Moreover, this philosophy is not merely an attempt to develop from within an encompassing Christian faith its inherent rationality. It is not simply a Christian philosophy, such as Gilson conceived it, that is, one which considers, from within the perspective of revelation, those truths revealed by God which can be known and confirmed by natural reason itself.[48] Although he emphasizes the intimate relationship between the truth of Christianity and the truth of his philosophy of spirit, and even acknowledges that the Christian religion is a necessary anticipation of his philosophy, in the final analysis it is in virtue of the truth of the latter that the former is judged to be true. The truth of Christianity as absolute religion rests upon the identity of its content, portrayed in the inferior representational form of contingent historical facts and events, with the content of philosophy of spirit. In the philosophy of spirit, this content is articulated in its appropriate form of rational necessity. In philosophy, we rise above the essentially receptive and representational form of religious faith to the absolute or divine viewpoint of speculative thought which expresses the rational necessity of the whole process of spirit's self-othering and self-reconciliation. From this divine perspective of philosophical thought, the life of religious faith is surpassed and comprehended as the penultimate stage in the accomplishment of divine self-knowledge.

Admittedly the generality of mankind may never rise above a religious appreciation of the truth about spirit as absolute reconciliation. They may experience a satisfaction in their simple religious faith which is adequate to their commonsense level of consciousness. This religious fulfilment is a valid human experience and by no means to be despised. (Recall Aquinas's comparable insistence that it is appropriate that even truths accessible to the philosophical reflection of a few, should be revealed in faith because they are required by all for salvation.) However, for Hegel, precisely because man is a thinking being he will not be fully liberated until through philosophical reflection he witnesses to spirit in the higher form of philosophy which discloses the rational necessity of the whole reconciling movement of the life of spirit. Only in this form is the fully adequate self-consciousness of spirit attained. 'In faith the true content is certainly already found, but there is still wanting to it the form of thought. All forms, such as we have already dealt with, feeling, popular ideas and such like, may certainly have the form of truth but they themselves are not the true form which makes the true content necessary. Thought is the absolute judge before which the content must verify and attest its claim.[49]

The mainspring of this itinerary of reconciliation, progressing as it does through religion to philosophy, is its transformation of the conceptions of both God and man within the more comprehensive notion of absolute spirit. God is now conceived as comprising finitude in himself as a necessary phase of his auto-constitution as spirit. Correlatively, man is no longer conceived as a contingent reality gratuitously 'divinized' by divine adoption but rather as 'divine' in his own right as a necessary feature of the development of the life of absolute spirit. The relationship between man and God is reciprocal, necessary not contingent, not one grounded in free creation but rather one of mutual implication. Traditional monotheism, according to which God utterly transcends the finite order, is itself transcended in this new encompassing philosophy of spirit. In this context, religion is envisaged not only as an activity of man but also as an activity of God himself, operating through finite religious phenomena, to achieve concrete awareness of himself. This awareness in its most appropriate form is accomplished by the elevation of religion to philosophy.

Remarks

There are various points on which one might take issue with this crucial Hegelian claim that philosophy presents in the superior form of rational necessity the same content as that expressed in religious affirmations. For example, one might argue that the project of expressing the content of Christianity in the form of rational necessity inevitably involves a distortion of the content itself. For the content of Christian revelation describes a sacred history of the free and unnecessitated communication of God with man which resists Hegel's claim that 'the true Christian content of faith is to be justified by philosophy, not by history'.[50]

The religious representation of particular historical events, as gifts of divine love arising solely from God's sovereign freedom, attributes to these events as such a significance which is irreducible to philosophical reformulation in terms of strict rational necessitation.[51] Hegel's attempt to effect such a reformulation can be seen as undermining the true religious representation of the Christian God by subordinating it to an ideal of philosophical explanation which is incompatible with the explicit content of this religious representation itself.

The content of Christian religious representation portrays humanity as basically receptive of the divine initiative of God's free and 'eventful' gift of salvation. Hegel's philosophy of spirit claims to transcend this human perspective on the finite-infinite relationship and to comprehend the relationship from a divine viewpoint through an adequate speculative re-enactment of it. However, if as he maintains, this divine viewpoint is accessible to man and if the divine self-knowledge which it involves is realized only through human philosophical consciousness, then the Christian religion is shown to be falsified in its content no less than in its form. For an essential feature of the content which is disclosed in Christian religious representation is that the whole finite order, in its entire reality, is a created order of existence, asymmetrically related to an ontologically independent divine creator by whom it has been divinely willed and personally 'intended' into existence.

It is not enough, from a religious standpoint, to claim that the finite order may be understood to be such that it can, in the person of man, intend a Trinitarian ideal of rationality. The finite order must itself be understood as freely intended by an actual divine Trinity. In other words, part of what the Christian religion as such affirms is the absolute ontological priority of God as an act of actually intending freedom rather than as an Hegelian secular Trinitarian ideal of rationality, which is capable of being intended through the philosophical resolve which wills pure thought. Hence, the Christian believer can argue that in Hegel's system the central content of religion has been either discredited or misrepresented in its philosophical reformulation and not, as Hegel would wish to maintain, merely purified.

The goal envisaged in Christian religious consciousness is human salvation through worship, service and love of a transcendent but personal God. It differs entirely from the teleology of a philosophy which envisages the concrete accomplishment, through rational human resolve, of a secular Trinitarian ideal of absolute spirit. As Paul Ricoeur remarked: 'A teleology carried out in Hegelian style does not have as eschaton, as final term, the sacred delivered in myth, cult, belief. Of itself what this teleology envisions is absolute knowing not faith; and absolute knowing bespeaks not transcendence, only the subsumption of all transcendence in a thoroughly mediated self-knowledge.'[52]

This 'subsumption of all transcendence in a thoroughly mediated self-knowledge' is further illustrated by the difference between the understanding of the relationship between God and man affirmed in Christian religion through divine revelation and its theological elaboration on the one hand and the new understanding of this relationship advanced by Hegel's philosophy of spirit on the other. Both approaches claim to provide a deeper understanding of the relationship than that which we might attain simply by way of our natural understanding. From Christian Revelation and its theological elaboration we learn that not simply are we contingent finite beings created freely by God but are also elevated freely by his love to partake of his divine life. For Hegel also we come to a deeper consciousness of our intimate relationship and ultimate identity with God's self-awareness than that afforded by the oppositional operation of our everyday natural way of understanding. For Christian religion, the new understanding is attained through faith in a supernatural divine revelation whose theological import exceeds any knowledge we might naturally or philosophically attain. However, for Hegel the new understanding of our divinity is attained only by going beyond religion and theology, through the resolve which wills pure thought, to a pure philosophy of spirit which adamantly rejects all unresolved duality and any a priori limitation of human reason.

In more general terms, it can be argued that Hegel's conception of philosophy, as ultimate wisdom which adequately comprehends the complete rational necessity of an all-embracing absolute spirit, can sustain its affirmation of God and religion only in virtue of a systematic ambiguity. For, as we have indicated, identifying properties of the God of monotheist religion such as 'absolute transcendence', 'unconstrained freedom', 'immutable infinite perfection' are used in such a radically transformed sense to describe the nature of absolute spirit that the continued use of the term 'God' in this context is perhaps more misleading than illuminating.

Undoubtedly, his remarkable system represents an intellectual tour de force. It can be seen as a model of what a system of philosophy would be like if one accepts the strict equivalence of human rationality and reality; that the real is the rational and the rational the real; that ontological asymmetry can be reinterpreted as logical co-relativity; that metaphysical causality can be reinterpreted as logical implication; that all external relations and distinctions can be internalized and unified; and that it is contradictory to speak of any intrinsic limitation of human reason.

Even those who, for reasons such as I have indicated, would not accept the Hegelian synthesis have been compelled by its challenging reformulation of traditional theological doctrine to reach beyond the formality of well-worn definitions to a keener appreciation of their inadequacy as expressions of the mystery which they seek to signify. Hegel's philosophy has unquestionably been a challenge to theological complacency and a powerful stimulus to refinement and renewal of theological understanding. One need only mention, as examples of such theological renewal in the light of the Hegelian challenge, the work of theologians such as Kierkegaard and Barth.

Paradoxically, however, and contrary to its author's intention, the Hegelian philosophical system has also been an influential source of various forms of contemporary atheism. Its attempt to reconcile the coexistence of finite and infinite in terms of an account of humanity as the necessary vehicle for God or absolute spirit to achieve concrete self-awareness enabled Feuerbach, and more effectively Marx, to reverse the perspective. They account for the affirmation of God as an expression of an alienated human nature which must be critically re-appropriated by exclusively human means. Here the coexistence of finite and infinite is reconciled, one might say, not vertically but horizontally in terms of the relationship between the individual person and her species-being. A comparable demythologization of the Hegelian absolute spirit is proposed in the existentialism of philosophers such as Sartre and Merleau-Ponty which repudiates, in the interest of individual human freedom, any idea of an absolute. Thus Merleau-Ponty remarks: 'The metaphysical and moral consciousness perishes at the touch of the absolute.'[53]

These various reactions to Hegel's remarkable philosophical achievement are not our immediate concern. What interests us here is its attempt to reconcile in a higher unified system the various kinds of philosophical and theological approaches to God which we have discussed in the previous chapters. Hegel does not approach the question of God simply phenomenologically from the perspective of human consciousness; nor simply metaphysically from the perspective of being; nor simply theologically from the perspective of divine revelation. Rather he seeks to integrate all three approaches into a new and superior one governed by the animating master concept of spirit understood as an active and all-embracing process of positing, differentiating and reconciling. In this new philosophy of spirit, all difference of approach, all distinctions of form and content, all alienation and opposition are recognized, acknowledged and reconciled in a concrete and unified consciousness which can be referred to truly and indifferently either as man's consciousness of God or God's consciousness of himself.

However, although the various approaches discussed earlier may thus be combined by Hegel in a higher philosophical unity, the objection remains that the unification is an artificial one which fails to respect the integrity of the different approaches thus unified. In particular, in order to be accommodated within the unified account, they are obliged to submit to a very different conception of God to that which their distinctive approaches proclaim. Thus the transcendence and immutable perfection which are defining characteristics of the God of monotheistic religions cannot readily be reconciled with a God who can become God only through the mediation of human consciousness.

Likewise, the God of revelation of whom theology speaks – and who discloses, as a gift exceeding all natural capacity and discovery, the gracious divinization of humanity – is difficult to reconcile with the claim that all eventful theological truth must be transformed into the form of rational necessity fully accessible to a human reason which has no limit.

Such misgivings about the outcome of the remarkable Hegelian enterprise incline us to reconsider the various approaches to God which we have previously outlined. We are prompted to explore whether a more modest account of the relationship between them is appropriate. Instead of seeking to integrate them into an altogether different and superior approach, namely the philosophy of absolute spirit, we might consider: What are their particular individual merits? Is one or some combination of them more satisfactory than others? Are they mutually exclusive or complementary and, if complementary, in what sense? These are issues which we shall address in the following chapters in an attempt to throw further light on the appraisal of the various approaches to God which we have discussed earlier in this work and bearing in mind our misgivings about the heroic Hegelian attempt to reconcile them in a higher unified system, namely, the philosophy of spirit.

Comparisons

Introduction

Having considered both the attraction and the hazards of Hegel's endeavour to provide an adequate, comprehensive and unified speculative approach to God, let us return to a fuller consideration of the various approaches which we have discussed earlier. Each of the approaches to God outlined in the first three chapters has its own particular attractions and its own particular difficulties. Let us re-examine them in the light of these considerations. I will discuss how they might be compared one with another in a way which may help to resolve or at least counteract their inherent difficulties and provide a broader more complementary account of their common objective, that is, to articulate the most satisfactory, or perhaps the least unsatisfactory, reflective approach to God. In this chapter, I will concentrate mainly on a comparison of the *philosophical* approaches we have considered, namely, the phenomenological and the metaphysical. In the next chapter, I will see how these interrelated approaches bear upon the *theological* approach which was considered in Chapter 3.

Phenomenology versus metaphysics

The great attraction, and indeed the great merit, of a phenomenological approach to God is that its primary object of attention is not some abstract impersonal notion of God but rather the God envisaged in the given phenomena of concrete religious experience. These experienced phenomena span a wide range of emotions, feelings and encounters. For example, they encompass emotions of awe, fear, amazement, existential anxiety. They encompass profound feelings of contingency and dependence, of ultimate concern, of dread, of confidence, of spiritual exaltation, of deliverance. They include intimations of transcendence, for example, in amazement or delight at the sublimity of nature; in the aesthetic impact of a great work of art; in acknowledging the absolute moral invocation of the vulnerable neighbour; in the conviction that somehow love triumphs over the impersonality of circumstance – even of death; in the sentiment of a consoling 'presence' of God in response to prayerful dispositions of need, dereliction, repentance, awe or adoration.

Such phenomena, associated with our sense of God, are considered, non-judgementally, by phenomenology precisely as they give themselves to human consciousness. They are not viewed reductively as happens in dismissive sociological, Marxist or psychoanalytical critiques.[1] They are perceptively described and comprehended as phenomena, affecting a naturally experienced religious disposition, which are worthy of consideration precisely as they give and show themselves to consciousness.

This domain of 'natural', irreducible sui generis, religious phenomena is dramatically surpassed by the domain of 'supernatural' phenomena accessible to, and affirmed in, the believer's act of faith and its theological elaboration.

These latter, although surpassing any phenomena which might be envisaged as commensurate with a natural religious awareness, are likewise accessible phenomenologically inasmuch and to the extent that they give themselves to and engage the believer's consciousness. Moreover, these phenomena are not just the ecstatic disclosures attained by the contemplative mystic. They include the lived beliefs of ordinary Christians, for example, their lived convictions about the Trinity, the Incarnation, the Sacramental Church and about their own divinization and supernatural goal.

Phenomenological description as such does not disclose distinctive prefiguration or proof of the objective truth of these faithfully held convictions. It describes them as they are given to religious belief, a belief affirmed as a matter of faith in the actuality of an historical Revelation. It is theology as the elaboration of this faith in an historical Revelation which elucidates and confirms it. Phenomenology is limited to disclosing the possibility, or non-impossibility, of such Revelation and, without any commitment to its objective actuality, to describing how it manifests itself as assured actuality to a believer's consciousness – to the eye of faith!

Undoubtedly the phenomenological approach has the great advantage of addressing the question of God from the 'first-person' perspective in which this question impinges most directly and intimately on human consciousness. It addresses the question of God inasmuch as he is an explicitly self-involving issue for any person's consciousness in her existential enquiry concerning her ultimate meaning and value. It provides illuminating description of an individual's religious route-finding quests through various compounds of intransigence and of how these quests are consciously resolved, most notably through belief in divine Revelation, by phenomena which are incommensurate with and transcend any natural expectation. Thus John

Caputo remarks: 'To speak in strictly phenomenological terms, the things that are not under our control, where we have run up against the limits of our powers, are the raw materials of religion, the stuff of which it is made, the occasion on which the name of God makes its entry.'[2]

This self-involving, first-person, perspective of phenomenology of religion endows this approach to God with a greater personal significance and existential immediacy than the more abstract approach of traditional metaphysics. The God attained in this perspective is a God-for-man, God inasmuch as he gives himself as illuminating the human condition. Caputo again: '*The* experience of God always comes down to *our* experience, and our experience is of a God of *experience*, a God who lends himself to experience.'[3]

Indeed a defining feature of this approach is its rigorous rejection of a metaphysical approach to God and of whatever is involved in any such approach whether realist or idealist. It rejects the 'supreme being' or 'first cause' of Aquinas, the 'sufficient reason' of Leibniz, the 'absolute spirit' of Hegel and even the 'transcendental subject' of Husserl's phenomenology from which it draws so much of its inspiration.

Central to this rejection of metaphysics is, as we have seen, the following claim:

> The phenomenological description of a given act and in particular the specification of its intentional content, must not rely upon the correctness of any *existence assumption* concerning the object(s) (if any) the respective act is about. Thus the *epoche* has us focus on those aspects of intentional acts and their contents that do not depend on the existence of the represented object out there in the extra-mental world.[4]

This implies that in the phenomenological approach there is no claim about God as he exists independently of our consciousness of him as creator, saviour, final end, etc. Phenomenologically, God may be described as given experientially as though existing in this way – but the hypothetical 'as though' never achieves, in phenomenology, the detached impersonal affirmation that this is how things are irrespective of our conscious awareness. He is affirmed only inasmuch as he is somehow given in terms of, and in relationship to, human religious experience. The move to an affirmation of trans-phenomenal actual existence requires a gear shift from phenomenology to theology.[5]

The human intimacy of the phenomenological approach to God is thus achieved at the expense of any ontological conclusion or presupposition about his existence as independent of its givenness in human consciousness. Of course the believer in her spontaneous attitude of belief and in her theological reflection on this belief is assured through her faith that God's reality is independent of her human consciousness of it. And even in the phenomenological description of the God of Christian Revelation as affirmed in faith he is described as disclosed to religious belief as though truly obtaining independently of this belief.

However, insofar as phenomenology itself is concerned, the correctness of this *existence assumption* is bracketed or suspended. The phenomenologist seeks to re-enact, sympathetically and imaginatively, in an ontologically neutralized manner, the faith-inspired convictions of the believer. In other words, for phenomenology as a *philosophical* approach to God, as distinct from a *theological* instrument, the *existence assumption*, although a feature of its description of religious belief in God, is understood phenomenologically as an assumption relative to and not independent of this religious experience. In the phenomenological account of the existence assumptions of religious experience, they are not understood as free-standing ontological affirmations. Rather they are understood phenomenologically as phenomena given immanently as appearing to human consciousness. They are affirmations which are always *quoad nos*, incapable, phenomenologically, of impersonal confirmation or reformulation as affirmations about what obtains independently *in se*. (To this the phenomenologist might reply that she declines this opposition between *quoad nos* and *quoad se*. She might argue that it is precisely the sort of opposition which can be defended only by espousing the sort of metaphysical perspective which it is a declared aim of phenomenology to call in question.)

This phenomenological approach to God, which relates the issue so effectively to human experience, discloses aspects of what an affirmation of God involves which are not otherwise accessible. It shows that such an affirmation as a human achievement relates inextricably in its meaning to the receptivity of first-person conscious experience. It reveals insights into aspects of the religious relationship as a cognitional bond which encompasses a range of experiences of the 'givenness' of God that are inexpressible in objective impersonal ontological terms about the relationship of a creature to her creator. Thus John Caputo remarks: 'With the withering away of metaphysics, which was given ample time to prove its worth and whose only result was an arid and reifying rationality that turned the world and human life into objects for instrumental reason, we are free to return to the nourishment of the old religious narratives.'[6]

However, as was indicated in Chapter 1, in the opinion of some philosophers this phenomenological approach to God as he is for human consciousness poses difficulties for an affirmation of his unqualified and unconditional transcendence. The basic objection is that by linking the affirmation of God so intimately to human experience, and concomitantly excluding as deceptive onto-theology all *metaphysical argument* about what exists beyond experience, the affirmation of God's absolute transcendence is thereby likewise precluded. Recall Jeffrey Kosky's remark: 'Phenomenality could be defined broadly as the appearing that remains in and for consciousness when all ecstatic openness to transcendence has been shut down or closed by the reduction. It is, in short, the field of immanence.'[7] There is no presumption that behind the tapestry of experience there is an objective metaphysical scaffolding, no implication of unsupported metaphysical sky-hooks sustaining the unfolding experiential drama.

It has been objected that whatever transcendence might be affirmed in this context will always be only a relative transcendence, a transcendence relative to human subjectivity, a transcendence contained within the field of immanence. The immediate existential appeal of a phenomenologically described affirmation of God as essentially God-for-man is haunted by the misgiving that as such he may be *only* God-for-man. Indeed, as we noted, Richard Kearney explicitly asserts that 'God can be God only if we enable this to happen.'

This assertion is harmlessly acceptable if we mean simply that God can be an effective feature of our lived experience only if we do not turn a deaf ear to the role which he might play in our experience. But does an affirmation of God involve more than this? Certainly, as I indicated in Chapter 1, phenomenologists of religion such as Ricoeur, Levinas, Kearney and Marion are insistent that their affirmation of divine transcendence does indeed involve more than a transcendence intrinsically conditioned by the a priori capacities of human subjectivity. They insist that commitment to the phenomenological principle of immanence does not preclude, from within this commitment, an affirmation of genuine and unconstrained divine transcendence. Let us recall, in a little more detail, how this insistence plays out, particularly in the thought of the philosopher to whom I devoted most attention in that chapter, namely, Jean-Luc Marion.

The key to Marion's rejection of the objection that in phenomenology an affirmation of divine transcendence is compromised by its irreducible relationship to subjectivity is his innovative description of what this relationship between transcendence and subjectivity involves. This description is implicit in his account of how in our experience of a saturated phenomenon, unlike the situation with more mundane experiences, intuition surpasses and annuls the intentional capacities of ordinary human subjectivity. The very idea of human subjectivity is transformed.

This transformation is accomplished in and by the given experience of transcendence itself. The meaning of human subjectivity is comprehended now, not as that to which transcendence is relative as the irreducible subjective pole of every experience, but as that which is essentially relative to the givenness of transcendence. In a dramatic claim, countering the prevailing phenomenological orthodoxy, Marion claims that in the saturated phenomenon of transcendence a new dimension of subjectivity is established, a 'given-to' subjectivity wholly relative to the bedazzling givenness of the experience of transcendence and therefore not imposing any a priori metaphysical constraints upon it. For him, as Kosky remarks, the primacy of the *ego's* intentional activity is replaced by 'a reversed intentionality where the *ego* finds itself subject *to* not the subject *of* a gaze (the givenness of saturated phenomena in Marion). The I no longer precedes the phenomena that it constitutes, but is instead called into being or born as the one who receives or suffers this intentionality.'[8]

This dramatic reversal of role for human subjectivity is verified both phenomenologically and theologically. The reversal is verified phenomenologically by the multiple evidence of saturated phenomena, the intuited givenness of which utterly exceeds the constitutive capacity of the conscious subject. It is verified theologically by theological thinking like that of Karl Barth which relies exclusively on God's unconditional self-revelation, a Revelation in no way metaphysically prefigured or anticipated, as is the case with Karl Rahner, in an account of our existential openness to, and anticipation of, this Revelation.[9] In both cases there is a robust rejection of metaphysics and its presumed onto-theological constitution. As Thomas Carlson remarks in his perceptive introduction to his translation of Marion's *The Idol and Distance*: 'Marion's theology and phenomenology alike will attack above all the characteristically metaphysical subjection of the absolute or unconditional – be it the Christian God specifically or the saturated phenomenon more broadly – to the preconditions and limits of human thought and language.'[10] The guiding idea in both cases is to liberate the approach to God from the idolatrous metaphysical tendency to limit an account of him to a concept of our own making such as 'supreme being', 'first cause' or 'sufficient reason'. Such liberation enables us to interpret the contemporary affirmation of the death of God, not as atheism, but as a rejection of the God of metaphysics. 'In taking its distance from all metaphysics, it therefore allows the emergence of a God who is free from onto-theo-logy; in short the "death of God" immediately implies the death of "the death of God".'[11] It makes way for an authentic reception of God's self-revelation as phenomenal visibility of the invisible, a negative experience of God as distant from any presumed human condition for experience of the divine, an experience of God as dwelling in inaccessible light. As Marion's theology surpasses metaphysics by freeing God's self-revelation from any limiting concept that seeks to subordinate it to the idolatrous conditions of thought so also his phenomenology surpasses metaphysics by liberating the phenomenon's self manifestation from any similar a priori conditions whether those of a thinking subject or a metaphysical God.[12]

However, the elimination of metaphysics from both disciplines raises some concern. The priority of 'the given' (*donation*) over the given-to (*adonne*) nevertheless requires the latter, however passively understood, in order for 'the given' to show itself as phenomenon. This 'given-to' is described as that which not only receives the given and enables it to show itself but also as that which *receives itself* from this given which it enables to show itself. This enabling given-to which converts what gives itself into what shows itself comes into play as a choice to move from pre-phenomenological obscurity to the light of phenomenal unconditional givenness – a choice which is itself a function or gift of the givenness it enables to show itself. 'Nothing of what gives itself can show itself except to *adonne* and through it. Not through constitution, anticipatory resoluteness, or exposure to the Other, but by the will to indeed see, originally derived from givenness itself.'[13] In this way, the Husserlian constituting and conditioning subject, the subject of everyday language and consciousness, is surpassed by a, logically antecedent but temporally subsequent, new level of subjectivity, a given-to, wholly relative to the givenness from which it derives. 'What phenomenology opposes to revelation – the *I* as origin – is perhaps not phenomenologically legitimate. Who is the *I*? is the *I* original or derived? . . . Far from the *I* restricting the possibility of a revelation phenomenologically, would not one have to venture that maybe the *I* can only attain its proper phenomenological possibility from a givenness that cannot be constituted, cannot be objectified and is prior to it – maybe even from a revelation?'[14]

But since this given-to human subject, which is required for the given to show itself, is a finite subject it can receive and show the given *as it gives itself* only in a limited manner in accordance with its own intrinsic finitude. Hence, the issue to which we have referred in Chapter 1 presents itself anew: 'Is not any transcendence thus disclosed, including a disclosure of divine transcendence, inextricably relative to the finitude of the given-to which witnesses to it – even if this given-to is understood as arising from what is given?'

According to Marion the givenness which discloses itself phenomenally to a witness as transcendent perfection does so indeed as given immanently to consciousness but appears therein as distant, withdrawn or absent from what we can effectively conceive. It is a givenness which shows itself as a transcendence revealed within immanence, showing itself therein as surpassing the constitutive capacity of thought. It is 'discovered as the instance par excellence of immanence'.[15]

In this account, all givenness and transcendence, indeed all religious phenomena, are contained within the sphere of immanence, to the exclusion of any ontological realism and metaphysical causality. 'All these lived experiences of consciousness would hence appear as phenomena by full right, at least to the extent that they are given to consciousness. When an allegedly adequate explanation is missing for them, that is to say, in fact their cause or sufficient reason, their legitimacy as phenomena is not thereby put into question, but only their objectivity beyond the limits of immanence.'[16] From this, it would appear that within phenomenology the domain of such phenomena, and in particular the bedazzling experience of God, can be said to be subjectively certain but cannot be said to disclose what is objectively true in the sense of existing as ontologically independent of our awareness.

But can this immanent bedazzling or bemusing experience of divine transcendence as awareness of that which is utterly distant and withdrawn from the range of conceptual comprehension be taken as a dependable revelation, even if only 'through a glass darkly', of God? Or instead of peering more closely at this allegedly unconditioned experience of an immanent transcendence, of a visible invisible, might it not be more appropriate to recognize this experience as a dependent cipher of an ontologically independent transcendent God, to whom one must argue metaphysically from the experienced cipher? In the final analysis, is the reliable affirmation of God's unconditional transcendence established phenomenologically by our intuitive immanent experience of it as absent and withdrawn, or must this experience itself be confirmed as a reliable cipher of this transcendence by having its implicit significance deciphered through a metaphysically grounded causal argument?[17]

It would seem that this is a question which cannot be resolved phenomenologically not least because there are unresolved issues about the nature and ontological significance of the allegedly absolute pre-phenomenological value of givenness in virtue of which, through a pre-phenomenological choice which is itself a function of this givenness, every phenomenon obtains. This problematic pre-phenomenological givenness is described enigmatically by Marion as an insistent power that 'makes the gift decide *itself* as gift through the twofold consent of the givee and the giver, less actors of the gift than acted by givenness'.[18]

From this phenomenological viewpoint, God and the self appear to obtain as reciprocal features of an internal relation – understood as a relation essential to and defining of its bearers – rather than as ontologically distinct substances one of which is wholly dependent for its existence upon the radically independent existence of the other. The concept of relation would appear to replace that of substance as the basic philosophical category. From this perspective, God and the self appear as phenomenological, not ontological, co-relative principles of conscious experience. Ontological considerations are transcended or absorbed. As Levinas perceptively observes: 'When Husserl denies that one can say that consciousness exists first of all and thereafter tends towards its object – he asserts, in reality, that the very *existing* of consciousness resides in thinking . . . He is concerned to deny that in the ontological structure of consciousness there is any reference to a foundation, to any nucleus which would serve as a scaffolding for intention; it is a matter of not thinking of consciousness as a substantive.'[19]

The issues involved here certainly appear to require meta-phenomenological consideration and analysis rather than simply phenomenological allusion. But it is precisely such consideration which is precluded by the perspective of immanence that the phenomenological reduction establishes. Perhaps this meta-phenomenological consideration can be more effectively pursued from the metaphysical perspective of ontological realism which is put out of play by a phenomenological approach to God?

Metaphysics versus phenomenology

Whereas the phenomenological approach to God highlights phenomena as given immanently to our conscious subjectivity, metaphysical realism emphasizes the objective consideration of beings as ontologically independent – as existing independently of our consciousness of them. This distinction between the viewpoint of subjectivity and an objective viewpoint, between an internal and an external standpoint, is not an absolute dichotomy. Although it emphasizes a very real difference, it is more a matter of comparative difference on a spectrum.

The internal phenomenological standpoint of subjectivity is not a purely subjective viewpoint. It aspires to intersubjective accord about phenomena and the discernment by imaginative variation of their essential meanings in the pure immanence of consciousness.

The external objective standpoint can never wholly absorb or encompass our initial subjectivity or personal perspective which it seeks to transcend. All our knowledge claims, including our claim to know how things are other than simply as objects of our consciousness, are abstractive human products or achievements as well as discoveries. Our scientific quest for objectivity, however successful, never entirely absorbs or eliminates the 'first-person' perspective from which it originates. As Thomas Nagel remarked, 'Realism underlies the claims of objectivity and detachment, but it supports them only up to a point'.[20] Moreover, metaphysical enquiry has an inherently existential or personal dimension inasmuch as it seeks to articulate the ultimate meaning and value not just of reality in general but of human existence in particular. Likewise any metaphysical affirmation of God as creator is not just like the impersonal affirmation of a natural cause. It has inescapable self-involving implications.

Nevertheless, it is undoubtedly true that a metaphysical approach to God, such as that of Aquinas, unfolds as an objective enquiry into the structure and implications of being itself in general. We intuit extra-mental being and consciously affirm it as that which exists independently of our consciousness of it. The fruit of this primary intuition is a pre-philosophical concept or apprehension of being which finds expression in the basic existential judgement 'this exists'. It signifies the transcendental unity and absolute character of being, its status as that which actually exists independently of our consciousness of it and of which everything we progressively experience and comprehend is a determination. Consciousness finds itself, in Seamus Heaney's felicitous phrase, 'under the gravitational pull of the actual', by which its finite achievement is measured rather than that of which it is the measure. This is the realist domain of the 'natural attitude', the cradle of metaphysics, from which phenomenology distances itself by way of *epoche* and phenomenological reduction.

The subsequent properly metaphysical analysis of the experienced diversity, analogical character, interrelationships and causal dependencies of the beings of our experience constitutes the context of the indirect metaphysical approach to the existence of God. It is an approach which is both realist and rationalist. It is realist in claiming that a world exists independently of our intentional representations of it. It is rationalist in its conviction that our abstractive representations and arguments can, in however limited and perspectival a manner, achieve objective truth about this order of finite beings as existing in itself independently of our consciousness of it.

In its arguments for the existence of God, this metaphysical approach certainly appeals to the, phenomenologically impugned, 'principle of causation' in its effort to establish the existence of God as transcendent creator of the order of finite beings. However, as we have indicated in Chapter 2, it does not, at least in the case of Aquinas, invoke the 'principle of sufficient reason' attributed to Leibniz, which Marion sees as integral to metaphysical arguments about God.

The principle of causation is important to a metaphysical argument because, since we can have no a priori knowledge of God, the question of his existence must be approached a posteriori through reflection on what is given to our experience. We raise the hypothesis of his existence, by way of nominal definition of him, as the transcendent cause of the given order of finite being. Metaphysical reflection seeks by way of indirect reasoning to establish that an affirmation of his existence as the infinite creator of the universe is a necessary consequence of the metaphysical analysis of the finite beings of which we have experience.

The argument proceeds by seeking to show that this order of finite beings, metaphysically conceived, is contradictory and impossible unless understood as radically dependent for its existence upon a transcendent 'infinite cause'.

The metaphysical argument for God as transcendent first cause of finite being, and the consequent identifying description of him as *Esse Subsistens*, infinite pure act of existence, enables further metaphysical description of the divine perfection. It enables description of him as the paradigm of all perfections such as knowledge and freedom, truth and goodness, – the absence of which would signify a limitation or lack. Further, it enables an account of various features of the basic asymmetrical relationship of creation which obtains between creatures and God.

In a word, the metaphysical approach to God proposes argued responses to the three main kinds of question which arise in a discussion about God: the question of the *existence* of God, the question of the *nature* of God and the question of the *coexistence* of creatures and God. It commends itself as an objective, largely impersonal approach which can engage rational debate between believers of different shades and degrees of religious conviction or indeed of none at all.

We have reached the appropriate point for a more detailed discussion of the relationship between a phenomenological and a metaphysical approach to God. We have already noted that at first sight they appear mutually exclusive. In final analysis is this all there is to be said?

The metaphysical approach is based upon an unequivocal affirmation of being as existing independently of our consciousness of it. It affirms the act of existence as the fundamental perfection in virtue of which all other determinate perfections obtain. In its approach to God, it recognizes the importance of an argued affirmation of him as creator exercising a unique form of causation. Its fundamental description of God is in terms of his infinite perfection of existence which we realize utterly exceeds our own understanding of being as intrinsically finite.

The phenomenological approach to God, at least as defended by Marion, its most influential contemporary exponent, is an approach to 'God without Being'. It suspends or brackets consideration of the pre-philosophical affirmation of being as transcending our consciousness of it which is characteristic of our natural attitude. It defines itself in opposition to a metaphysical approach to God which it considers idolatrous. In particular it is critical of any metaphysical appeal to causation which it considers incompatible with its own affirmation of the self-sufficient givenness of phenomena.

Likewise in some of its formulations, for example that of John Caputo, its commitment to the principle of non-contradiction is somewhat selective. He is concerned to defend the possibility of the impossible. For, he maintains, we experience God, and can describe him phenomenologically, in our experience of the impossible. 'For God is given in the experience of the impossible.'[21] An existential experience of 'the impossible' is a positively possible one unlike the merely negative idea of logical contradiction which is characteristic of the onto-theology and which he rejects. 'But by "the impossible", I hasten to add, I do not mean a simple contradiction, the simple *logical* negation of the possible, like (*p* and not *p*), which is a cornerstone of the old onto-theology . . . I am resisting all *a priori* logical and onto-theological constraints about the possible and the impossible in order to work my way back into the texture of the phenomenological structure of experience.'[22]

Phenomenology and metaphysics

These contrasting accounts of a phenomenological and a metaphysical approach to God are certainly very different. Nevertheless it is worth considering further whether they are as radically mutually exclusive as some of their respective proponents maintain, or whether perhaps they are in some important respects similar and even complementary.

One such consideration is the comparison between a phenomenological account of the givenness of phenomena, particularly of saturated phenomena, and a realist metaphysics of the intuition of being, which describes it as an awareness of being as given asymmetrically to consciousness; given as transcending and remaining ontologically independent of this dependent consciousness. A comparison of the 'being-given' of phenomenology with the 'given-being' of metaphysics may indicate the sort of complementarity which is, perhaps, involved.

Marion's elucidation of the fundamental principle of phenomenology – that everything originarily offered in intuition be accepted as it presents itself – enables him to develop his distinctive phenomenology of givenness. This phenomenology undermines the primacy of the Husserlian constituting or transcendental subject and its implicit metaphysical idealism. In this repudiation of metaphysical idealism, metaphysical realism can find common cause with Marion's phenomenology.

However, although he thus repudiates the ego as irreducibly constitutive of all phenomena, particularly of saturated phenomena, and argues that the reverse is the case – the *I* becomes constituted and experiences itself as a *me* 'deprived of the duties of constitution' – he, nevertheless, is equally dismissive of metaphysical realism. This he sees as involving a combination of epistemological naiveté and a complicated ontological baggage of substances and causes, to 'account for' the phenomena of consciousness.

It would be difficult to deny that an account of cognition provided in metaphysical realism, such as that advanced by Aquinas, involves rather technical appeal to the causal influence of extra-mental substances or beings upon cognitive subjects or beings. Moreover, the ability of these subjects to attain knowledge is described as dependent upon ontological cognitive powers and dispositions which characterize the substantial form or distinctive nature of the knower, that is, which expresses what it takes for it to exist as the sort of cognitive subject or substance it is.

Such an account is more an ontology of knowledge than an epistemology in the post-Cartesian sense. It accepts that our knowing is an immanent activity which originates and terminates *within* the conscious substance or agent itself but which attains an object of knowledge that is *external* to and transcends asymmetrically this cognitive subject or substance. It seeks to provide an account of how this can be so, of this mystery of consciousness as ontological immanence and intentional transcendence.[23] It does so through its metaphysical account of the analogical natures, dispositions, powers and operations of the distinct finite beings or substances, the knower and the known, which enable a realist interpretation of knowledge as intentional awareness of that which exists independently of it. Metaphysical realism maintains in its account of knowledge that although it undoubtedly involves such ontological mediation in terms of faculties, activities, etc. of the knower, there is no mediation at the level of consciousness which attains immediate awareness of mind-independent reality. It is 'an internal act of awareness of a cognitive substance which attains a limited but effective intellectual grasp of the organized structure of the external world'.[24]

Such a realist description of the ontological conditions of cognition is an aspect of the broader account of our primary affirmation of being and the subsequent analysis of the metaphysical meaning of finite and infinite being that we outlined in the metaphysical approach to God in Chapter 2. It is more an external account of cognition in terms of being than an internal account of it in terms human consciousness which is characteristic of the explicitly non-metaphysical phenomenological approach to God such as that developed by Marion.

The phenomenological approach can argue that such a metaphysical account of knowledge in terms of an ontology of cognition is inappropriate and insufficiently critical to account for the indubitability of knowledge, particularly with regard to religious phenomena. The critical epistemological question, it claims, is prior to all metaphysics. The naïve natural attitude which underpins such metaphysical realism should, it is argued, be subjected to phenomenological reduction, a liberating 'leading back' to the bedrock of immanence.[25] However, if it is true to say that there are valuable insights available from a phenomenological approach which are absent from an exclusively metaphysical one, it can likewise be argued that a phenomenological approach has certain metaphysical implications which are not accessible within the limits of an exclusively phenomenological description.

The phenomenological approach is situated within the context of the relationship between subject and object. It views the subject in its relationship to objectivity and the object in its relationship to subjectivity. Being is 'reduced' or 'led back' to the co-relation between subject and object.

The metaphysical approach provides a complementary perspective to this by arguing for the ontological considerations which elude it. Reflecting upon the primary judgement of existence, it argues that subjectivity obtains to disclose objects not just as objects of consciousness but in their self-possessed being. As one commentator remarks: 'The necessary pre-condition of the relation between subject and object is the co-existence of the being which is subject with the being which is object.'[26] The affirmation of this precondition suggests that there is a certain complementarity between the 'being-given' (or 'givenness') of Marion's phenomenology and the 'given being' of Aquinas's metaphysics. The being of the phenomenon, it can be argued, is more than its undoubted 'being-given' to consciousness. It is also the trans-phenomenal ontological setting in and from which it is given to consciousness. The 'phenomenal' appearance of things is apprehended as the appearing or self-manifestation within experience of their extra-mental reality itself. The phenomenon is the manifestation of a structured reality which is accessible to us and partly understood by us. It can be argued (as I will in the concluding chapter) that the objective ontological affirmations of metaphysics provide the theoretical truth conditions of what is described and asserted phenomenologically as given to conscious subjectivity.

For Aquinas, as we have seen, being is not just an object of consciousness constituted by an empirical or transcendental ego. It is given to a cognitive subject capable of receiving or apprehending it as transcending that subject's consciousness of it. This, as I have mentioned, involves an invocation of a metaphysical account substance, cognitive capability, asymmetrical causality, etc., all of which are aspects of the transcendental perfection of being.

For Marion, givenness (*donation*) is accorded the absolute character which Aquinas accords to being. As one commentator perceptively observes: 'His *donation* is as comprehensive as *esse* is for St Thomas: the analogy of being is retrieved as an analogy of donation.'[27] Givenness gives and manifests itself as phenomena in our consciousness as subjects. But, our reality as subjects, as the given-to, is itself seen as a gift of givenness. It is as given-to by givenness that we exercise our role of phenomenalizing the manifestations of givenness.

Givenness or the fact of being-given immanently to consciousness plays a comparable role in Marion's phenomenology to that of the external givenness-of-being to consciousness in Aquinas's metaphysics. But their difference in consequences, when considered individually, is so significant as to seem irreconcilable unless some conception of their complementarity is seen to be required in virtue of their individual incompleteness and mutual implication which derive from their contrasting subjective and objective standpoints.

Whereas the transcendence of being vis-à-vis consciousness is affirmed by metaphysics, Marion tells us that the result of the phenomenological reduction is 'to suspend all transcendence precisely in order to measure what is thus given in immanence'.[28] He insists, however, that this does not preclude the phenomenological consideration of anything whatsoever which is genuinely given to consciousness including religious phenomena, and indeed the transcendent God himself – provided they are not considered in terms of the objectifying categories of metaphysical causes and principles and reasons. All the lived experiences given to consciousness appear autonomously as phenomena in their own right. Their 'legitimacy' is not put in question by the absence of an explanatory reason or cause but only their objectivity beyond the limits of consciousness.[29] 'To return to things themselves amounts to recognizing phenomena as themselves without submitting them to the (sufficient) condition of an anterior authority (such as thing in itself, cause, principle, etc.). In short it means liberating them from any prerequisite other than their simple givenness to which consciousness bears witness before any constitution.'[30]

One can appreciate that in accepting the option for immanence involved in the phenomenological reduction one is, by definition or choice as it were, excluding the appeal to ontological substances, principles and causal explanation characteristic of metaphysical argument. One finds oneself in a virtual domain of phenomenological experience where everything is more seamlessly and immediately interwoven in cognitional interconnections than is the case in the metaphysical domain of individual substances acting upon, and reacting to, each other in very real relationships of causal influence and dependence. One might say that one is operating in the more polite and civilized world of phenomenological implication than the blunter more untamed natural world of metaphysical causality!

Nevertheless, one wonders how Marion might respond to the claim that what he maintains, unless it is understood as only one perspective requiring a complementary metaphysical account, could be construed as a version of neo-Humean empiricism. For just as he describes phenomena in terms of a givenness which phenomenalizes itself immanently in a passively registered conscious experience so likewise Hume's account of our knowledge is based exclusively upon the passive awareness of data which are given in conscious experience. Like Marion, he draws the consequence that from this perspective there is no justified basis for an affirmation of the objective existence of either substances, causes or indeed, in his case, God – although he holds that we may continue to acknowledge them by way of natural belief or outlook.

It is useful to make this comparison if only to discern not simply the anti-metaphysical similarity of these two positions but also to highlight a basic difference. Whereas for Hume the given of experience is confined to the data of sense experience such as sounds, colours, tastes, etc. for Marion givenness has a much broader and deeper import. Indeed among its richest expressions, the saturated phenomena, religious phenomena such as beliefs, volitions of charity, visions, 'presences', etc. reappear in philosophy as lived experiences of consciousness, *facts* justified de jure since given *in fact*.[31] He claims that what is transcendent to direct experience is nevertheless manifested phenomenally in experience. 'The so-called religious lived experiences of consciousness give intuitively, but by indication, intentional objects that are directly invisible: religion becomes manifest and revelation phenomenal . . . phenomenology would be the method par excellence for the manifestation of the invisible through the phenomena that indicate it – hence also the method for theology.'[32]

For Marion, revealing the invisible through the phenomena that indicate it is strikingly accomplished in all instances of saturated phenomena and in instances of religious phenomena in particular. However, it is also a feature of his phenomenology more generally – according to which all givenness, initially invisible, becomes eventfully manifest in the phenomena which indicate it through the reciprocal phenomenalizing of the given and the given-to. 'Each phenomenalizes the other as the revealed, which is characterised by this essential phenomenal reciprocity, where seeing implies modification of the seer by the seen as much as of the seen by the seer.'[33]

The delicate task in all of this is for phenomenology to explain just how the given visible phenomena 'indicate' the invisible givenness of which they are said to be an indication. This requirement is particularly acute in the case of religious phenomena where the unconditional givenness which they allegedly indicate is God 'whom no man has seen'.

When this issue is addressed by metaphysics, the phenomena which are said to be visible indications of the invisible God can be described as finite ontological ciphers of the divine transcendence which are deciphered by indirect causal argument to show that the phenomena in question are impossible and even contradictory unless understood as dependent upon an infinite creator. Such metaphysical argument with its appeal to causation and metaphysical first principles is, as we have seen, precluded by a phenomenology of immanence such as that advocated by Marion. It must provide a different kind of account of how given religious phenomena indicate the invisible God.

For Marion, givenness, in a general sense, shows itself by projecting or crashing itself onto the screen of consciousness of the given-to who, in virtue of his resistance to this impact, transforms it into visibility. The extent of this phenomenalization depends upon the measure of the resistance of the given-to to the brute shock of the given. The resistance of the given-to does not actively fashion or determine what is given but rather forces the given to show itself to a greater or lesser extent. I have indicated in Chapter 1 how he illustrates this resistance by the suggestive example of what happens with electricity when the restriction of the movement of electrons in a circuit dissipates part of their energy as light or heat.[34]

Following from this general view about givenness, he elaborates his characteristic account of saturated phenomena whose visibility is occluded by the bedazzling intuition of their excess of givenness which overwhelms our attempts to conceptually contain them. There is no metaphysical subjection of their unconditionality to constitutive preconditions of human thought. Only the passive resistance of the finite given-to can partially transmute this excess into an indication or presentation of what is immeasurable.[35] In the context of these saturated phenomena, he situates the possibility of the being-given of 'God', both the 'God of the philosophers and the scholars' and the 'God' of Revelation, 'the God of Abraham, of Isaac, and of Jacob'.[36]

The phenomenological figure of 'God' as the being-given par excellence entails an absolute mode of presence which saturates all horizons. It offers a luminous shadow of 'God', not as metaphysical ground or cause but as being-given absolutely, more than any other being-given, a bedazzling being-given without horizon, limit or restriction. 'It voids the saturated horizons of any definable, visible thing. The absence or unknowability of "God" does not contradict givenness but on the contrary attests to the excellence of that givenness.'[37]

It would seem that Marion's strategy is to articulate a reflection on the essential nature of a saturated phenomenon as an appearance that is of itself, and starting from itself, and whose possibility is not subject to any prior determination. This reflection develops initially from our common intuitive experience of various instances of such phenomena, for example, the experience of an unpredictable historical event, or a painting which because of excess of intuition can be viewed but not constituted, or the dazzling invisible gaze of a loved one bearing down upon my own.[38] From this initial reflection upon our experience of saturated phenomena one can develop an account of the essential nature of such phenomena as inclusive of the *possibility* of a phenomenal experience of absolute and unconditioned givenness. By itself phenomenology can describe this saturated phenomenon of the being-given of 'God' as a genuine possibility: 'not only as a possibility as opposed to actuality but, above all, as a possibility of givenness itself.'[39] However, it only provides an account of the genuine representation or 'essence' of this saturated phenomenon of 'God', that is, just of its intrinsic possibility of givenness and not directly of its factual givenness. 'More than phenomenological analysis, the intuitive realization of that being-given requires the real experience of its givenness, which falls to revealed theology.'[40]

The phenomenological description of 'God' as the genuine *possibility* of unconditional and irreducible being-given par excellence, extrapolated from our varied experiences of saturated phenomena, could never anticipate that or how this possibility is concretely realized, as it has been historically, in the Christian Revelation of the absolute being-given of God as unconditional love. It is this acclamation of God as unrestricted self-giving love rather than as metaphysical *Esse Subsistens* which animates, in different ways, both Marion's theology and phenomenology.

He suggests that phenomenologically this *possibility* of 'God' described as the saturated phenomenon which indicates unconditional 'being-given' par excellence can be best pursued by thinking about that idea which, for Anselm, Descartes and indeed Levinas, was a most perspicuous example of a saturated phenomenon, namely, the incomprehensible, ego-relativizing, idea of infinity. For 'recognizing saturated phenomena comes down to thinking seriously "that than which none greater can be conceived [*aliquid quo majus cogitari nequit*]" – which means thinking it as a final possibility of phenomenology.'[41]

For Marion the saturating power of this idea of infinity is not that it provides an adequate concept of God from which we can deduce his existence. It is rather that it is an idea of him as one of whom we cannot have a proper concept since it is an idea of him as utterly transcending our capacity to conceptualize him. 'If we know that God is, we attain this knowledge by means of the concept that we have no concept of Him, rather than through the concept that we do.'[42]

Moreover, as Anselm appreciated, this idea of infinity is described more appropriately in terms of qualitative rather than quantitative greatness – a description whereby the rather indeterminate idea of 'that which is greater (*majus*) than anything conceivable' is determined by the idea of 'being better (*melius*) than anything conceivable'. That which is greatest is specified as the greatest good, summum is explicated as summum bonum.

The idea of infinity, of 'that which is greater (majus) than anything comprehensible' already indicates a transcendence which goes beyond the relative comparisons available within the transcendental limits of the power of thought. It indicates an absolute comparative or a superlative – that is, the greatest good (summum bonum).[43]

Moreover, for Marion, thinking thus, like Anselm, about 'God' as the incomprehensible supreme good necessitates that thought; not limit itself to its conceptual and representational functions but also engage its desire in the process and bring to bear the function of love. 'If it is a question of knowing God as *melius* and supreme good, thought must not lean on the impossible concept of an inaccessible essence, but rather on its own desire, and thus deprived of any other recourse, on its love.'[44]

Marion's original reflection upon Anselm's famous argument dovetails nicely with the guiding idea of his theology that charity or love (not being) is the most distinctive characteristic of God and that he is more assuredly attained by our loving desire than by our metaphysical speculation.

The saturated phenomenon of transcendent superlative goodness, overwhelming our conceptual capacity and engaging our loving desire, provides us with a shadowy or dazzling indication of the genuine possibility of God as goodness and love. It provides an assurance that God so indicated by this saturated phenomenon is a *genuine possibility* of givenness and not, as a phenomenology which accords an absolute priority to transcendental subjectivity might contend, an impossibility. This genuine possibility of givenness finds historical realization in that incomprehensibly wonderful excess of donation – the Christian Revelation.

This claim that the phenomenological indication of God as transcendent supreme goodness discloses a genuine possibility of givenness liberates Marion from the charge of theological fideism on the one hand and from the need to offer metaphysical arguments for the existence of God on the other. The reality of God as supreme goodness is adumbrated *philosophically*, that is, by way of a phenomenology of the possibility of such givenness disclosed in our experience of the saturated phenomenon which we name 'the idea of infinity'. The profound, and philosophically unsuspected, significance of this possibility of God as supreme goodness is disclosed *theologically* in the historical Christian Revelation of the actuality of God as self-giving love who has incorporated us into his divine life of love.

This is an approach which, unlike some exclusively theological accounts of our knowledge of God, claims to accord due significance to both reason and faith, to the God of the philosophers and the God of Abraham, of Isaac and of Joseph.

However, some misgiving persists about this elegant claim that the proposed indication of God as absolutely supreme goodness is a *genuine or positive possibility* of givenness. For this claim would appear either to assume or make a matter of definition his real existence or make it somehow an instance of direct experience, however qualified shadowy or bedazzling. For an absolutely supreme goodness which is not a reality would be a contradiction in terms and therefore an impossibility of givenness rather than a positive or genuine possibility of it. If we are entitled to affirm the genuine or positive possibility of an absolutely supreme goodness we are ipso facto entitled to affirm its reality. For unless it were real, it could not be positively possible. The problem is that we are not entitled to affirm a priori that an absolutely supreme goodness is positively possible, that is, non-contradictory until we are aware that it is indeed a reality and, therefore, not contradictory. The most we can claim before we are aware that it is indeed a reality is that it is negatively possible, that is, we don't know whether it is positively possible or positively impossible.

For a metaphysical realist, we come to know that God envisaged as absolutely supreme goodness is positively possible by proving his reality as transcendent cause of the world rather than claiming his reality on the basis of an a priori awareness of its positive possibility. Marion, self-excluded from the route of metaphysical proof, and also from a claim to an abstract a priori conceptual comprehension of the divine essence, must rely on an appeal to a bedazzling or shadowy experience of God ('who remains incomprehensible, not imperceptible – without adequate concept, not without giving intuition') to transform our initial awareness of his negative possibility into positive possibility.[45] Such an experience, however dazzling, blinding or shadowy, occurs, it would seem, as an intuitive apprehending, not of some trace of divinity, but of God himself!

This appeal to a self-authenticating human experience of God revives the issue, touched upon in Chapter 1, about how or whether the transcendence of a humanly experienced God, however obscure the experience, can be more than a relative transcendence, a transcendence for us? There would appear to be a substitution here of an awareness of the existence of God, known immediately but indistinctly in experience, for the metaphysical claim that the existence of God is known only implicitly in experience. For metaphysics, it is a mistake to understand 'implicit' as 'blurred' or 'indistinct' as there is no direct experience whatsoever of God however indistinct or blurred. The claim that his existence is known implicitly in experience means that his existence can be established as creator by indirect causal argument from features of the world which we do know directly. And this claim to implicit knowledge of his existence can be reliably affirmed only when this existence has been explicitly established through such an argument.[46]

I will return to this persistent nagging question in the conclusions of my final chapter. These will develop the suggestion broached in this one that the metaphysical and phenomenological approaches to God are complementary rather than mutually exclusive. In the next chapter, I will discuss how both approaches are needed to serve different requirements of a Christian theological approach to God.

Relationships

Introduction

In this chapter, I want to bring together and develop some implications of the observations which have emerged from the dialogue in previous chapters between various approaches to God. Particular attention will be devoted to the relationships between a theological approach to God and the two philosophical approaches considered in previous chapters.

The central idea animating this reflection is that the metaphysical and phenomenological approaches to God each play a distinctive and irreducible role in giving due significance to an important distinction within Judeo-Christian Revelation. It is a distinction which has a crucial bearing upon the elaboration of a theological approach to God and our relationship to him. This is the distinction between our natural status as creatures dependent upon an infinite creator and our supernatural status as divinized by God's love to participate, through Christ's saving action, in his divine life.

With regard to this distinction, the question which presents itself is how the respective roles of metaphysics and phenomenology should be availed of in developing a theological understanding of it.

The revealed truth which we are seeking to elucidate can be summarized as follows: God created us as free agents called to respond to an invitation to participate in his divine life of self-giving love. However, through the countervailing self-assertiveness of our freedom, this invitation could have been and has in fact been rejected. Nevertheless, because of God's constant love in our regard, manifested in the incarnation, redemptive life and death of Jesus Christ, the consequences of this rejection have been absolved and the enabling supernatural invitation to a divinized sharing in God's own self-giving love has been reaffirmed.

The two aspects of this revealed truth, creation and divinization, must be given due weight in a balanced theological elucidation of it.

First, there is the fact that our fundamental reality, our natural condition, is a condition of being created. The great foundational revealed mystery of Judeo-Christianity and of monotheism generally is that the entire finite world, including human existence, is a created world. 'In the beginning God created the heavens and the earth' (Gen. 1.1). 'He is the God who made the world and everything in it' (Acts 17, 24). Our condition as created beings is ontologically prior to our supernatural divinization into God's life. We are not 'naturally' part of God's life. We are creatures just as much as the mountains, the sea, the animal kingdom or any other natural phenomenon – lovingly created indeed but not thereby a part of God's own life.

The second aspect of this central revealed truth is that we have been created to enjoy a divine destiny beyond the natural capacity of any creature, namely, to be conscious partakers of God's own life and love.

The view which I propose to consider, already indicated in Chapter 3, is that whereas metaphysics provides theology with an appropriate tool to develop an informative account of our natural condition as creatures dependent upon an infinite creator, phenomenology is methodologically more appropriate to a theological discussion of our divinization into God's life. The successful outcome of either depends upon not neglecting the justified claims of the other and understanding them as complementary, or at least compatible, aspects of the overall initiative.

Creation

In principle, knowledge that like the whole domain of finite being we are created beings, radically dependent for our existence upon God affirmed as infinite creator, is naturally accessible to us through metaphysical reflection. Undoubtedly such philosophical knowledge about God as infinite creator of finite being, rather than as merely a superior or divine agent of change in already existing beings, might not have been readily acquired independently of the doctrine of creation proclaimed historically in the beliefs of the major monotheistic religions.

For classical Greek philosophy (as indeed for contemporary scientific method), the de facto existence of the domain of finite material being is a non-problematic assumption and the objective is to understand its deepest intrinsic characteristics – not its very existence. As Bertrand Russell once famously remarked about the universe: 'I should say that the universe is just there, and that's all.'[1] Classical Greek philosophers would have agreed!

Nevertheless, consequent upon monotheist religious belief in creation, there has been a persistent philosophical tradition which argues that this belief can be rationally confirmed and elucidated by metaphysical argument. This conviction has deepened and transformed what has been the animating aim or intention of metaphysics since ancient times, namely, to elucidate the ultimate meaning and value of being in general and of human existence in particular – to understand their nature, appearance, activity and purpose.

The identification of some ultimate divine reality or agent such as a Platonic 'Idea of the Good', an Aristotelian 'Self-Thinking Thought' or a Neoplatonic 'One' played an important role in this Greek endeavour. However, the role of this divine reality was envisaged, not as creator, but rather as exemplar perfection, finite artificer or final cause. In such a conception, God is assumed to be an integral part, albeit the best part, of the cosmos. His efficacious activity is one of transforming that which is already and eternally there rather than one of initiating the cosmos absolutely into existence.

In the context of Judeo-Christian belief in divine creation, this metaphysical aim or intention is extended to enquire, not just about the formation, emanation, nature and interactive causality of finite beings, but about their very existence. This distinctive character of the revealed truth of creation has been elucidated theologically and philosophically by a transformative adaptation of Greek metaphysical thinking about causality and change.

The routine objection that Christian belief was corrupted by this influence of Greek metaphysics is, in my opinion, very wide of the mark. It is much more plausible to maintain that Greek metaphysics itself was profoundly transformed and brought to a new level of significance by its adaptation to articulate the Christian doctrine of creation. For although the Judeo-Christian doctrine of creation has a primarily religious significance, it is a doctrine that has profound ontological implications. These implications, as metaphysically formulated, are important to its theological elaboration. These include the existence and transcendence of God and the asymmetrical real relationship of total dependence of finite beings upon his creative will – not just for their nature but for their very existence. Creation makes things not just to be the sort of things that they are but, more fundamentally, to be rather than not to be.

One feature in particular which is common to belief in creation and metaphysical explanation is the idea of causality. Although what the fullness of revelation discloses dramatically surpasses what is involved in the metaphysical interpretation of the biblical idea of creation nevertheless this interpretation articulates an irreducible feature of this biblical idea. It articulates the truth that, as creator, God is the cause of the world – admittedly in a very much more profound sense than the intra-mundane efficient causality operative within experience – but still undeniably a cause in however a unique and analogical sense. The status in virtue of which we are enabled to be, and be what we are, and act as we do is our existence as creatures whose very existence is wholly dependent upon the creative causality of an utterly transcendent God.

It is such ontological considerations, bearing upon the actual existence of things, which a metaphysical approach to God can seek to elucidate and rationally confirm more effectively than a phenomenological approach. For the doctrine of creation is incomprehensible without these rather substantial ontological claims about various kinds of existence other than existence for human consciousness. It affirms, at least implicitly, the infinite plenitude of divine existence and the finite but real and manifold existence of creatures existentially dependent upon this divine being – whether or not this dependence is consciously acknowledged or this divine being is consciously worshipped.

When referring to our relationship to God, an appeal to a unique and analogically developed concept of causality is not, as is so often proclaimed, an example of metaphysical idolatry. It is a theologically appropriate elucidation of the revealed truth of our creaturely existence.

The fundamental distinction in Christian belief between God and the world, including ourselves, is real and is expressed in terms of creation or divine causality. This distinction involves a non-reciprocal relationship between us and God – an ontologically real relationship in our case but only a notional relationship in the case of God (arising from *our* way of thinking). Unless this real distinction is given its full weight in terms of our relationship of radical existential dependence upon divine creative causality, a distorted account of both our fundamental condition and of God's transcendence seems inevitable.

Undoubtedly this creaturely status is not a defining feature of the nature or essence of anything. The created nature and activity of anything is the same nature and activity that we can think about and conduct experiments upon without any reference to its being created. Being a created dog does not mean being a different kind of thing to just being a dog. Coming to be as a created thing is not a matter of something becoming a different kind of thing. *That* kind of 'becoming' is the becoming which is a characteristic effect of finite causality, that is, the change of something already existing into something different, for example, the change of a living person into a corpse which a bullet can effect.

Creation is the action of originating the universe absolutely, whether temporally or eternally – to exist and evolve as the sort of cosmos it is (whatever that may be) – rather than changing something pre-existing into something verifiably different. Knowing that the universe is created is no help in deciding anything about quantum physics or evolution!

Creation accomplishes the finite participation in real existence of something as distinct from its mere possibility or its obtaining only as an object of consciousness. Considered thus as a finite participant in actual existence (as distinct from non-existence or merely notional existence), any being can be understood as dependent upon God's creative causality. Hence, Aquinas can remark that although being created does not enter into the definition of a thing nevertheless being caused may follow from its reality as a concrete instance of a particular finite nature participating effectively in the perfection of actual existence.[2] Of course this causal dependence is not evident and must be established by way of indirect metaphysical argument which seeks to establish it by disclosing the contradiction involved in its denial.

However, as we have seen, in virtue of its characteristic method of reduction, phenomenology abstracts from the consideration of whether or how things might exist other than as for, and correlative to, human consciousness. A phenomenological approach necessarily involves as its non-negotiable touchstone the *epoche* or phenomenological reduction.[3] As such, it brackets out of consideration the dimension of extra-phenomenal existence which underpins the appeal to metaphysical causality in elucidating an account of God as creator of the world in general and of human existence in particular. For such an appeal, as we have seen, is based not just on a consideration of what a thing is, its nature or essence, but precisely upon its actual existence as the sort of thing that it is.

In the light of the *epoche*, the context of phenomenological enquiry becomes that of the perceptive description of given phenomena and the elucidation – through careful description and techniques of imaginative variation – of their essential natures, conditions of possibility, significations, modalities, noematic-noetic structures, etc., but not of their objective existence beyond the limits of cognitional immanence. It is the context of logical implication rather than ontological causality, a gentler world of 'as if' rather than the existentially obdurate historical world of distinct beings tending to act, or being impeded from acting, variously and vigorously as cause and effect. By way of sporting analogy, one might say that a phenomenological description of a game of football as personally experienced by a keen supporter contrasts greatly with a subsequent impersonal objective analysis of it by the team manager!

This world of phenomenology is 'tone deaf' to an objective affirmation of God, elaborated in irreducibly metaphysical terms, affirming the independent excellence of his being and the omnipotence of his causality. Such considerations, even if not positively denied as idolatrous, are deemed to be surpassed by an authentic phenomenological elucidation of the deeper self-involving truth of Christian Revelation that God is love. They are seen as the relic of an outdated philosophical vision failing to connect meaningfully with the standpoint and language of contemporary philosophical and theological discourse.

Thus, as we have seen, Richard Kearney subscribes 'to that new turn in contemporary philosophy of religion which strives to overcome the metaphysical God of pure act and asks the question: what kind of divinity comes after metaphysics? . . . How we may overcome the old notion of God as disembodied cause.'[4] God's *esse* is refigured as the 'loving possible' who depends on us to be.[5] And Marion seeks to explore the significance of God beyond the limiting metaphysical horizon of 'being' and to develop a phenomenology liberated from the presupposition of causal dependence. 'Under the title *God Without Being*, I am attempting to bring out the absolute freedom of God with regard to all determinations, including, first of all the basic condition that renders all other conditions possible and even necessary – for us humans – the fact of Being.'[6] Also to return to things themselves amounts to recognizing phenomena themselves, 'without submitting them to the (sufficient) condition of an anterior authority (such as thing in itself, cause, principle, etc.)'.[7]

However, this methodological abstraction from discussion of 'existence' other than as immanent to human consciousness does not ipso facto dispense from the consideration of such ontological issues which are indeed posed by the idea of creation. However preliminary, the account of God as infinite being and as transcendent creator of the finite world should not be ignored or dismissed as the misleading discourse of a bygone metaphysical age. For it corresponds faithfully to a fundamental truth of Christian Revelation that the world we experience is a divine creation. A metaphysical account takes seriously and seeks to elucidate perceptively the significance of the objective existence and dependent character ascribed to the world in the biblical creation story. It highlights an aspect of revelation outside the ambit of or 'bracketed' by phenomenological considerations. It seeks to address it explicitly and thereby to provide a level of understanding of it which is methodologically precluded by phenomenology from its sphere of enquiry.

I have indicated in Chapter 2 an example of just such a metaphysical account of these ontological considerations in the thought of Thomas Aquinas. We saw how it provides a developed analysis of finite beings as composite structures of essence and existence radically dependent, not just for their disposition, but for their actual existence upon a creator God.[8] Moreover this God, affirmed through indirect argument as unique cause of finite being, is not just the 'supreme being' in the totality of finite being but transcends this order entirely as an infinite plenitude and intensity of being whom we can indicate only indirectly as incomprehensible pure act of existence, *Esse Subsistens.*

Obviously a metaphysical account of finite being as dependent upon the creative causality of infinite being does not provide the full or the deepest meaning of the doctrine of creation. It is more comprehensively considered in terms of a theology of redemption and divinization, and in this context phenomenology as a method of theological enquiry has a crucial contribution to make. But the fact remains that the doctrine of creation, even if considered in the deeper theological context, does have ontological implications and these ontological implications are elucidated by a metaphysics of being in a way which provides a level of understanding irreducible to phenomenological description.

This metaphysics of being is not, of course, a prerequisite of faith. It is very likely the case that most believers accept as 'a matter of faith' the essential doctrine of creation and its affirmation of the existence of both creatures and God. They require no metaphysical arguments about the ontological implications of the doctrine. Also, as 'Christian philosophers' such as Gilson have argued, the metaphysical reasoning is more likely to fully convince somebody who is already a believer than somebody who is not.

Nevertheless, the possibility and indeed the reliability of such a metaphysical approach is an important consideration in any account of the relationship between faith and reason which attributes a positive role to natural reason in this relationship. Such an account argues that the profoundly self-involving theological account of the great biblical truth of creation can, to some extent, be confirmed by a philosophical itinerary which originates in an impersonal analysis of the existence and nature of the finite beings given in human experience but intuited as independent of this experience. Unlike theology, which originates in divine revelation, metaphysics reflects in an a posteriori way upon the rational implications of what is first given in pre-reflective lived experience. Thus Aquinas points out the theological account begins with the word of God and proceeds to an account of his creation whereas philosophy begins with the effects of this creation and works back to their divine source.[9]

Nor need this metaphysical approach to God be dismissed, in a manner so common today, as exemplifying the idolatrous onto-theology described by Heidegger. The characteristics ascribed to metaphysics, construed as onto-theology, include: (1) that God, is part of the object of metaphysics and is properly spoken of as a being among beings albeit the supreme being; (2) that God is the efficient cause and explanation of all beings; and (3) as founding cause of all beings God is *causa sui*, his own founding cause.

As we have seen in our discussion of Aquinas, none of these characteristics are necessary to a metaphysical approach to God. God is certainly not 'a being' in our basic metaphysical understanding of 'a being' as that in which the act of existence is determined to a particular form. That is why we speak of God not as 'a being' but as incomprehensible infinite act of existence, *Esse Subsistens,* 'beyond the range of all existing beings'.[10]

Similarly, although God is certainly the cause of all finite beings he is so, not in the univocal sense in which finite beings, causally related by way of efficient causation, are mutually interdependent, but only in the unique sense in which as its creator he transcends the order of finite being which stands in an asymmetrical relationship of dependence upon him. Creatures are dependent upon God but this relationship is non-reciprocal. The coming to be as freely created which really characterizes finite being does not involve any real alteration of God's infinite being.

As for the suggestion that God is somehow the cause of himself, Aquinas not only dismisses the suggestion as involving a contradictory pre-existence of God to his own existence but also because the existence of God is the precondition of everything whose existence must be caused.[11]

In the second edition of *Dieu sans l'etre*, Marion includes an interesting chapter on Thomas Aquinas in which he agrees that none of the above defining characteristics of onto-theology applies in the case of Aquinas. 'The thought of Thomas Aquinas is not at all an instance of onto-theologically constituted metaphysics, at least as understood in the strict sense postulated by Heidegger.'[12]

However, Marion goes further than absolving Aquinas from a charge of onto-theology. He suggests that he should be understood as agreeing with Marion's own position about the inappropriateness of any approach to an affirmation of God by way of metaphysical or ontological speculation about being, beings or their existence (*esse*). For Marion, it is a mistake to persist in the belief that we can make progress in knowledge about God starting from what we think we know about 'being'. Instead of trying to think metaphysically about God in terms of being, we should think theologically about being in terms of God.[13] He argues that the Thomist affirmation of existence (*esse*) is properly understood only in terms of the mystery of divine transcendence and the infinite distance of creatures from God. Also we must urge, as a genuinely Thomist claim, that the *esse* or infinite act of existence which we attribute to the transcendent God has nothing in common with what we know and understand by the term 'being'.

Hence, for Marion, it can be said that Aquinas agrees with his distinctive view that the God we affirm is a God without being, at least in any sense in which we claim to know and understand being. To speak of the *esse* attributed to God, we must think theologically and beyond all metaphysical or ontological categories.[14] When we speak of the irreducibility of the divine *esse* to any determinate essence or concept, we signify its profound unknowability. In attributing *esse* as the first name of God, Aquinas means primarily that God is called *esse* only nominally and not according to the manner in which we understand it.[15] As pure act of existence, involving no trace of the composition which characterizes our metaphysical understanding of being, the divine *esse*, like God himself, is unknown by us. It is known only as unknowable – unlike the *esse* of any finite being of which metaphysics forms a concept to render it essentially knowable.[16] Marion's overall conclusion is that, in accord with what he himself maintains, any authentic interpretation of Aquinas's affirmation of the divine *esse* excludes all references to being as we know it, whether metaphysically or otherwise. To affirm the divine *esse* is to affirm God without being. To speak of the divine *esse* is to speak of God only negatively as not pertaining in any way to our understanding of being.[17]

Marion's interpretation of Aquinas's account of the divine *esse* as of exclusively theological significance and as having no metaphysical import is both interesting and insightful but ultimately unconvincing.

It is certainly the case for Aquinas that although we can know the existence of God in the sense that we know that the proposition 'God exists' is true, we can have no knowledge of it in the sense of comprehending the divine act of existence itself. We know that 'there is infinite act of existence' is a proposition which has real reference, although we do not directly know that to which it refers. We can know that there is infinite being but we do not know the *esse* which is this being. Likewise it is true that for Aquinas strictly speaking and in final analysis, existence (*esse*), and all its characteristic perfection, pertain primarily to God and only in a secondary and derivative manner to creatures.[18] Further, he observes that the way in which we use terms to signify things always has a connotation of finitude which God's existence transcends.[19] In their real application, terms such as '*esse*' or 'being' as metaphysically conceived by us signify what is proportionate to our intellect, namely particular determinate finite participations in the perfection or act of existence. Therefore, God as infinite existence is indeed beyond our intellectual comprehension or way of signifying the perfection of existence.[20]

All of these observations accord with Marion's view that when we speak about God's existence, his *esse*, we refer to what exceeds anything we can know and understand from within the horizon of our metaphysical discourse about being and that this view also represents Aquinas's position. In this sense one is entitled to maintain that to affirm 'God without being' is not only true but true for Aquinas also. Theology, not metaphysics, is the appropriate context for discussion of the God of Judeo-Christian belief.

However, this is only half the story. Certainly for Aquinas when we try to speak of the divine existence we find ourselves 'in a state of confusion' and 'when we remove from him even "being" as found in creatures' he remains for us 'in a kind of shadow of ignorance'.[21] But we attain this *bouleversement* as an outcome of metaphysical reasoning. Thus he remarks: 'The manner in which our intellect knows *esse* is the manner in which it is found in lesser things from which our knowledge is obtained, and in these things *esse* is not subsistent but [finitely] inherent. However, by reasoning it discovers that there is something which is *Esse Subsistens*.'[22] We come to affirm God as *Esse Subsistens* by way of metaphysical causal argument. In the order of knowledge 'finite being' and 'cause' are logically prior to 'infinite being' since we come to know that infinite being or *Esse Subsistens* exists by proving his existence as the creator of finite being. 'Knowledge of the existence of God is not at all self-evident to us but can be demonstrated from his effects which we do know.'[23]

When discussing how names such as 'being' or *esse* can signify God, Aquinas distinguishes between what is signified and our way of signifying it. The perfection signified is indeed properly predicated of God. However, our way of signifying this divine perfection is always defective because terms such as 'being' and *esse* insofar as we know and understand them always retain the connotation of finitude which characterizes the realities which are the proper and direct objects of our knowledge.[24] We come through metaphysical argument to the realization that the terms we predicate of God have a deeper significance than our initial understanding of them and that what is initially signified in our use of the terms is, paradoxically, dependent upon what is signified in their deeper and, for us, uncomprehended positive meaning.

Our realization that there is this deeper meaning of the term *esse*, exceeding our positive comprehension, is derived from our understanding of it in the context of our initial metaphysical analysis of finite being and the indirect metaphysical reasoning which establishes the causal dependence of such being on infinite being. Aquinas is unambiguous in affirming that it is by way of such metaphysical reflection that we can come to our affirmation that God truly exists as infinite being or *Esse Subsistens* even though we have no direct or positive comprehension in this life of this plenitude of perfection.[25]

Even though we have no comprehension of the *esse* predicated of God, we know that such attribution is appropriate because *esse* designates the act in virtue of which any real perfection obtains as real and is thereby distinguished from non-being or intentional being or merely possible being.[26] In metaphysics we ascribe being only to what actually exists.[27] Clearly *esse* in this sense of real or actual perfection is properly ascribed to God even though we cannot understand what is thereby signified. (At least we understand what it is that we cannot comprehend and why we cannot!)

To affirm real being independently of *esse* is metaphysically a contradiction in terms.[28] Consequently if we are to speak of God as real, as we must to affirm him as creator of finite being, he must be understood to realize in a unique non-finite way the perfection of *esse*.

As we noted in Chapter 2, it is this firm grasp of the truth that actually exercised *esse* is the fundamental characteristic of all real being which provides Aquinas with a sure norm for distinguishing ontological being such as God and his creation enjoy from merely apparent or imaginary beings such as blindness, bank overdrafts, dragons, triangles, etc.[29] By metaphysical reflection it is established that only, and all, that which in some manner is an expression of the act of existence, *esse*, is real being. The knowledge that God exists as *Esse Subsistens* is an accomplishment of our natural reason, a metaphysically demonstrable truth and as such not an article of faith – even though it may be held on faith by those who do not know of, follow or care about metaphysical argument.[30] It is clear that for Aquinas such metaphysical reasoning, even though it culminates in the affirmation of what exceeds its comprehension, plays an indispensable role in elaborating the ontological implications of the doctrine of creation and developing a rational confirmation of it. In this way, it contributes fundamentally, and more effectively than can phenomenology, to the theological understanding of the first aspect of the important distinction with which we commenced our discussion in this chapter. This is the distinction between our status as mere creatures like any other and our status as divinized participants in God's own life. It is in elucidating the irreducible ontological implications of our status as creatures that metaphysical enquiry can make its characteristic and immensely valuable contribution to Christian theology.

The situation is very different when one comes to consider the second aspect of the important theological distinction we seek to elucidate, namely, our divinization into a life beyond any natural capacity. Here, I suggest, the role of phenomenology, particularly as developed by Jean-Luc Marion, can play an illuminating methodological role.

Divinization

The central Christian truth we are trying to elucidate is stated very succinctly in *II Peter*, 1,4: 'In making these gifts, he has given us the guarantee of something very great and wonderful to come: through them you will be able to share in the divine nature.' By this gracious gift, or gift of grace, God has enabled and revealed to us a higher and more personalized knowledge of him than that available through natural reason.[31]

Metaphysical categories, impersonally articulating various ontological dimensions of this divine initiative, are inadequate to describe all that it involves. They can throw light upon certain implications of it, for example, how the divinizing gift of grace presupposes our essentially non-divine created nature (*gratia praesupponit naturam*), or how it perfects but does not destroy this nature (*gratia perficit naturam, non tollit*). Such considerations might intimate what could be termed the 'emergent' character of grace, its non-deducibility from and irreducibility to created nature. But inasmuch as this suggests comparison with natural instances of alleged emergence such as life from chemistry or thought from biological life, it fails to get to the heart of the matter of what is affirmed.

For the heart of the matter is the claim that by God's freely bestowed self-giving love we are graced or divinized, beyond any natural capacity of *ours*, to share in and partake of *his* nature and thereby eventually, through this participation, to know him as he knows himself. We are deified in order to know and love God in a divine way.

Here it becomes appropriate to speak of the creation of a personal relationship, a partnership or friendship, between man and God.[32] One might say that the level of discussion has been notched up from a metaphysics of creation to a theology of divine love.

In seeking to elucidate this astonishing claim that we are not just creatures but loved by God into a personal relationship of friendship with him, we are impelled to reach beyond the impersonal metaphysical characterization of God as creator. The equality which is a prerequisite of friendship surpasses the analysis in terms of asymmetry which is the defining characteristic of our relationship with God as creatures. It is no longer adequate to speak of an unbridgeable chasm between God as he is in himself and God-for-me which is appropriate when we speak of our status as creatures. Creatures, as such, cannot be loved by God – only benevolently and providentially cared for. As Herbert McCabe puts it: 'God cannot, of course, love us as creatures, but "in Christ" we are taken up into the exchange of love between the Father and the incarnate human Son, we are filled with the Holy Spirit, we become part of the divine life. We call this "grace". By grace we ourselves share in the divine and that is how God can love us.'[33]

God in this personal relationship is a God known and loved by way of a grace-enabling faith – a God as he is for human consciousness. The relevance of a phenomenological approach to this personal relationship becomes evident. The relationship can be elucidated by a phenomenological account of it in which the ontological distinction between God as he is in himself and as he is for me is 'bracketed' or 'phenomenologically reduced' – 'led back' to a deeper truth. The ultimate truth about God and ourselves which such a phenomenological approach to what is given in Revelation can bring into intelligible focus is not, as metaphysics accomplishes, that he is creator but that he is charity or love – that it is no longer adequate to speak in terms of the distinction between God as he is in himself and as he is for us. Likewise, it highlights, not that we are creatures, but that we are freely gifted into this divine love. There is no unsurpassable barrier to participation in this love other than those which we may consciously impose.

This approach discounts the significance of any metaphysical speculation about 'being' and 'causality' in an approach to God. Such onto-theological speculation is, it is claimed, what has led to the contemporary conviction of the death of God. This metaphysical God, fashioned according to the preconditions of human thought, is declared deservedly dead. Its demise prepares the ground for a more authentic phenomenologically articulated affirmation of God.

The importance ascribed by phenomenology, particularly that of Jean-Luc Marion, to what is given or gives itself immediately to our consciousness provides us with a methodological approach with which to explore, non-metaphysically, the significance of the astonishing gift from the Father, through Christ, of our divinization – the gift we call the Holy Spirit.

Marion, as we have seen, emphasizes that any phenomenon which shows itself in experience primarily gives itself. There is, he claims, a certain absoluteness or irreducibility about this givenness of a phenomenon, at least to the extent that we do not need to seek its cause or sufficient reason. He likes to cite, and takes with the greatest seriousness, Husserl's 'principle of principles' which posits that 'every originarily giving intuition is a source of right for cognition'. Everything that gives itself originarily in intuition is attested through itself, without the background of a reason yet to be given. 'Far from having to give a sufficient reason, it is enough for the phenomenon to give itself through intuition according to a principle of sufficient intuition.'[34]

Of course what gives itself in our experience commonly gives itself to us as inscribed within a conditioning horizon and is therefore led back to an 'intentional' *I* or subject which to some extent limits and constitutes the given phenomenon which shows itself in experience. Hence, the possibility of an absolutely unconditioned and irreducible intuited givenness appears implausible. However, for Marion as we have seen, this constitutive role of the conscious subject is not an absolute precondition of givenness. There are given experiences in which the given-to subject plays no active constitutive role. These are phenomena, he argues, in which intuition, far from being overdetermined by conscious intention, gives '*more, indeed immeasurably more* than intention ever would have intended or foreseen'.[35] These, as we have seen, he calls 'saturated phenomena'.

Marion's brilliant identification and description of instances of saturated phenomena, as bedazzling intuitions in which what is experientially given surpasses conceptual comprehension or anticipation, prepares the way for a phenomenological treatment of the Christian Revelation of the gift of God's love for us.

A saturated phenomenon is a phenomenon in the fullest sense of the term. For 'it alone truly appears as itself, of itself, and starting from itself, since it alone appears without the limit of a horizon and without reduction to an *I*.'[36] As such it can be called a revelation in a purely phenomenological (not a theologically revealed) sense.[37] Examples of such phenomena are found in truly *seeing* – rather than interpreting – a work of art, in attending to the dazzling invisible gaze of a loved one and, most perspicuously, in thinking Anselm's 'that than which none greater can be conceived' or Descartes's 'idea of infinity' as the final possibility of phenomenology.[38]

From the perspective of saturated phenomena, the constituting primacy of the *I* or subject is called in question. In this context, the subject is rather a recorder or witness of the impact of a given intuition which has precedence over any subsequent attempt to describe it conceptually. One might even say that far from the subject actively constituting the given phenomenon, it itself is constituted or reconstituted by what is given. 'Far from being able to constitute this phenomenon, the I experiences itself as constituted by it. It is constituted and no longer constituting because it no longer has at its disposal any dominant point of view over the intuition which overwhelms it.'[39]

The approach recalled in the preceding paragraphs envisages the possibility of a phenomenological elucidation of the Christian Revelation of God's love for us and the personal relationship with him which it establishes. There is no question here of phenomenology deducing or proving the reality of such a revelation. The intuitive realization of its actually being-given in fact requires the real experience of its givenness. This is unavailable simply through phenomenological reflection. It falls to rational theology to elucidate this real experience of Revelation as historically given actuality.[40] However, phenomenology through its technique of imaginative variation and its reflection on the essential character of saturated phenomena can provide an outline template of its possibility.

God as self-giving love, revealed in theology, and the saturated phenomena of phenomenology are each identified by the characteristic of a givenness which is independent of any metaphysical causation and of any objectifying limits or preconditions imposed by human subjectivity. Following the guiding thread of the non-objective givenness or being-given that is characteristic of the saturated phenomena which we have experienced, we can seek to push phenomenological imaginative enquiry to its ultimate possibility. We can envisage as a genuine possibility a givenness or saturated phenomenon par excellence, corresponding to the 'that which is greater than anything which can be thought' God of the philosophers. Phenomenological reflection on saturated phenomena can disclose the possibility, or at least the non-impossibility, of experiencing a saturated phenomenon of such philosophically unpredictable, unconditional and irreducible excellence that it would be a genuine revelation were it to obtain. 'In fact the saturated phenomenon can mark, by rendering visible to excess, the paradoxically unmeasured dimensions of possible givenness – which nothing stops or conditions.'[41]

The aim would be to provide by means of phenomenology a rational or philosophical approach to God which is independent of a metaphysics of being or traditional *metaphysica specialis*. 'The question then becomes: What (if any) phenomenal face can the "God of the philosophers and the scholars assume? More, precisely, what phenomenon could claim to offer a luminous shadow of this "God" so as to correspond to the being-given's relief of being?'[42]

Marion argues that we can envisage the possibility that God is given and allows to be given more than any other being-given. The phenomenological figure of 'God' as the possible being-given par excellence is a being-given absolutely and without reserve, invisible to objectifying consciousness, incommensurate with any other being-given and irreducible to any constituting *I*. 'It alone appears without the limits of a horizon, or reduction to an *I* and constitutes itself, to the point of *giving itself as a self*.'[43] The *I* which experiences this being-given par excellence, far from constituting it by an objectifying gaze finds itself in the counter-experience of being itself constituted, given over to (*adonne a*), or called (*interloque*) into dedicated relationship with this being-given par excellence whose invisible gaze visibly envisages me and loves me. By pushing the phenomenological intention to its ultimate possibility we open up the possibility of a phenomenology of religion.[44]

This phenomenological approach envisages, on the basis of our experience of particular saturated phenomena, the ultimate possibility of givenness as a 'luminous shadow of God'. This possibility is the possibility of a saturated phenomenon in the second degree encompassing in the most perfect manner all modalities of saturating givenness. It is a model of phenomenality, a possibility which represents the most imaginative and daring expression of phenomenological rationality. It remains, however, only a possibility – envisaged by pushing the idea of phenomenological givenness to its ultimate consideration. Indeed one might wonder, as Marion himself appears to, whether it could have come to be entertained without the promptings of theological knowledge antecedently obtained about Christian Revelation – much as the metaphysics of creation, though not logically dependent upon, may have been prompted by awareness of the biblical story of creation.

What is involved here is an enquiry into what would be required of phenomenology in order to respect the possibility of divine revelation. For Marion, the issue comes down to a simple alternative. Should we limit the possibility of how God might appear to within the limits of some unquestioned and intangible framework of metaphysics or even to phenomenology a la Husserl, or should one enlarge the possibility of phenomenology to embrace the possibility of the sort of manifestation which is raised by the affirmation of divine Revelation.[45] For phenomenology this possibility, of course, remains just that – the possibility of an intimated but unknown and undefinable actual revelation.

Marion argues that the manifestation of Christ, as described in the New Testament, can be interpreted phenomenologically as the paradigm phenomenon of revelation, the ultimate exemplar of every possibility of saturated phenomenon, a saturated phenomenon of the second degree.[46] Should such divine self-manifestation actually obtain, phenomenology, understood as respect for whatever gives and shows itself from itself, must expand its understanding of saturated phenomena to include the unique compounded saturation of intuition which such revelation involves.[47]

There is a certain parallel between a theology of Christian Revelation and a phenomenology of givenness which enables phenomenology to operate as the method of theology but not of course as the originating disclosure of its factual history, its actuality or its meaning.[48] 'Phenomenology offers a method . . . for the manifestation of the invisible through the phenomena that indicate it – hence also the method of theology.'[49] What is vaguely adumbrated by phenomenology as a philosophical possibility is brought to unpredictable light and is confirmed as historically actual through faith 'in the unsurpassable primacy of Christian Revelation'.[50] This faith in the

Christian Revelation of God's self-giving love for us discloses a truth which is accessible only through this faith in the dependable and irreducible actuality of what the revelation discloses. It is not accessible to natural reason even in its broadest phenomenological speculation about what might be the ultimate instance or revelation of a saturated phenomenon.

Nevertheless the truth thus disclosed in Christian Revelation does lend itself admirably to methodological elaboration in terms of the phenomenological description of saturated phenomena. This, as we have seen, highlights how an intuitive excess of being-given or givenness, surpassing the domain of constituted objects, can itself, as the self that it is, constitute the recipient of this givenness as a given-to which is called to make manifest and be a living witness to the being-given. God's divine love in our regard and the personal relationship with him which it establishes is aptly described in these terms. He is the loving self-givenness par excellence who, revealing himself to us in Christ through the grace of faith, freely constitutes us as partners or sharers in his divine life. Through this gift of faith he becomes manifest to us as he truly is in himself, namely, a loving God-for-us. The metaphysical distinction between God as he is in himself and as he is for us is surpassed in the revealed knowledge of our personal relationship with him. We in turn as the given-to of God's love are thereby enabled and invoked to witness to this love in our relationship with him and our neighbour.

Such an elucidation of Christian Revelation by phenomenology involves the epoche or 'reduction' which is a defining characteristic of phenomenological method. This reduction, the non-negotiable touchstone of phenomenology, ascribes an unconditioned origin to whatever gives itself originarily in intuition. Whatever gives itself thus, manifests itself as ultimately coinciding with its phenomenal immanence to consciousness.[51] The intuited phenomenon, as that which shows itself immanently to consciousness from itself and not as an effect or on the basis of something other than itself, is taken as the fundamental self-justifying source of cognition.[52]

This means, as we have seen, that it abstracts from or brackets consideration of the ontological status of God and creatures and of any metaphysical relationship of causality between them. 'On the contrary, it could be that givenness can arise only once causality has been radically surpassed, in a mode whose own rationality causality does not even suspect. It could be that givenness obeys requirements that are infinitely more complex and powerful than the resources of efficient causality.'[53]

Nor, as phenomenology, does it aspire to deduce or verify the historical actuality or truth of Christian Revelation. To repeat, it considers the account of the manifestation of Christ as revealed in the New Testament only as a possibility of phenomenal revelation. But, it maintains that should such an historical revelation of God, manifesting himself from himself, be otherwise known, for example, by way of faith in the given theological Revelation, a duly extended phenomenology of saturated phenomena would be the appropriate means to elucidate the import of this Revelation.

In virtue of its characteristic reduction, phenomenology considers the manifestation of the divinity of Christ as a phenomenon given immanently to human consciousness which transforms human consciousness from an objectivizing *I* into a witness to this divine being-given. It is interested in describing this Christian God as the phenomenon par excellence of self-giving love who relates humankind to himself in a divinized relationship of equality. The God so described as immanent to human consciousness is not the radically independent *Esse Subsistens* of metaphysics. It is God as he in himself (freely) is for humans, that is, a self-giving love whose givenness becomes manifest through those whom it enables to bear faithful witness to it. In this manifestation, the distinction between God in himself and as he is for us is surpassed. It is thus that God manifests himself immanently in our conscious experience as the intuitively given saturated phenomenon par excellence, a givenness which is absolutely unconditioned and irreducible to any constituting *I* or predetermining concept.

However, one might wonder, yet again, how this phenomenological account of divine revelation as a non-objectifiable saturation of intuition, given immanently to human consciousness in accordance with the strict requirement of phenomenological reduction, affects our understanding of God's transcendence? If immanent to consciousness in this way, in what sense can God be said to be transcendent? Do not the misgivings aired in previous chapters about divine transcendence being rendered relative to human subjectivity resurface here?

However, Marion insists that in this phenomenological elucidation of divine revelation God's transcendence is not compromised but rather confirmed and rendered more significant for us by the immanentism which is a consequence of the 'reduction'. His transcendence is affirmed, non-metaphysically, in our phenomenal awareness of him as surpassing all conceptual objectivization – in his 'visibility' as intrinsically invisible. 'The absence or unknowability of "God" does not contradict givenness but on the contrary attests to the excellence of that givenness. "God" becomes invisible not in spite of givenness but by virtue of that givenness.'[54]

Instead of a metaphysical account of divine transcendence in terms of creature and creator, what this approach proposes is an interpretation of this transcendence elaborated in the light of the unforeseeable personal relationship between man and God disclosed in Christian Revelation. The attempt to predetermine, by metaphysical argument, an account of divine transcendence, or indeed any other divine attribute, is here radically criticized. It is replaced by one in terms of God's self-giving love and our divinized relationship with him disclosed only and irreducibly by revelation. This givenness of God which appears truly as itself, of itself and starting from itself is identical with its phenomenal manifestation to our consciousness by means of the faith which it enables. As such it is not relativized by its immanence to our consciousness. On the contrary, it relativizes our consciousness as a function of it: 'a subjectivity or subjectness entirely in conformity with givenness – one that is entirely received from what it receives, given by the given, given to the given.'[55] It manifests itself as a rejection of any idolatrous philosophical 'subjection of the divine to the human conditions for the experience of the divine'.[56] Indeed one might say that the true depth of divine transcendence is available only through the faith experience in which the metaphysical opposition of creature and creator is itself transcended in the Revelation of God as self-giving love in our regard.

God's transcendence is confirmed precisely in and by his immanent manifestation to human consciousness as uncontainable and unobjectifiable by it. Our problem about the phenomenological understanding of divine transcendence is seen to derive from the attempt to predetermine the nature of this transcendence metaphysically. It is dissolved when we appreciate that this is a misguided attempt to judge the self-authenticating givenness of phenomenology in terms of an allegedly prior and more fundamental metaphysical perspective.

The phenomenological distance which God manifests from our all too human constructions and preoccupations is, paradoxically, the primary figure of his faithful presence. The contemporary proclamation of the death of the God of metaphysics is, for Marion, an appropriate clearing of the scene to facilitate a welcome of God who manifests his presence only in paternal distance from such metaphysical presumption. Thus Thomas Carlson remarks: 'The God of Marion's Christian revelation is . . . the God whose generous love surpasses all knowledge or understanding. That love is exercised primarily through paternal distance, which, precisely and only as distance, opens the only true space for filial relation.'[57]

Divine transcendence understood thus in phenomenological, rather than metaphysical, terms indicates an immanent experiential presence of God to consciousness as a dazzling saturated intuition which cannot be looked at or surveyed because it is utterly unobjectifiable. (Recall the helpful illustration of the invisible gaze of a loved one, certainly experienced but irreducible to the face which is seen.) From an objective point of view, therefore, one can say without contradiction, that the divine saturating phenomenon reveals nothing that can be seen.[58] Indeed it reveals its real presence in experience precisely as withdrawal and distance from the world of naturally comprehended things or objects. It gives itself experientially from itself alone to the faithful witness whom it enables to manifest and reciprocate, in her imperfect finite way, the unconditional and all-surpassing self-giving love which God is. Viewed phenomenologically, divine transcendence is not an impersonally affirmed objective ontological state of affairs, but a self-involving faith experience of the immanent presence of God as loving paternal distance – an experience most perceptively described, and proposed for our example, in gospel accounts of Christ's relationship with God his Father.

Of course God really exists but this is a trivial assertion by comparison with what characterizes him as given in revelation, namely, that he is unconditional love, a love into which we are called and enabled to participate in. 'If to begin with "God is love" then God loves before being. He only is as he embodies himself – in order to love more closely that which and those who, themselves have first to be. This [is a] radical reversal of the relations between Being and loving, between the name revealed in the Old Testament (Exodus 3:14) and the name revealed more profoundly though not inconsistently, by the New (First Letter of John, 4:8).'[59]

One might well agree with Marion that to know that God is love is to know something more profound than to know simply that he exists. But even if she is not a metaphysician a Christian might be surprised to learn that; 'God loves before Being. He only is as he embodies himself.' She would, I suggest be more convinced by the metaphysical judgement that there is no real distinction in God between his divine attributes such as his being and his love, neither of which we comprehend. The idea of a God 'that loves before being' not only does not describe a profound truth but rather an impossible metaphysical contradiction. For the metaphysical claim that the act of existence is the principle of all real perfection actual or potential and that God is the infinite expression of this act of existence upon whom all finite beings depend for *their* existence is certainly in accord with Christian belief – even though one may, like Marion, decline to avail oneself of this metaphysical perspective.

The affirmation that God is self-giving love, which can be elucidated so effectively in phenomenological idiom, need not be viewed as incompatible with a metaphysical account of God's infinite being described as *Esse Subsistens* or unrestricted act of existence.

Such avoidance of a metaphysics of being as an approach to God may rest, I suspect, upon a mistaken but understandable belief that ultimately 'being' can only signify finite being, so that the idea of 'infinite being' (such as not only Aquinas but also Descartes and Levinas affirm) must be understood as indicating the possibility of something more profound than being, namely, the truth that God is love. But we have seen in our account of Aquinas's metaphysics that although our way of signifying being (*modus significandi*) always represents finite being, this does not preclude that the perfection thereby signified (*quod significatum*) can be realized in God in an infinite manner as *Esse Subsistens* – a perfection incomprehensible to us but in him identical with his essential nature as unrestricted love. In the conclusions provided in the following chapter, we will discuss further how this congruity between a metaphysical conception of God as infinite being and a phenomenological conception of him as unrestricted self-giving love may be envisaged.

Conclusions

Introduction

Finally, I come, in the light of the indications of the preceding chapters, to formulate some conclusions about the strengths and limitations, the differences and complementarities of the three approaches to God which we have considered – the phenomenological, the metaphysical and the theological. These conclusions, of a rather general nature, are obviously capable of further development and comparison with other approaches.[1] However, precisely in virtue of their generality they may have the advantage of providing an overview or road map of the main features which must be taken into account in negotiating the very complex landscape which they traverse.

The first point to note is that both the metaphysical and phenomenological approaches are each, in their inspiration and development, philosophical undertakings of natural reason. They differ fundamentally from one another, and from theology, in virtue of their very different animating concepts or first principles. These are the intuition and affirmation of being as independent of human consciousness in the case of metaphysics, and the self-justifying phenomena given immanently to human consciousness in the case of phenomenology. The theological approach, by contrast, has as its inspirational origin and abiding presupposition the actuality of the revealed word of God accepted in faith as such.

Although metaphysics and phenomenology each has its own distinctive approach to God, they both also claim to play an important methodological role in the elaboration of a theological approach. Each considers that they are the appropriate philosophical instrument for this task and that the claims of the other approach are either inadequate or misguided, or both. One might usefully contrast them as seeking to address the issue in one case from an external or objective viewpoint and in the other from a more internal or subjective one – although this distinction is more a matter of degree than absolute difference.[2]

External and internal viewpoints

The metaphysical approach unfolds as an enquiry into the nature of being its various categories and properties, its analogical character and absolute value. It adopts an impersonal stance and seeks to express, as far as possible, the objective order of things as seen, not from a personal self-involving viewpoint, but dispassionately as if from 'a view from nowhere'. It is an approach whose claim to objectivity and detachment is supported by an underlying realist epistemology which affirms that our awareness extends beyond what is merely an object of our consciousness to knowledge of what exists independently of our awareness. It is committed as metaphysical enquiry to exploring the ultimate meaning and value of being understood as 'that which exists' – and it understands truth to be fundamentally an accordance, however incomplete, of our affirmations with that which exists.

In this exploration it seeks to determine the objective ontological structure of finite being, to establish its created dependence upon God identified as infinite being, and to develop an account of their coexistence. It maintains that a comprehensive discussion of creation cannot bracket out or ignore these metaphysical assertions about the ontological status of creatures and God and their relationship in which its enquiry culminates.

One of its criticisms of the phenomenological approach is the disinclination or inability of the latter to address such ontological issues, which for metaphysics are crucial to a philosophical approach to God. Indeed metaphysics would claim that it is clear that in several ways phenomenology itself presupposes these ontological affirmations. Thus, for example, the phenomenological reduction itself abstracts from the natural pre-philosophical attitude by a conscious exercise of selective inattention which brackets the issue of the independent existence of things affirmed in the natural attitude. It can proceed only by acknowledging that this ontological issue has not been adequately addressed by phenomenology otherwise than to dismiss it out of hand as 'a trap'.

Likewise if, as Marion insists, the being-given, which the enabled conscious subject manifests phenomenally, is anterior to and precedes this phenomenal manifestation, there is an issue to be addressed about the ontological status of this pre-phenomenological donation or *self-giving self* which the *self* as phenomenalized manifests indirectly and ultimately coincides with.[3] Metaphysically, activity presupposes existence and flows from it. Hence, if that which shows itself must first of all give itself then 'that which gives itself' must exist in order to do so. Its 'giving itself' cannot be disassociated from its 'being itself' except perhaps by means of the metaphysically disputed abstraction of the epoche or phenomenological reduction.

Similarly, there are ontological implications in Marion's appeal to the existence of a *pre-phenomenological* act of the will (albeit enabled by God) to account for the way in which what gives itself shows itself through the given-to which renders it manifest or phenomenal.[4] Providing an account of the existence of this pre-phenomenological power of willing is an ontological issue which by definition surpasses the goal of phenomenological explanation. Nor is it clear that there are no meta-phenomenological issues involved in the various analogical levels which 'the subject' assumes in the passage from constituting to constituted *ego*.

Likewise, the insistence that phenomenology as a method can play a role in the theological development of Christian Revelation only on the presupposition of the historical actuality of this revelation, which as such is inaccessible to phenomenology, has ontological implications which, again by definition, are beyond the scope of phenomenology to determine. Indeed, as one commentator remarks, 'to privilege phenomenology as the sole or even as the primary path of thinking is a metaphysical decision that can turn against phenomenology itself; and that in theology can actually lead to a distortion of the biblical phenomena'.[5]

Again, when Marion affirms that 'God is, exists, and that is the least of things', one may wonder is there an inadequate distinction here between the grammar of the proposition 'God exists' and the metaphysical affirmation of God as *Esse Subsistens*?[6] Certainly the proposition 'God exists' is trivial in the sense that it doesn't tell us anything about the divine perfection. But this is certainly not so in the case of the metaphysical affirmation that God is *Esse Subsistens*.

These are examples of what I have called the ontological complex of sustaining threads which constitute the obverse side of the meaningful pattern manifested directly on the phenomenological tapestry accessible immanently to consciousness. A consciously metaphysical approach will argue that such indications of trans-phenomenal reality have ontological implications which must be taken into account. Otherwise, it argues, one is banished to a mystifying Alice-in-Wonderland world where instead of, as usual, seeing a cat without a grin one sees a grin without a cat.

Such line of argument would claim that the objective ontological affirmations of metaphysics are a necessary counterpart to what phenomenology describes as given immanently to conscious subjectivity. This claim is particularly relevant to any affirmation of an experience of divine transcendence.

Any such affirmation implies, in the first instance, what may be called its *'assertability conditions'* – that is, the experiential conditions which must obtain to validate an affirmation of an experience of divine transcendence. In the validation of such an affirmation these conditions will include those which exceed any conditions involved in a purely naturalistic account of the alleged experience. Such naturalistic accounts which reductively dismiss any scientifically irreducible dimension of the alleged experience are found in some versions of human sciences such as sociology, anthropology and psychology – operating what Ricoeur calls their characteristic 'hermeneutic of suspicion'.

The experiential *assertability conditions* which, in the case of an affirmation of divine transcendence, resist and exceed any such reductive naturalistic understanding are perceptively depicted in Marion's account of saturated phenomena. These, as we have seen, are phenomena given in a bedazzling intuition as exceeding our conceptual capacity to originate, intend or adequately comprehend them. As such they are phenomenally verifiable non-naturalistic conditions of an assertion of divine transcendence. They are experiential phenomena in virtue of which divine transcendence is either adumbrated as a genuine possibility (e.g. in the intimation of infinite goodness given in our idea of 'that which is greater than anything conceivable') or actually experienced, through the gift of faith as historically realized in the all-surpassing Christian Revelation.

However, from the perspective of phenomenology, what these experientially 'saturating' conditions of an assertion of divine transcendence signify is deemed to be somehow immanent to conscious subjectivity. Thus considered, in the light of the phenomenological reduction or epoche, they are viewed as intrinsically relative to, though not derived from, this subjectivity. They are viewed as essentially co-relative to it. They do not consider or inform us about any objective existence intrinsically independent of their immanent presence to consciousness. Even the believer's conviction that the divine transcendence, which he experiences and affirms, enjoys an existence intrinsically independent of his awareness of it is, from a phenomenological perspective, reductively contained within the context of immanence. The independent existence which as believer he affirms is considered by phenomenology only as so appearing to him. As Husserl remarked, *'True being, therefore, whether real or ideal, has significance only as a particular correlate of my own intentionality,* actual or potential'.[7]

However, the convinced believer is unlikely to be satisfied with this phenomenologically reduced interpretation of his belief. He is more likely to consider it a diminution or unwarranted bracketing of the existential import signified by his belief rather than a critical refinement of it. A more adequate account of the believer's insistence upon the intrinsically independent transcendent existence of God requires a more fundamental perspective. This is one in which the experiential *assertability conditions* which enable the phenomenological assertion of divine transcendence are complemented by what may be called the particular *theoretical truth conditions* of this assertion. These are the ontological conditions or requirements which are elucidated metaphysically as the necessary counterpart of the phenomenological intimation or affirmation of divine transcendence.

Having argued against the dissolution by human sciences of any possible reality reference of our sense of God by showing what counts as an irreducible experience of divine transcendence and how such experience is discerned (e.g. by way of saturated intuition), a further issue arises. Is it the transcendent God himself who is given in our experiential sense of God? Or is it an effect or cipher of his transcendent reality which must be deciphered metaphysically? Or is it perhaps only an hallucination or illusion? In other words, beyond the *assertability conditions* of the affirmed experience, there remains the issue of the *theoretical truth conditions* which must obtain if the assertion of the experience is to be more than just that – however sincere, or convinced. It seems to me that this further question, in effect a metaphysical issue, is not only legitimate but also necessary. It seems unreasonable not to look for an ultimate explanation of how an allegedly dependable and irreducible experience of divine transcendence is possible. If we seek theoretical explanations even of unproblematic 'natural' experiences, surely it is reasonable to look for an explanation of a 'saturating' experience which exceeds our constitutive capacity and comprehension? (Perhaps, a helpful illustration, from the history of science, of this distinction between assertability and theoretical truth conditions is the differing pre-Copernican and post-Copernican theoretical accounts – one geocentric and the other heliocentric – of the same experiential astronomical observations. More simply, there is a clear distinction between the phenomenological description of a visual experience and the theoretical account of it in terms of neurological science.)

There is a tension, if not a downright contradiction, inherent in any phenomenological assertion of an experience of divine transcendence as both unconditional and also as co-relative to human subjectivity, a finite subjectivity however graciously transformed. This tension can be mitigated and perhaps even resolved by considering it in a wider metaphysical context. In this wider metaphysical context, the phenomenological indication of divine transcendence is appraised as an experienced finite cipher, trace, saturated impression or effect of an ontologically independent *non-experienced*

God. In a word, what is experienced phenomenologically is not divine transcendence but a cipher trace, effect, etc. of this divine transcendence which can mediate our assertion of the ontologically transcendent God. In this mediated indirect affirmation of divine transcendence, God can indeed be said unproblematically to be the origin of our 'sense of God'. How these phenomenal ciphers, traces, effects, etc., which can mediate our assertion of the non-experienced transcendent God, are to be interpreted is a further question. But however addressed, whether in terms of natural theology or simply in terms of the evidence of faith itself, the requirement remains for a metaphysical assertion of the ontological reality of God's transcendent existence as intrinsically independent of any phenomenological evidence for it. His immanence in creation, whether experienced or otherwise, must be understood in terms of his ontological transcendence – rather than the reverse.

A further feature of a metaphysical approach to God, such as we have seen defended by Aquinas, is its confidence in the capacity of natural reason to play a significant role in the justification of the free commitment of faith. This it does not only by elaborating the theological meaning and value of the truths held on faith but also by establishing through its own ability certain truths about the created nature of finite being, about the existence and nature of God and about the manner of their coexistence. It maintains that although such truths are accessible in the theological elaboration of divine revelation and are usually known in that way, they are also in principle, and often in practice, knowable by philosophical reflection and argument.

Moreover, a metaphysical approach is convinced that the concepts and language developed in its impersonal objective understanding of being are appropriate in the theological elaboration of revealed truths of faith which exceed the natural capacity of reason, for example, fundamental truths with profound ontological significance concerning the Triune God, the incarnate God, the real Eucharistic presence and the sacramental life of the church. The impersonal objective language through which we express our metaphysical comprehension of being serves to express the ontological significance of such truths, their accord with what actually exists, rather than what is only religiously experienced, poetically expressed or imaginatively signified.

In sharp contrast to this 'external' objective metaphysical point of view, a phenomenological approach to God, such as we have seen defended by Marion, adopts a distinctly more 'internal' and subject-oriented perspective. It elaborates its account exclusively in terms of that which gives itself, from itself and independently of anything other than itself, to human consciousness. It is only as immanent to the consciousness of a gracefully enabled subject that Christian Revelation can manifest itself as the saturated phenomenon of grace which it is. The God which one talks of here is not some abstract first cause, known by indirect metaphysical argument from finite beings, but God as he is in himself for us, a God who reveals himself experientially to us from himself as self-giving love of us.

This approach rejects all metaphysical speculation as an unwittingly idolatrous attempt to impose preconditions of human thought upon what could count as a manifestation or knowledge of God. Unlike metaphysics, as phenomenology it makes no supra-phenomenal ontological claims. As a philosophical approach to God, and in particular with reference to what might be known about the God of Christian Revelation, it confines its attention to articulating how such a divine manifestation would be phenomenologically possible if it were otherwise known to actually obtain. It does not, like metaphysics, claim to prove the existence of God as 'creator' or infinite being. It is through its imaginative concentration and optimization of the various modes of saturated intuition, which overflow any objectifying ambition of human consciousness, that it outlines this phenomenological possibility of God. The saturated intuitions which we experience, such as a painting that enraptures me, or the invisible gaze of face which I love, adumbrate the possibility of a religious experience of an invisible gaze which envisages and loves me. 'Recognizing saturated phenomena comes down to thinking seriously "that than which nothing greater can be conceived (*aliquid quo magus cogitari nequit*)" – which means thinking it as a final possibility of phenomenology.'[8]

In proposing itself as the appropriate methodology for Christian theology, phenomenology concentrates primarily not on the fact of creation to which metaphysics claims access, but on the great Christian truth, available only through divine gift or revelation, that God is self-giving love who loves us and has divinized us into his own life. Here, the theological account of God's revelation, as a loving givenness which enables us to manifest it and witness to it, is elaborated phenomenologically in terms of saturated phenomena.

This elaboration in phenomenological terms of the central Christian truth that, more fundamentally than ontological *self-possession,* God is expressive *self-giving* love highlights the insight that 'being-given' or 'donation' is more fundamental than the affirmation of 'being' prioritized by metaphysics.[9]

The subject-centred and self-involving revelation that the believer is divinized into God's life of self-giving love is the origin and continuing focus of a phenomenologically articulated Christian theology. It seeks to chart the profoundly interpersonal relationship of givenness between God as self-giving love for us and we who are thereby empowered with this love to respond and witness to it by our love of him and our neighbour. God as thus revealed to us in interpersonal terms is experienced immanently as the dazzling saturated phenomenon par excellence. It is an experience always of God as he is for us – a God of whom everything we affirm such as his goodness, truth and love, his closeness and distance, his presence and absence, his immanence and transcendence are all interpreted phenomenologically as they give themselves to our consciousness. They are not affirmed metaphysically as various objective modalities of his independently self-possessed act of existence.

This theological utilization of a phenomenologically oriented approach, focused 'subjectively' on the revelation of God as loving givenness, views metaphysical discourse and assertions about the objective order and modalities of being as inadequate and inappropriate in a theological articulation of this fundamental revelation of the loving interpersonal relationship of givenness and response established by grace between God and ourselves. Its external objective viewpoint cannot do justice to the drama of interiority which our divinization by God's love accomplishes. It might be of some use if we were discussing simply a God who might be known, through natural reason as well as revelation, only as a divine creator. God, thus considered, might be discussed in metaphysical language as the omniscient, omnipotent and infinite creator of an order of radically dependent finite beings. But for phenomenology, as developed by Marion, such a God, whom one would do well to fear and obey, might at most be seen as a provident and benevolent master of the universe including ourselves. He is the God rejected by much contemporary atheism. He is not the God who loves us, known only through Revelation, and best described theologically in phenomenological terms as givenness who fashions us immanently as his witness.

Needless to say, a proponent of the relevance of metaphysics as providing both a rational justification of some revealed truths and a valuable interpretative resource for theology generally will dispute this phenomenological rejection of it. She will argue that not merely the fact of creation but also the revealed truth of God's love of us and our divinization into his life can, and indeed should, be described objectively in the light of the metaphysical understanding of the act of existence as the source of all real perfection. The metaphysical discourse which objectively describes modalities and properties of being such as substance, relation, person, virtue, activity and receptivity, unity and diversity, love, truth, goodness and beauty are, it would be argued, not only appropriate but also required to explicate theologically the real significance and ontological density of various divinely revealed truths. These include the great revelation that God loves us, a truth which involves the requirement to describe our transformed ontological condition as not only creatures but also divinized into fellowship in God's own life.

Moreover, a theology open to metaphysical considerations will be concerned to emphasize that God is not only a God who is manifested in the believer's loving response and witness to him which his self-givenness enables. He is also God who exists in his own right independently of whether or not we believe in him or make him manifest phenomenally by our loving response. Indeed our metaphysician would argue that this ontological claim is implicit in Marion's own central motif according to which 'What *shows itself* first *gives itself* – This is my one and only theme'.[10]

It appears therefore that the phenomenological and metaphysical approaches to God and their respective relationships to Christian theology are very different and each understands itself in opposition to the other. As systematic approaches, each is animated by a different theme. They march to different tunes. Phenomenology prioritizes givenness manifesting itself immanently to human consciousness as saturated phenomenon. Metaphysics prioritizes the affirmation of being as that which exists absolutely and independently of human consciousness. Insofar as they each claim to be the philosophically ultimate, appropriate and comprehensive approach to God, they appear to glide through each other without establishing any effective contact.

However, our discussion has, I believe, shown that although each may be appropriate neither is either adequate or comprehensive. They need each other; for each identifies and elucidates important features which the basic orientation of the other overlooks.

Complementarity

The metaphysical approach seeks, as far as possible, to provide an external impersonal objective 'view from nowhere' to issues concerning the existence, nature, and coexistence of God and finite beings. It resorts to the resources of a metaphysics of being to elucidate the truths of Christian Revelation whether accessible to or beyond the reach of natural reason.

The phenomenological approach considers these issues as they present themselves internally to the believer's subjective (not subjectivist) self-involved consciousness of the graced interpersonal relationship in which he stands to God. It has recourse to the powerful idea of the saturated intuition through which a loving givenness and a responsively enabled given-to mutually phenomenalize each other in essential phenomenal reciprocity.[11] In this mutual phenomenalization, the situating God and the situated self appear as reciprocal and co-relative elements of an internal relationship rather than as metaphysically distinct substances one of which is ontologically dependent for its existence upon the other.

As has been indicated in Chapters 5 and 6, the difference between the two approaches is highlighted by their differing accounts of divine transcendence. In metaphysics this transcendence is understood impersonally and objectively as involving a radical asymmetry between God and his creation. This is an asymmetry which emphasizes God's ontological unrelatedness to and radical independence of his creation, which is understood as really related to him as wholly dependent. It is only in terms of this objective relationship of total dependence upon the creative activity of an ontologically transcendent God that one can speak metaphysically of God's immanence in his creation. Metaphysically, God's immanence in creation is affirmed only in terms of and as relative to his transcendence.

By contrast, in Marion's phenomenology, this metaphysical understanding of divine transcendence and immanence appears to be reversed. The affirmation of divine transcendence is situated *within* the context of its alleged immanence to human consciousness. It is an epistemological rather than a metaphysical conception of divine transcendence. In this conception, God's independent transcendence of the intrinsic resources of our conscious subjectivity is certainly maintained. Nevertheless, it is affirmed only as related to this conscious subjectivity which it paradoxically enables to phenomenalize it as a saturating experience of divine transcendence.

Within this context of what is immanent to consciousness, the affirmation of divine transcendence is intuited as cognitively related to, but underived from, the finite human subjectivity which sustains this consciousness. Here the asymmetry of divine transcendence, which in metaphysics is described in ontological terms, is interiorized within the sphere of immanence. It is described in terms of a saturated phenomenon which is intuited as exceeding the intrinsic constitutive or originating resources of the human subjectivity to which it is cognitively related as to that which enables the phenomenalization of it as divine transcendence. Divine transcendence is affirmed as an affection of human consciousness, given within the immanence of conscious subjectivity and recognized as transcendent because it exceeds the intrinsic resources of this consciousness. In a word, whereas in metaphysics divine immanence is understood ontologically in terms of divine transcendence, in phenomenology this transcendence is understood epistemologically in terms of God's immanence to human consciousness in a saturated intuition to which the subject of this intuition finds itself relativized.

This phenomenological approach to divine transcendence in terms of God's immanence to human consciousness opens an illuminating subject-oriented approach to the revealed truth that we are graced or divinized into personal friendship with God and to cognitive participation in his own life of unrestricted love. However, the metaphysician will, with justification, point out that the more objective ontological approach to divine transcendence must also be accommodated to give due weight to the equally veridical revelation of our condition as a radically dependent creation. Here, indeed, we find a striking example of the incompleteness and complementarity of both an internal or subjective standpoint and an external or objective one.

The two different approaches are embodied in different modes of discourse just as the language in which we express our conscious aesthetic delight in a beautiful sunset is relatively independent of the technical scientific language in which we might describe its neurological concomitant.[12] The two modes of discourse represent two different stances vis-à-vis our experience. One is internal and intentional-subject related. The other is external and impersonally objective. They are mutually exclusive in the sense that they cannot be simultaneously entertained.

This seeing the world differently does not imply that the metaphysician and the phenomenologist see different worlds or that one viewpoint is reducible to the other by way of simple translation or elimination.

They retain a certain autonomy vis-à-vis one another; each attaining significant insights but at the expense of abstraction from the insights of the other. This, however, should not exclude the attempt to explain or enlighten what is problematic in one approach in terms of the insights of the other. Each in their differing mode of discourse is an abstract, partial, conceptual expression of our concrete experience. Neither is identical with or a complete replica of this experience. However, their abstract character which enables their differing stances and discourses also constitutes the basis for a discussion of their compatibility and complementarity.

The ontological insights of metaphysics will never generate the awareness disclosed to a conscious subject's personal intuition of a saturated phenomenon conveying an experience of divine transcendence. It does not attain the perspective of phenomenological conviction. Similarly, phenomenology will never disclose the ontological implications of its conscious experience – implications from which it methodologically abstracts. But this mutual inhibition should not preclude comparative consideration of the two approaches with a view to discerning to what extent they imply one another as valid and complementary abstract expressions of our concrete experience.

That these two approaches to God, the external and the internal, each conveying crucially important insights, do not coalesce into a unified viewpoint is a consequence of the finite nature of our knowledge of things. It is just a further illustration of the more general difficulty in every branch of knowledge of ever-totally reconciling external and internal perspectives. As Thomas Nagel explains, if one could show how the internal and external standpoints can be developed and modified to take each other into account and together govern our thought about everything one would have a unified world view. However, 'instead of a unified world view, we get the interplay of these two uneasily related types of conception and the essentially incompletable effort to reconcile them'.[13] This of course does not imply that we should not strive to bring these very different approaches into relationship and to demonstrate that each provides us with truths which are overlooked or methodologically abstracted from if not precluded by the other. There is much to be gained from a consideration of the extent of their complementary difference. For example, the ontological distinctions and affirmations of the metaphysical approach temper any tendency of the phenomenological to identify our created divinization with God's uncreated divinity. Likewise the phenomenological account of our intuitive saturating awareness of a God who surpasses all objectivization and conceptual containment tempers any metaphysical tendency to consider its objective 'view from nowhere' as identical with God's knowledge of things.

The objective and subjective or external and internal standpoints represent, in all areas of knowledge, different and irreducible ways of accessing truth. The temptation is to embrace one to the exclusion of the other.

From the external or objective standpoint, we seek as far as possible to describe and understand a world as it exists independently of our pre-philosophical personal perspective on it. It operates effectively in the natural sciences. It also sustains a metaphysics which not only affirms the truth of extra-mental existence but also seeks by reflective impersonal argument to lead this existence to its ultimate truth.

However, this impulse towards a wholly objective and unified understanding in every sphere can lead us into error by seeking to apply a single model of objectivity to all problems. We can fall prey to false objectifications which involve us in various forms of reduction, elimination or annexation of evident features of reality. Reality is addressed as exclusively what can be described objectively. As Nagel observes, the paradigm of such reality is often taken to be the world described by physics by which we have attained the greatest detachment from a personal perspective on the world.

But precisely as such, physics must leave undescribed the subjective nature of the mental processes, however intimately associated with physical brain activity, involved in our formulation of physics itself. The subjectivity of consciousness is as irreducibly real as matter or energy or space or time and its fundamental reality is a condition of doing physics or, indeed, metaphysics or anything else.[14]

Conversely, to an internal or subjective standpoint it may be pointed out that my perspectival conscious awareness of the world implies the reality of physically describable impersonal processes, and metaphysically describable objective ontological principles which as such are inaccessible to the subjective standpoint. They are not directly part of our pre-scientific or pre-metaphysical view of things. They are not projections or elaborated descriptions of our immanent phenomenological experience of things. But they are realities (e.g. physiological processes and ontological structures), adduced by objective scientific and metaphysical enquiry, without which, whether we advert to it or not, we could not have a subject-centred phenomenological standpoint, or any other one either! Merleau-Ponty may make phenomenological sense when he affirms that, viewed from the perspective of conscious subjectivity, I am not the outcome of my physical and cultural antecedents since, on the contrary, such considerations are the outcome of my conscious intentionality which enables a world to appear and exist for me. However, it is at least equally true that this phenomenological perspective is accessible to us only in virtue of trans-phenomenological physical and cultural antecedents accessible, not phenomenologically, but only if at all by way of objective scientific enquiry. When you experience an unexpected even 'saturating' sharp pain in your chest you consult a physician not a phenomenologist!

Because the external and the internal viewpoints are never wholly reducible to one or the other, we must accept that a totally unified philosophical approach to God is unavailable. However, we should hardly find this surprising or disconcerting. Recognizing the finite and diversified nature of our knowledge, we can press on with the quest for the ever-vanishing goal of a more unified overview which fosters appreciation of the particular significance and mutual complementarity of the various irreducibly distinct approaches to God.

Perhaps, for example, the parallel alluded to in the previous chapter, between Marion's analogical understanding of *donation* or givenness and Aquinas's analogical understanding of *esse* might usefully be explored further. Perhaps the 'being-given' of phenomenology and the 'given being' of metaphysics can be helpfully interpreted as expressing two informative but complementary versions, inverse and obverse, of the same encompassing reality? The 'being-given' affirmed of our phenomenological experience is how reality appears from the immanent internal subjective standpoint of human consciousness. The 'given being' affirmed or 'consented to' metaphysically is how the same reality appears from an external objective impersonal standpoint. They are both dependable, but mutually irreducible, standpoints. One might allude again to the illustrative example of the complementarity between the subjectively engaging view of the meaningful imagery depicted on the front of a tapestry and the objectively discernible structured weave of the sustaining threads which scientific examination of the back of the tapestry discloses.

The phenomenon as that in which the 'being-given' manifests itself to conscious subjectivity is more than a mere datum of consciousness. It is a manifestation of the 'given being' which gives or discloses itself to consciousness – a self-possessed being whose component principles and ultimate foundation are matters for objective metaphysical consideration beyond any subject-oriented phenomenological description of what is consciously experienced. The delusion is to expect to achieve a totally unified philosophical approach. But we are at least relieved of the requirement to achieve our own tailored version of the great Hegelian system which, as argued in Chapter 4, seeks unavailingly to combine in a single philosophical tour de force a completely unified account of the metaphysical, phenomenological and theological approaches to God.

Interaction of theology and philosophy

Finally, a few words specifically about the theological approach to God – although it has been a constant backdrop as an unthematized criterion in our discussion of the adequacy of the different philosophical approaches. As we noted in Chapter 3, theology is the elaboration of truths revealed by God, and held on faith. These truths are held by way of divinely enabled faith because they characteristically surpass what we can know by natural reason. As such, for the believer, theology is an infinitely richer source of knowledge of God than is available in any philosophical system.

However, an appropriate use of our reason is required in order to unfold theologically the wealth of meaning and value contained in Christian Revelation about God and our supernatural relationship with him. Theology is a systematic attempt to understand what God has told us. It is an endeavour of human reason to come to terms with knowledge which is beyond its own intrinsic capability, knowledge attained through a gift of faith.

In this theological endeavour to understand what God has told us, one finds different views, not only about the nature of religious faith, but also about the appropriate (or inappropriate) use of philosophical reason in the undertaking. Such considerations influence the shape and course of different theological systems. We have seen, for example, how the different theologies of Thomas Aquinas and Karl Barth reflect very different appraisals of the role of reason in the theological enterprise. Here again, we are reminded that although all theology affirms the revealed word of God as its source, its elaboration is a selective cognitive activity of fallible finite beings who even in theology can only know in a finite human way. We know the word of God but not as God knows it, that is, as he knows himself in knowing the Word of God (– a Word which for us is made flesh in the mystery of the Incarnation which invokes but also eludes both phenomenological and metaphysical comprehension.)

Certainly theology, because of the divine source of the supernatural truth which animates it, can claim to be a more comprehensive approach to God than any philosophical endeavour. But, inasmuch as it involves varying appraisals of the instrumental scope and role of philosophical reason in its systematic elaboration, it is incapable of a unique and definitive formulation. The same dichotomy of external and internal viewpoints, which affect the broad philosophical options to which it can have recourse in its systematic interpretation and elaboration of revealed truth, affect the terms in which this theological interpretation will be formulated. Thus, for example, we have seen how the impersonal, objective standpoint of his metaphysical ontology affects Aquinas's theological account of how the foundational truths of faith are best elucidated and justified. (Even though he will eventually relativize the significance of his remarkable impersonal objective theological system as mere straw in comparison with what he glimpsed subjectively in a moment of mystical ecstasy.)[15]

Likewise, for Marion, his distrust of metaphysics and his phenomenological philosophical conviction orients him to a Barthian rather than a neo-Thomist theology.[16] His theological standpoint starts exclusively from the fact of God's unconditional revelation. It involves no metaphysical preconditions or demonstrations. It is one in which a phenomenology of saturated phenomena describing various non-objective manifestations of givenness both actual and possible, serves as a non-probative methodological instrument for the theological interpretation of the God of Revelation as a self-giving love who enables our personal self-involving response and witness.

However, the variety of theological elaborations of Christian Revelation is a result not only of the different philosophical methods invoked. It is also, and more basically, a consequence of the comparative theological significance ascribed by theologians in the course of human history to different components of revelation. To appreciate the difficulty of maintaining a balanced account of revealed truths, one need only advert to the enthusiasms which have inspired the many theological views deemed unorthodox or heretical by various church authorities, councils and magisteria.

In this study, we have highlighted just two fundamental truths of Christian Revelation: (1) that all finite being is created; (2) that God loves us and that we are thereby enabled not merely to obey him but to love him as divinized sharers of his life. These are the touchstones of Christian belief which establish the claims of theology to embody an approach to God and of God to us, which utterly surpasses the range of philosophical discovery.

There is of course the delicate question of how these fundamental truths should be understood or prioritized in relation to each other in a theological elaboration of them. The typically Judeo-Christian belief in creation is obviously historically prior in biblical terms. But is it a more fundamental theological consideration than the belief that God is love and that we are divinized into this love? Here again the tension between an external objective standpoint and an internal self-involving standpoint makes its presence felt.

From an external objective standpoint, one might argue that being created is a precondition of being graced or gifted with divine life and therefore is the foundation from which a systematic theology should be developed into an account of God's redeeming love.[17]

From an internal personal standpoint, the most significant theological consideration is the revelation of God's love for us. From this standpoint, the belief in creation can be interpreted as a consequence of this eternal love of God for us.

It would be difficult to maintain that either approach, considered on its own terms, is wrong or inappropriate. But it can be argued that each is essentially an incomplete elaboration of revelation and needs to be complemented by the insight and emphasis of the other. Thus the external standpoint emphasizes that our divine life is a gift and not an intrinsic feature of our created nature which is its objective precondition. Its theological significance is elucidated, from this standpoint, in ontological terms of re-creation or re-generation as a result of which the essence of the soul is endowed with a new spiritual being disposing it as capable of the vision of God, a vision anticipated in acts of faith and charity in this life.[18] The internal standpoint emphasizes that the astonishing revelation of our divinized involvement in God's love, *accepted as a revelation*, is not just an item of objective information but a personally enabled response in faith to this love. The theological elaboration of this internal subjective standpoint will be developed more in experiential self-involving terms of interpersonal encounter and response than in terms of objective ontological principles.

This theological diversity of perspectives from which the richness of revelation can be elaborated reinforces and is reinforced by the similar diversity of philosophical approaches to God which we have considered. Thus the theological articulation of the biblical revelation of creation will have influenced in a transformative way metaphysical speculation on the ultimate origin of the world, and this in turn provides an interpretative context for a more developed theology of creation. Likewise there is a reciprocally reinforcing influence of the revelation that God is a self-giving love which enables our love of him, and the enabling givenness of saturated phenomena described in Marion's phenomenology. Marion, of course, insists upon the distinction between theology as faithful elaboration of revelation accepted as historical actuality and phenomenology as exploration of the ultimate possibility of saturated phenomenon. However, as Thomas Carlson observes, his theology and his phenomenology inform one another profoundly.[19]

General conclusion

These remarks about various approaches to God, both theological and philosophical, lead us to a rather untidy, even banal, but possibly salutary general conclusion. It is that, unlike Hegel, we have no comprehensive or uniquely adequate approach to God. Certainly, we can say that theology has a justified claim to provide more comprehensive and more assured knowledge about God and our relationship with him than any purely philosophical approach. But this claim is justified only to the extent that the theological system in question is faithful to the revelation it articulates and is aware that it is never the adequate or only possible faithful expression of the revelation it seeks to understand. It may be a true understanding of revelation but never an adequate or exhaustive one. It is always only the limited expression of one finite effort, utilizing one or more than one of a variety of philosophical standpoints, to understand what God has told us. The theologian will do well bear in mind what Newton remarked about his own scientific endeavours: 'I seem to have been like a boy playing on the seashore, and diverting myself in now and then finding a smoother pebble or a prettier shell than ordinary, whilst the great ocean of truth lay all undiscovered before me.'[20]

This appraisal applies with even greater force to the various philosophical approaches to God. Individually they may provide true and valuable knowledge about the existence and nature of God, about our coexistence with him, and about the mode in which he might manifest himself if he exists. As different philosophical approaches to God, they will reach different or at least differently ordered and hopefully complementary conclusions about what can be known about him. But they cannot attain the revealed truth about God which by definition exceeds the scope of natural reason.

However, it is worth mentioning one particular claim about which both a metaphysically and a phenomenologically based philosophy might agree with one another and with an important theological contention. It is the claim that natural reason is able to understand the meaning of what is adhered to as true by faith. In view of their differing internal or external standpoints, they may differ in their account of the discourse in which this meaning should be expressed. But they would agree that it is grace and the will to adhere personally to the accessible meaning disclosed in revelation that transform this naturally understandable meaning into the response of faith. Faith does not disclose a new dimension of meaning in revelation which is inaccessible to the non-believer. It effects a new responsive relationship of a believer to a meaning accessible to believer and unbeliever alike – and therefore open to mutual discussion. Faith involves an assent to the truth of what without it one can understand but not assent to.

I mentioned that the rather untidy conclusion that the various approaches to God which we have considered are incomplete and irreducible but complementary may after all be a salutary one. For it can foster a fitting intellectual humility and engender a more open-minded and ecumenical spirit with regard to the great themes they investigate concerning the existence, nature and coexistence with us, of the God who created us and loves us. It illustrates that in order to advance a viewpoint it is not necessary to absolutize it and denigrate others which approach the same issues from another perspective. We might do well to recall that we still use the complementary terminologies of waves and particles when discussing the behaviour of much more mundane phenomena such as radiation and light. Or, more broadly, as Stephen Hawking remarked recently about theoretical physics generally: 'It could be that the physicist's traditional expectation of a single theory of nature is untenable, and there exists no single formulation. It might be that to describe the universe, we have to employ different theories in different situations . . . that is acceptable so long as the theories agree in their predictions whenever they overlap, that is, whenever they can both be applied.'[21]

The analogy of this remark with what we have suggested about the interrelationships of various approaches to God is obvious. This is not an apologia for relativism but a realistic and charitable recognition that we are each seeking to achieve, to the best of our finite ability and resources, some limited understanding about limitless truth, goodness and being.

A final word on the ambiguity, mentioned on the opening page, of our title *Approaching God*. Is it a matter of us approaching God or God approaching us? In the case of metaphysics, it seems clear that it is a case of us approaching God through natural reason exploring the ultimate metaphysical implication of our affirmation of being. Likewise, it seems clear, that in theology we have a case of God approaching us through the Revelation of his love for us.

The situation is less clear in phenomenology with its concentration on the self-giving manifestation of God to human consciousness. On the one hand it is theologically critical of claims of philosophical reason to establish, through its own resources and presuppositions, metaphysical truths concerning the existence of God as infinite being. Our assured knowledge concerning the actuality of God and of his love in our regard depends upon his approach to us through his gracious revelation which is best elaborated theologically in phenomenological terms. As philosophy, phenomenology approaches God – not in order to establish his existence and nature but rather to clear the philosophical space and delineate the terminology in which he can be appropriately welcomed should we otherwise become aware (through Revelation) of his actuality and intention in our regard. As Samuel Beckett might have remarked, it is an attentively prepared waiting for a God who may approach us.

Notes

Introduction

1 Cf. Georges Van Riet, *Philosophie et Religion* (Paris: Nauwelaerts, 1970), 188.
2 Cf. Patrick Masterson, *Atheism and Alienation; A Study of the Philosophical Sources of Contemporary Atheism* (South Bend: Notre Dame UP, 1972; Dublin: Gill and MacMillan, 1972; London: Penguin, 1973).
3 Cf. Patrick Masterson, *The Sense of Creation* (Aldershot: Ashgate, 2008), 127.

Chapter 1

1 For an excellent general introduction to philosophy of religion, cf. Brian Davies, *An Introduction to the Philosophy of Religion,* 3rd edn (Oxford: Oxford UP, 2004).
2 H. Dumery, *The Problem of God in Philosophy of Religion*, trans. C. Courtney (Evanston: Northwestern UP, 1964), 7.
3 Ibid.
4 Cf., for example, W. James, *The Varieties of Religious Experience* (London: Fontana Library edn, Collins, 1960); N. Smart, *The World Religions,* 2nd edn (Cambridge: Cambridge UP, 1998).
5 Dan Zahevi, 'Phenomenology', *The Routledge Companion to Twentieth Century Philosophy,* ed. Dermot Moran (London: Routledge, 2008), 674.
6 Cf. ibid., 673.
7 Martin Heidegger, *Basic Problems of Phenomenology*, trans. A. Hofstadter (Bloomington: Indiana UP, 1982), 21.
8 Cf. Zahevi, 'Phenomenology', 670.
9 Ibid., 678–9.
10 Martin Heidegger (citing Goethe's *Maxims and Reflections* n.993), *Basic Writings from Being and Time (1927) to The Task of Thinking (1964),* ed. David Farrell Krell (London: Routledge Keegan Paul, 1978), 385.
11 Cf. Richard Kearney, *Strangers, Gods and Monsters* (London: Routledge, 2003), 24.
12 Cf. ibid., 23.
13 Ibid., 22.
14 Cf. Richard Kearney, *Anatheism: Returning to God after God* (New York: Columbia UP, 2010), 52–3, 182–3.
15 Kearney, *Strangers, Gods and Monsters,* 105.

16 Ibid., 16–18.
17 Cf. ibid., 106–10 and *The God Who May Be* (Bloomington: Indiana UP, 2001), 69–79.
18 Cf. Kearney, *The God Who May Be*, 76.
19 Ibid., 29–30.
20 Ibid., 30.
21 Cf. ibid., 2.
22 Ibid., 4.
23 Emmanuel Levinas, *Totality and Infinity*, trans. A. Lingis (Pittsburgh: Duquesne UP, 1969), 78.
24 Cf. ibid., 183.
25 Ibid., 78–80.
26 Cf. Paul Ricoeur, 'Experience and Language in Religious Discourse', R. Janicaud, J. F. Courtine, J. L. Chretien, M. Henri, J. L. Marion and P. Ricoeur, *Phenomenology and the Theological Turn – The French Debate*, trans. B. Prusak and J. Kosky (New York: Fordham UP, 2000), 127.
27 Ibid.
28 Cf. ibid., 127–8.
29 Cf. ibid., 128.
30 Ibid.
31 Cf. Jean-Luc Marion, *The Visible and the Revealed*, trans. M. Gschwandtner (New York: Fordham UP, 2008), 127.
32 Jean-Luc Marion, 'In the Name', *God the Gift and Postmodernism*, ed. John Caputo and Michael Scanlan (Bloomington: Indiana UP, 1999), 39.
33 Cf. ibid., 40.
34 Cf. Edmund Husserl, *Ideas,* trans. W. Boyce Gibson (New York: Collier, 1962), I–24.
35 Marion, 'In the Name', 41.
36 Jean-Luc Marion, 'The Event the Phenomenon and the Revealed', *Transcendence in Philosophy and Religion*, ed. James E. Faulconer (Bloomington: Indiana UP, 2003), 99.
37 Ibid., 102.
38 Ibid., 103.
39 Cf. Marion, *The Visible*, 42–4.
40 Marion, 'In the Name', 40.
41 Cf. ibid., 39.
42 Cf. Marion, 'The Event', 97–101 and *The Visible*, 42–4.
43 Cf. James Faulconer, *Transcendence in Philosophy and Religion*, 7.
44 Cf. Marion, 'The Event', 99–101.
45 Ibid., 104.
46 Cf. Hussel, *Ideas,* I–24.
47 Marion, *The Visible*, 5.
48 Cf. ibid., 7.

49 Cf. John Smith, *Experience and God* (New York: Oxford UP, 1968), 167.
50 My account of this objection is indebted to Roger Chambon, *Le monde comme perception et realite* (Paris: Vrin, 1974), 82–91.
51 Husserl, *Ideas,* I–30–2.
52 Chambon, *Le monde,* 88–9.
53 Marion, 'In the Name', 40.
54 I am indebted to Marlene Zarader for her discussion of this difficulty in Marlene Zarader, 'Phenomenology and Transcendence', *Transcendence in Philosophy and Religion,* 106–19.
55 Marion, *The Visible,* 44.
56 Zarader, 'Phenomenology and Transcendence', 115.
57 Ibid., 116.
58 Marion, *The Visible,* 123.
59 Cf. Marion, 'The Event', 98.
60 Ibid., 99–100.
61 Ibid., 100–5.
62 Ibid., 102–3.
63 Cf. Marion, *The Visible,* 68.
64 Marion, 'On the Gift', *God the Gift and Postmodernism,* 70.
65 Cf. Marion, *The Visible,* 6.
66 Zarader, 'Phenomenology and Transcendence', 116–17.
67 Marion, 'On the Gift', 70.
68 Marion, *The Visible,* 100.
69 Cf. ibid., 21–2.
70 Cf. Marion, 'On the Gift', 70.
71 Marion, *The Visible,* 62.
72 Cf. ibid., 63.
73 Ibid., 47.
74 Marion, 'In the Name', 104.
75 Cf. Marion, *The Visible,* 121.
76 Cf. Marion, 'The Event', 103–4.
77 Cf. John Caputo, 'The Experience of God and the Axiology of the Impossible', *Religion after Metaphysics,* ed. M. Wrathall (Cambridge: Cambridge UP, 2003), 123–45.
78 Cf. ibid., 123.
79 Ibid., 143.
80 Dominique Janicaud, 'The Theological Turn of French Phenememology', *Phenomenology and the Theological Turn,* 103.
81 Cf. John Caputo's perceptive discussion of these contrasting views in *God the Gift and Postmodernism,* 1–19 and 185–222.
82 Cf. Maurice Merleau-Ponty, *Eloge de la Philosophie* (Paris: Gallimard, 1958), 38.
83 Jacques Derrida, 'On the Gift', *God the Gift and Postmodernism,* 75.

Chapter 2

1 Thomas Nagel, *The Last Word* (New York: Oxford UP, 1997), 3.

2 Cf. David Papineau, *Reality and Representation* (Oxford: Blackwell, 1987), 10.

3 John Searle, *The Construction of Reality* (London: Penguin, 1995), 165.

4 Cf. Thomas Aquinas, *Commentary on The Metaphysics of Aristotle,* trans. J. Rowan (Chicago: Henry Regnery, 1961), Bk 5, lectio 9, n.889.

5 Oliver Blanchette, *Philosophy of Being* (Washington: Catholic UP, 2003), 85.

6 St Anselm, *Prosologion,* trans. A. Mc Gill (London: MacMillan, 1968), 6.

7 Cf. ibid., 6–7.

8 Cf. Immanuel Kant, *Critique of Pure Reason,* trans. Norman Kemp-Smith (London: MacMillan, 1933), A592–A602.

9 Cf. Plato, 'Phaedo', *The Dialogues of Plato,* trans. B. Jowett (London: MacMillan, 1892), par. 75.

10 Cf. Aristotle, *Metaphysica,* trans. W. Ross (Oxford: Clarendon Press, 1928), Bk 10, ch. 1, 1052b.

11 Cf. St Augustine, *De Trinitate* (Paris: Bibliotheque Augustinienne, 1955), Bk 8, ch. 3.

12 'Qoumodo autem sciret intellectus, hoc esse ens defectivum et incompletum, si nullam haberet cognitionem entis absque omne defectu', St Bonaventure, *Itinerarium Mentis in Deum* (Rome: *Omnia Opera,* Quaracchi edn, 1891), t. 5, ch. 3, par. 3.

13 Rene Descartes, 'Meditations III', *A Discourse on Method, Meditations, and Principles,* trans. J. Veitch (London: J.M.Dent, 1912).

14 Thomas McPherson, 'Finite and Infinite', *Mind,* vol. 66 (1957): 379–80.

15 A. Farrer, *Finite and Infinite* (London: Westminister Press, 1943), 14–15.

16. Mark Pontifex and Ian Thretowan, *The Meaning of Existence: A Metaphysical Enquiry* (London: Sheed and Ward, 1953), 42–3.

17 Arthur Little, *The Platonic Heritage of Thomism* (Dublin: Golden Eagle Books, 1949), 194.

18 Cf. G. Isaye, *La theorie de la mesure et l'existence d'un maximum selon saint Thomas* (Paris: Beauschene, 1949), 79.

19 J. Marechal, *Le point de depart de la metaphysique* (Bruxelles: Lessianum, 1949), 378–80 (my translation).

20 Cf. Patrick Masterson, 'La definition du fini implique-t-elle l'infini?' *Revue Philosophique dde Louvain,* t. 62 (1964), 39–68.

21 Cf. Marion, *The Visible,* 58.

22 Ibid.

23 Isaye, *La theorie de la mesure,* 79.

24 'There is a subtler form of reifying abstraction, too, one which amounts to a reification of a human ideal. This occurs when one confuses the transcendent infinity of God with the limit ideas normally used for conveying the unlimited and inexhaustible character of our aspirations

towards the true, the good, and the beautiful.' Albert Dondeyne, *Contemporary European Thought and Christian Faith*, trans. Ernan Mc Mullan (Pittsburgh: Duquesne UP, 1958), 19.

25 Thomas Aquinas, *Summa Theologica*, trans. English Dominicans (London: Eyre and Spottiswisoode, 1964–74), I, q.2, a.1, ad3. (Hereafter, *S.T.*)

26 'It should not be thought that the uncreated truth is the proximate principle by which we understand and judge: rather, we know and judge by a light with which we are naturally endowed.' Thomas Aquinas, *In Librum Boethii de Trinitate Expositio* (Turin: Marietti, 1954); *Proem.* q.1, a.3, ad1 (my translation).

27 *S.T.*, I, q.86, a.2.

28 'In material things, the term "infinite" is applied to that which is deprived of any formal term. And form being known of itself, whereas matter cannot be known without form, it follows that the material infinite is in itself unknowable.' *S.T.*, I, q.86, a.2, ad1.

29 Cf. Leo Sweeney, 'l'infini quantitative chez Aristote', *Revue Philosophique de Louvain*, t. 58 (1960), 505–28.

30 *S.T.*, I, q.7, a.1.

31 Thomas Aquinas, *Scriptum Super IV Libros Sententiarum*, lib. I, d.43, q.1, a.1. (Hereafter *In 1 Sent.*)

32 Thomas Aquinas, *Summa Contra Gentiles*, English trans. *Summa Contra Gentiles, On the Truth of the Catholic Faith*, 5 vols, trans. A. Pegis, J. F. Anderson, V. J. Bourke and C. J. O'Neil (New York: Doubleday, 1955–7), Bk 1, ch. 28. (Hereafter, *S.C.G.*)

33 Thomas Aquinas, *Quaestiones disputatae de potentia* (Turin: Marietti, 1965), q.7, a.2, ad9. (Hereafter, *De Potentia*.)

34 '*Esse* is innermost in each thing and most fundamentally inherent in all things since it is formal in respect of everything found in a thing.' *S.T.*, I, q.8, a.1.

35 *De Potentia*, q.7, a.2, ad9.

36 'What is common to a multitude of things is not anything apart from this multitude except in thought alone . . . Much less therefore is common existence (*esse commune*) anything apart from all existing things except in the intellect only.' *S.C.G.*, Bk 1, ch. 26.

37 'Since any given form is determinative of its act of existence (*esse*) none of them is existence itself but rather has existence.' Thomas Aquinas, *Expositio in librum Boetii de hebdomadibus* (Turin: Marietti, 1954), lectio 2, n.34. (Hereafter, *De Hebd.*)

38 *S.T.*, I, q.3, a.4.

39 'In every composite there must be act and potency. For several things cannot become absolutely one unless among them there is something in act and something in potency.' *S.C.G.*, Bk I, ch. 18.

40 *S.T.*, 1, q.8, a.1. Cf. also *De Potentia*, q.7, a.2, ad9.

41 *S.T.*, 1, q.50, a.2, ad4. Cf. also *De Potentia*, q.2, a.1.

42 'The truth is that the First Cause is beyond being inasmuch as its existence is infinite. For being is called that which participates in a finite way in existence and this is what is proportionate to our intellect whose proper object is "that which is" as *III De Anima* observes. Wherefore our intellect can know only that which participates in existence: but the essence of God is his existence and therefore beyond our comprehension.' Thomas Aquinas, *In Librum de Causis Expositio* (Turin: Marietti, 1955), lectio 6, n.175. (Hereafter, *In Lib. De Causis.*)

43 Cf. *In 1 Sent.*, d.8, q.2, a.1.

44 Thomas Aquinas, *In VIII Libros Physicorum Expositio* (Rome: Leonine edn, 1884), Bk 3, ch. 8, n.13.

45 *S.T.,* 1, q.6, a.4.

46 Thomas Aquinas, *In Librum Beati Dionysii de Divinis Nominibus Expositio* (Turin: Marietti, 1950), ch. XI, lectio 3, n.921. (Hereafter *In de Div.Nom.*)

47 Cf. *S.C.G.,* Bk 1, ch. 26.

48 Cf. *De Potentia,* q.7, a.2, ad7.

49 'Since we have no knowledge of the essence of God his existence is certainly not self-evident but requires proof.' Thomas Aquinas, *Quaestiones Disputatae de Veritate* (Turin: Marietti, 1949), q.10, a.12. (Hereafter, *De Veritate.*)

50 'A creature is said to be perfected by what pertains to its completed nature ... (and) by being contained within certain specific limits.' *In de Div. Nom,* ch. 13, lectio 1, n.964.

51 *In Lib. De Causis,* lectio 22, n.378–9.

52 Cf. Patrick Masterson, *The Sense of Creation,* chs 5–7. I suggest that the data of such arguments disclose significant ciphers of the sort of asymmetrical relationship between God and the world, the relationship whereby the world is wholly dependent upon God but he is in no way dependent upon it. It is these experiential ciphers of transcendence which provide the basis for indirect arguments for a divine creator.

53 Anthony Kenny, *Reason and Religion* (Oxford: Blackwell, 1987), 84.

54 *S.T.,* 1, q.3, a.4, ad2.

55 'For some have said that all such names, although they are applied to God affirmatively, nevertheless have been brought into use more to express some remotion from God, rather than to express any thing that exists positively in Him. Hence they assert that when we say that God lives we mean that God is not like an inanimate thing; and the same applies in like manner to other names; and this was taught by Rabbi Moses.' *S.T.,* 1, q.13, a. 2.

56 *De Potentia,* q.7, a.2, ad9.

57 '"*Esse*" is said to be the act of a being precisely inasmuch as it is being. It is that in virtue of which something is said to be an actual being in the

natural order of things.' Thomas Aquinas, *Quaestiones Qoudlibetales* (Turin: Marietti, 1949), lectio 9, q.2, a.3.

58 Cf. Thomas Aquinas, *De Ente et Essentia* (Paris: Roland-Gosselin edn,1948), ch. 1.

59 *De Veritate,* q.21, a.2.

60 *In 1 Sent.,* d.43, q.1, a.1; *De Potentia,* q.1, a.2.; *S.T.,* 1, q.4., a.2.

61 *Quaestiones Quodlibetales,* lectio 7, q.1, a.1, ad1.

62 Thomas Aquinas, *In Libros Peri Hermeneias Aristotelis Expositio* (Turin: Marietti, 1964), lectio 14, n.197.

63 *In Lib de Causis,* lectio 6, n.175.

64 Thomas Aquinas, *De Substantiis Separatis* (Turin: Marietti, 1954), lectio 7, n.49.

65 Cf. *S.C.G.,* Bk 1, ch. 43.

66 Cf. ibid, ch. 26.

67 Cf. *De Veritate,* q.10, a.11, ad10.

68 *De Potentia,* q.7, a.2, ad.7.

69 Cf. *S.C.G.,* Bk 1, ch. 30.

70 Cf. *S.T.,* 1, q.29, a.3, ad4 and *In II Sent.,* d.3, q.1, a.1, ad1.

71 Cf. *S.T.,* 1, q.29, a.3, ad4.

72 Cf. *In de Div. Nom.,* ch. 5, lectio 2, n.661.

73 Cf. *S.C.G.,* Bk 3, ch. 52 and *S.T.,* 1, q.11, a.3.

74 *S.C.G.,* Bk 1, ch. 28.

75 Cf. *S.T.,* 1. q.32, a.1; 1, q.19. a.4 and *S.C.G.,* Bk 2, ch. 25.

76 *S.T.,* 1, q.3, a.5, ad2.

77 Cf. *S.T.,* 1, q.61, a.1.

78 Cf. *S.T.,* 1, q.4, a.3, ad3.

79 Cf. *S.T.,* 1, q.6, a.4.

80 *S.T.,* 1, q.44, a.3.

81 H. Thibaut, *Creation and Metaphysics: A Genetic Approach to Existential Act* (The Hague: M. Nijhoff, 1970), 58.

82 'That which I call *esse* is the actualising principle of every act and therefore the perfection of every perfection.' *De Potentia,* q.7, a.2, ad9.

83 *S.C.G.,* Bk 3, ch. 69.

84 Cf. ibid.

85 *S.T.,* 1, q.44, a.1, ad1.

86 Cf. H. Thibaut, *Creation and Metaphysics,* 68.

87 Cf. *S.C.G.,* Bk 3, ch. 70.

88 Cf. *S.T.,* 1–2, q.19, a.5.

89 Cf. *S.C.G.,* Bk 1, ch. 11.

90 Cf. *S.T.,* 2–2, q.81, a.3.

91 Cf. Denys Turner, *The Darkness of God: Negativity in Christian Mysticism* (Cambridge: Cambridge UP, 1995).

92 Cf. *S.C.G.,* Bk 1, ch. 8.

93 *In 1 Sent.,* d.8, q.1, a.4.

Chapter 3

1 Jean-Luc Marion, *God without Being: Hors Texte*, trans. Thomas Carlson (Chicago: Chicago UP, 1991), 2.
2 Van Riet, *Philosophie et Religion*, 16–17.
3 These remarks are indebted to the perceptive summary of Barth's account of the relationship between faith and reason provided by Henri Bouillard, *The Logic of the Faith*, trans. M. Gill (Dublin: M.H. Gill and Son, 1967), chs 4 and 5, cf. also his masterly 3 volume *Karl Barth* (Paris: Aubier, 1957).
4 Karl Barth, *The Epistle to the Romans*, trans. E. Hoskyns (London: Oxford UP, 1933), 143–4.
5 Karl Barth, *Credo*, trans. J. S. McNabb (London: Hodder and Stoughton, 1936), 11–12.
6 Ibid., 40.
7 Bouillard, *The Logic of the Faith*, 100.
8 Karl Barth, *Dogmatik im Grundriss* (Munich: Kaiser, 1947), 42–3. Translated in Bouillard, *The Logic of the Faith*, 101.
9 Karl Barth, 'A Presupposition of the Proof: The Name of God', *The Many-Faced Argument*, ed. J. Hick and A. McGill (London: Macmillan, 1968), 123–4.
10 Cf. Bouillard, *The Logic of the Faith*, 95.
11 Cf. Sebastian Matczak, *Karl Barth on God* (New York: Alba House, 1962), 284–92, and Bouillard, *The Logic of the Faith*, 101; K. Johnson, *Karl Barth and the Analogia Entis* (London: T&T Clark, 2010): 13–81; K. Diller, 'Karl Barth and the Relationship between Philosophy and Theology', *The Heythrop Journal*, vol. LI (2010): 1035–52.
12 *S.C.G.*, Bk 1, ch. 11.
13 *S.C.G.*, Bk 3, ch. 4.
14 Cf. Van Riet, *Philosophie et Religion*, 75.
15 Ibid., 75–6.
16 Cf. *S.C.G.*, Bk 3, ch. 40.
17 M. D. Roland-Gosselin, 'De la connaissance affectif', *Revue Scientifique de Philosophie et Theologie*, t. 27 (1938), 22.
18 'But in knowledge by faith the operation of the intellect is found to be most imperfect as regards that which is on the part of the intellect (although it is the most perfect on the part of the object), for the intellect in believing does not grasp the object of its assent.' *S.C.G.*, Bk 3, ch. 40.
19 *S.T.*, 1, q.2, a.2, ad1.
20 *S.T.*, 1, q.1, a.1.
21 'The defect acquired from the origin is not acquired through any subtraction or corruption of any good that human nature possesses from its own principles, but through the subtraction or corruption of something that was added to nature.' *In II Sent.*, d.33, q.2, a.1.

22 'The end to which the human being is ordained – namely the happiness which consists in the vision of God – is beyond the power of created nature, for it is connatural only to God . . . So it was fitting that human nature be so instituted as to have not only what was due to it from its natural principles, but also something further by which it might easily reach its end . . . When a turning away from this end was brought about by sin, it all ceased to exist in human nature, and Man was left in possession of only those goods which followed from his natural principles.' *In II Sent.*, d.30, q.1, a.1.

23 Martin Luther, *Lectures on Genesis*, ed. J. Pelican (St Louis: Concordia Publishers, 1958), 187.

24 'The gifts of grace are added to nature in such a way that they do not destroy it, but rather perfect it. So too the light of faith which is imparted to us as a gift, does not do away with the light of natural reason given to us by God. Rather, since what is imperfect becomes a representation of what is perfect, what we know by natural reason has some likeness to what is taught to us by faith.' Thomas Aquinas, *In librum de Boethii de Trinitate Expositio* (Turin: Marietti, 1954), q.2, a.3.

25 Cf. Van Riet, *Philosophie et Religion*, 77.

26 Cf. ibid., 96.

27 Herbert McCabe, *God Still Matters*, ed. Brian Davies (London: Continuum, 2002), 7.

28 Marion, *God without Being*, XX.

29 Ibid., XXI.

30 Marion, *The Visible*, 7–8.

31 Marion, *God without Being*, XXIV.

32 Cf. ibid., ch. 4. Cf. also Philip Roseman, 'Postmodern Philosophy and Jean-Luc Marion's Eucharistic Realism', *Transcendence and Phenomenology*, ed. Peter Coulter and Conor Cunningham (London: S.C.M. Press, 2004), 84–110.

33 Husserl, *Ideas*, Bk 1, par. 24.

34 McCabe, *God Still Matters*, 8.

35 Cf. Ludwig Feuerbach, *The Essence of Christianity*, trans. George Elliot (New York: Harper and Row, 1957), ch. 1.

36 McCabe, *God Still Matters*, 9–10.

37 Martin Heidegger, 'The Onto-Theo-Logical Constitution of Metaphysics', *Identity and Difference*, trans. Joan Stambaugh (Chicago: Chicago UP, 2002), 68–73.

38 Cf. Paul Ricoeur, *Philosophie de la volonte* (Paris: Aubier, 1960), t. II, vol. 2, 25 and 257.

39 Jeffrey Kosky, 'Translator's Preface: The Phenomenology of Religion: New Possibilities for Philosophy and for Religion', *Phenomenology and the 'Theological Turn'*, 114.

40 Cf. Husserl, *Ideas*, Bk 1, par. 58.

41 Levinas, *Totality and Infinity*, 28.

42 Ibid., 78–80.

43 Ibid., 293.

44 I have described how this suggestion can be further developed in *The Sense of Creation*, 80–4.

Chapter 4

1   I elucidated this theme throughout Patrick Masterson, *Atheism and Alienation: A Study of the Philosophical Sources of Contemporary Atheism* (Dublin: Gill and MacMillan, 1971). This chapter on Hegel is a somewhat revised version of chapter 3 of that book reproduced here by permission of the publisher.

2   Edmund Husserl, *Cartesian Meditations*, trans. D. Cairns (The Hague: Martinus Nijhof, 1968), 4.

3   Descartes, *Meditations III*, 196.

4   Cf. Marion, *The Visible*, 58.

5   Cf. Immanuel Kant, *Critique of Practical Reason*, trans. T. Abbott (London: Longmans, 6th edn, 1909), 221–2.

6   Immanuel Kant, *Religion within the Limits of Reason Alone*, trans. T. Greene and H. Hudson (New York: Harper Torchbook, 1960), 157.

7   Friedrich Hegel, *On Christianity: Early Theological Writings*, trans. T. Knox and K. Kroner (New York: Harper Torchbook, 1961), 69–71.

8   Ibid., 176.

9   Ibid., 212.

10 Ibid., 247.

11 Ibid., 313.

12 The chief source of the following account of Hegel's discussion of God and religion is his *Lectures on the Philosophy of Religion*. They comprise courses given at various times between 1821 and 1831 and compiled posthumously from his own notes and copies of the lectures made by some of his students. Quotations in this chapter are from the English edition *Lectures on the Philosophy of Religion*, 3 vols, trans. E. Spiers and J. Sanderson (London: Routledge and Keegan Paul, 1895). (Hereafter, *Philosophy of Religion*.) This translation is a composite work conflating material from the various versions of the Lectures and was the only English edition available when the original version of this chapter was published. I have retained the quotations as translated in this edition. However, anyone wishing to pursue the sequence of Hegel's thought through a comparison of the various individual versions of the Lectures should consult the recently published three-volume translation – F. G. Hegel, *Lectures on the Philosophy of Religion*, ed. Peter C. Hodgson (Oxford: Oxford UP, 2007–8).

13   Cf. Friedrich Hegel, 'The Logic of Hegel', *The Encyclopaedia of the Philosophical Sciences,* trans. W. Wallace (Oxford: Oxford UP, 1873), par. 6. (Hereafter, *Encyclopaedia Logic.*)

14   Quentin Laeur, *Hegel's Concept of God* (New York: SUNY Press, 1982), 328.

15   *Philosophy of Religion,* vol. 1, 174.

16   Ibid., vol. 3, 164.

17   Ibid., vol. 1, 200.

18   Ibid., vol. 1, 198.

19   Ibid., vol. 1, 199–200.

20   *Encyclopaedia Logic,* par. 163.

21   *Philosophy of Religion,* vol. 1, 198.

22   Thomas Aquinas, *In Peri Hermeneias,* lectio 14, par. 21.

23   *S.T.,* 1, q.19, a.3 and *S.T.,* 1, q.44, a.4.

24   *In Peri Hermeneias,* lectio 14, par. 22.

25   Cf. *S.T.,* 1, q.3.

26   *Philosophy of Religion,* vol. 3, 98.

27   Cf. *S.T.,* 1, q.10.

28   *Philosophy of Religion,* vol. 3, 1.

29   Ibid., vol. 3, 37.

30   Ibid., vol. 3, 10.

31   Ibid., vol. 3, 42.

32   For a penetrating version of such an interpretation, cf. Georges Van Riet, 'Le Probleme de Dieu chez Hegel: Atheisme ou Christianisme?' *Revue Philosophique de Louvain,* t. 63 (1965), 354–418. Cf. also, Emil Fackenheim, *The Religious Dimension of Hegel's Thought* (Bloomington: Indiana UP, 1967), chs 5–7.

33   *Philosophy of Religion,* vol. 3, 71.

34   James Collins, *The Emergence of Philosophy of Religion* (New Haven: Yale UP, 1967), 279.

35   Friedrich Hegel, *Berliner Schriften* (Hamburg: Meiner, 1956), quoted in translation by Laeur, *Hegel's Concept of God,* 134.

36   'The rise of thought beyond the world of sense, all this transition is thought and nothing but thought . . . Animals make no such transition. They never get further than sensation and the perception of the senses, and in consequence they have no religion.' Hegel, *Encyclopaedia Logic,* par. 50; cf. also, *Philosophy of Religion,* vol. 1, 160–72.

37   *Philosophy of Religion,* vol. 1, 206.

38   Cf. ibid, vol. 1, 142–5.

39   Friedrich Hegel, *The Phenomenology of Mind,* trans. J. B. Baillie (New York: Harper, 1967), 229–67.

40   *Philosophy of Religion,* vol. 2, 340.

41   Ibid., vol. 2, 209–19.

42   Ibid., vol. 2, 211.

43 'The conscious perception of the unity of the soul with the Absolute,
    or the reception of the soul into the bosom of the Absolute, has not yet
    arisen. Man has as yet no inner space, no inner extension, no soul of such
    an extent as to lead it to wish for satisfaction within itself, but rather it is
    the temporal which gives it fullness and reality.' *Philosophy of Religion*,
    vol. 2, 213.
44 Ibid., vol. 3, 76–7.
45 'This death is love itself, expressed as a moment of God, and it is this death
    which brings around reconciliation. In it we have a picture of absolute
    love. It is the identity of the Divine and the human, it implies that in the
    finite God is at home with Himself, and this finite as seen in death is itself
    a determination belonging to God. God has through death reconciled the
    world, and reconciled it eternally with Himself. This coming back from
    the state of estrangement is His return to Himself, and it is because of it
    that He is Spirit.' *Philosophy of Religion,* vol. 3, 96.
46 Ibid., vol. 3, 138.
47 Ibid., vol. 1, 247.
48 Cf. E. Gilson, *Le philosophe et la theologie* (Paris: Fayard, 1960).
49 *Philosophy of Relgion,* vol. 3, 148.
50 Ibid., vol. 3, 121–2.
51 Cf. Roger Vancourt, *La Pensee religieuse de Hegel* (Paris: Fayard, 1965),
    104–6.
52 Paul Ricoeur, *De l'Interpretation* (Paris: Seuil, 1965), 505–6; trans. Laeur,
    Hegel's Concept of God, 4.
53 Maurice Merleau-Ponty, 'Le metaphysique dans l'homme', *Sens et
    non*-sens (quoted in translation by Laeur, *Hegel's Concept of God*, 4)
    (Paris: Gallimard, 1961), 167.

Chapter 5

1 'What has made us more cautious in defining with absolute certainty, the
   origin of the sense of God, is the realization that *a priori*, in behavioural
   terms alone, the possibility cannot be excluded that God is the origin
   of the sense of God – a possibility which to Tylor, Durkheim, and Freud
   was simply inadmissible.' John Bowker, *The Sense of God: Sociological,
   Anthropological and Psychological Approaches to the Sense of God* (Oxford:
   Oxford UP, 1973), 16.
2 John Caputo, 'The Experience of God and the Axiology of the Impossible',
   Religion after Metaphysics, ed. Mark Warthall (Cambridge: Cambridge
   UP, 2003), 139.
3 Ibid., 128.
4 C. Beyer, 'Edmund Husserl', online, *Stanford Encyclopaedia of Philosophy*
   (2007).

5   'But', it may be asked, 'does not this theological gear-shift from phenomenology not also "un-bracket" what the phenomenological reduction achieves and hence have unavoidable ontological implications?'

6   John Caputo and Gianni Vattimo, *After the Death of God* (New York: Columbia UP, 2007), 75.

7   Jeffrey Kosky, *Phenomenology and the Theological Turn*, 114.

8   Ibid., 116.

9   Cf. Jean-Luc Marion, *Being Given: Towards a Phenomenology of Givenness,* trans. Jeffrey Kosky (Stanford: Stanford UP, 2002), 367.

10 Thomas Carlson, '"Introduction" to J-L Marion', *The Idol and the Distance,* trans. and intro. T. Carlson (New York: Fordham UP, 2001), xvi.

11 Jean-Luc Marion, *God without Being*, xxi.

12 Cf. T. Carlson, Introduction to *The Idol and the Distance*, xix.

13 *Being Given*, 307.

14 *The Visible*, 14.

15 *Being Given,* 117.

16 *The Visible*, 5–6.

17 As Jean-Yves Lacoste remarks: 'Signs and symbols may always be pseudo-signs and pseudo-symbols. And we may eventually take leave of pure perception, and ask reasoning to come to the help of the party, to decipher them.' Jean-Yves Lacoste, 'Perception, Transcendence and the Experience of God', *Transcendence and Phenomenology,* 6.

18 *Being Given*, 112.

19 Emmanuel Levinas, *En decouvrant l'existence avec Husserl et Heidegger* (Paris: Vrin, 1967), 98. Cf. also Quentin Meillassoux, *After Finitude: An Essay on the Neccesity of Contingency*, trans. Ray Brassier, (London: Continuum, 2008), 1–27.

20 Thomas Nagel, *The View from Nowhere* (New York: Oxford UP, 1986), 4.

21 John Caputo, 'The Experience of God', *Religion after Metaphysics,* 132.

22 Ibid., 123–4.

23 Cf. Desmond Connell, 'Substance and Subject', *Essays in Metaphysics* (Dublin: Four Courts Press, 1996), 25–42.

24 Cf. A. Lisska, 'Medieval Theories of Intentionality', *Analytical Thomism: Traditions in Dialogue,* ed. C. Patterson and J. Pugh (Aldershot: Ashgate, 2006), 156.

25 Cf. Van Riet, *Philosophie et Religion*, 28.

26 Connell, 'Substance and Subject', 40.

27 J. O'Leary, 'A Trojan Horse in the Citadel of Phenomenology', *Givenness and God,* ed. L. Leask and E. Cassidy (New York: Fordham UP, 2005), 137.

28 *The Visible*, 60.

29 Ibid., 5–6.

30 Ibid., 5.

31 Ibid.

32 Ibid., 7–8.

33 *Transcendence in Philosophy and Religion,* 102.

34 Cf. ibid, 101–3.

35 Ibid., 102.

36 Cf. *The Visible,* 63–4.

37 Ibid., 63.

38 Cf. ibid., 47.

39 Ibid., 64.

40 Ibid.

41 *The Visible,* 48.

42 Jean-Luc Marion, *Cartesian Questions: Method and Metaphysics,* trans. and ed. Jefrey Kosky (Chicago: Chicago UP, 1999), 157.

43 'Transcendence requires a superlative, whereas the transcendental limited itself to, and was limited by, the comparative. But the *summum bonum* also influences what it has left behind, leaving its mark on it, by overdetermining the *majus* by a *melius,* which, so to speak, colours "the greatest" for us by the light (or the shadow) of the absolutely best.' Marion, *Cartesian Questions,* 153.

44 Marion, *Cartesian Questions,* 154.

45 Marion, *God, the Gift,and Postmodernism,* 39.

46 Cf. Aquinas, *S.C.G.,* Bk 1, ch. 11.

Chapter 6

1 Bertrand Russell, 'A Debate on the Existence of God', *The Existence of God,* ed. John Hick (London: MacMillan, 1964), 175.

2 'Though the relation to its cause is not part of the definition of a thing caused, still it follows, as a consequence, on what belongs to its essence; because from the fact that a thing has being by participation, it follows that it is caused. Hence such a being cannot be without being caused, just as a man cannot be without having the faculty of laughing.' *S.T.,* 1, q.44, a.1, ad.1.

3 Cf. Marion, *Transcendence in Philosophy and Religion,* 99.

4 Kearney, *The God Who May Be,* 2–3.

5 Cf. ibid., 111.

6 Marion, *God without Being,* xx.

7 Marion, *The Visible,* 5.

8 'The act of being, as such, is caused by creation which presupposes nothing; because nothing can pre-exist that is outside being as such. By makings other than creation, this being or such being, is produced; for out of pre-existent being is made this being or such a being. It remains that creation is the proper act of God.' *S.C.G.,* Bk 2, ch. 21.

9 Cf. *S.C.G.,* Bk 1, ch. 11.

10 *In Peri Hermeneias,* lectio 14, par. 197.

11 Cf. *De Ente et Essentia,* ch. 5.
12 Jean-Luc Marion, *Dieu sans l'etre* (quote from Marion's French text) (Paris: PUF, 2002), 315 (my translation).
13 Cf. ibid., 321–2.
14 Cf. ibid., 322.
15 Cf. ibid., 321.
16 Cf. ibid., 324–6.
17 Cf. ibid., 329.
18 'For as a creature has *esse* only as it originates from the first being so likewise it is called being only inasmuch as it resembles the first being. And similarly with wisdom and all other such perfections ascribed to creatures.' *In 1 Sent,* Prologus, q.1, a.2, ad2.
19 Cf. *In Lib. De Causis,* lectio 6, par. 161.
20 'The First Cause is beyond being inasmuch as he is infinite act of existence itself. For being is said to be that which participates in existence, *esse,* finitely and this is what is proportionate to our intellect, whose object is "that which exists" as is noted in III *De Anima.* Whence our intellect can grasp only that which of its nature participates in existence; but the divine nature is his existence itself, and therefore beyond our comprehension.' *In Lib. De Causis,* lectio 6, par. 175.
21 *In 1 Sent.* d.8, a.1, ad4.
22 *De Potentia,* q.7, a.2, ad7.
23 *S.T.,* 1, q.2, a.2.
24 *In Lib. De Causis,* lectio 6, par. 161.
25 Cf. *S.T.,* 1, q.32, a.1.
26 *De Potentia,* q.7, a.2, ad9.
27 *S.T.,* 1, q.5, a.1, ad1.
28 'It is impossible that there be any being that does not have existence, *esse.* De Veritate,* q.21, a.2.
29 Cf. *De Ente et Essentia,* ch. 1.
30 *S.T.,* 1, q.2, a2, ad2.
31 Cf. the brief but excellent account of this theme in Rudi Te Velde, *The 'Divine Science' of the Summa Theologiae* (Aldershot: Ashgate, 2006), ch. 6.
32 Thus Aquinas remarks: 'God alone deifies, bestowing a partaking of the Divine nature by a participated likeness.' *S.T.,* 1–2, q.112, a.1; and again: 'Since there is a communication between man and God, inasmuch as He communicates His happiness to us, some kind of friendship must needs be based on this same communication . . . the love which is based on this communication is charity; wherefore it is evident that charity is the friendship of man for God.' *S.T.,* 2–2, q.23, a.1.
33 McCabe, *God Still Matters,* 7.
34 Marion, *The Visible,* 21.
35 Ibid., 32.
36 Ibid., 45.

37 Ibid., 46–7.
38 Cf. ibid., 47–8.
39 Ibid., 44.
40 Cf. ibid., 64.
41 Jean-Luc Marion, 'Sketch of the Saturated Phenomenon', *Phenomenology – Critical Concepts*, ed. Dermot Moran (London: Routledge, 2004), 25.
42 *The Visible*, 61–2.
43 *Being Given*, 219.
44 Cf. *The Visible*, 48.
45 Cf. *Being Given*, 242.
46 Cf. ibid., 234–47.
47 Cf. ibid., 246–7.
48 Cf. ibid., 367.
49 *The Visible*, 7–8.
50 Marion, *The Idol and the Distance*, 20.
51 Cf. *Transcendence in Philosophy and Religion*, 88.
52 Cf. *The Visible*, 21; also, 'Hence phenomenology goes unambiguously beyond metaphysics in the strict sense that it gets rid of any *a priori* principle in order to admit givenness, which is originary precisely insofar as it is *a posteriori* for the one who receives it.' *Transcendence in Philosophy and Religion*, 57.
53 *The Visible*, 62.
54 Ibid., 63.
55 *Being Given*, 270–1.
56 *The Idol and the Distance*, 6.
57 T. Carlson, 'Translator's Introduction', *The Idol and the Distance*, xvii.
58 Cf. *Being Given*, 243–4.
59 *God without Being*, xix–xx.

Conclusions

1 Comparison, for example, with the approach influential in Anglo-Saxon philosophical circles, loosely referred to as Wittgensteinian Fideism, which has interesting similarities with the phenomenological approach. I have discussed this approach in *The Sense of Creation*, ch. 4.
2 For a perceptive account of this distinction between subjective and objective viewpoints across a wide range of philosophical issues, cf. Nagel, *The View from Nowhere*, 1–108.
3 'If manifestation perhaps proceeds from the given, then the given has to precede it: . . . The *self* of what shows *itself* would then manifest indirectly that it gives *itself* in a more fundamental sense.' Marion, *Transcendence in Philosophy and Religion*, 88.

4 'At the birth of the visible (at the conversion of what gives itself into that which shows itself), there comes into play a pre-phenomenological and pre-rational obscurity, the choice or refusal of "the great reason" . . . of unconditioned givenness . . . The gifted, inasmuch as finite, has nothing less than the charge of opening or closing the entire flux of phenomenality.' Marion, *Being Given*, 306–7.

5 O'Leary, 'The Gift a Trojan Horse in the Citadel of Phenomenology', 137–8.

6 Cf. *S.T.*, 1, q.3, a.4, ad2.

7 Edmund Husserl, *The Paris Lectures*, trans. Peter Koestenbaum (The Hague: Martinus Nijhoff, 1967), 23.

8 *The Visible*, 48.

9 'One might legitimately ask whether every phenomenon, inasmuch as it appears, does not, at least initially, dispense with Being – a phenomenon without Being. Consequently, phenomemology could free itself absolutely not only from all *metaphysica generalis (ontologia)*, but also from the question of Being *(Seinsfrage)* . . . General metaphysics, as *ontologia*, thus would have to yield to a general phenomenology of the givenness of any being-given . . . The relief of metaphysics (here of general metaphysics) goes all the way to this radical point.' *The Visible*, 57–8.

10 *Being Given*, 5.

11 For an effective treatment of this theme, cf. Philip Pettit, 'A sensible perspectivism', *The Philosophy and Politics,* ed. M. Baghramian and A. Ingram (London: Routledge, 2000), 60–82.

12 'Each phenomenalizes the other as the revealed, which is characterized by this essential reciprocity, where seeing implies the modification of the seer by the seen as much as the seen by the seer. The given-to functions as the revelatory of the given and given as the revelatory of the given-to.' *Transcendence in Philosophy and Religion*, 102.

13 Nagel, *The View from Nowhere*, 3–4.

14 Cf. ibid., 7–8. In a similar vein, Merleau-Ponty remarks: 'All that I know of the world, even by science, I know from a viewpoint which is mine, or from an experience of the world without which the symbols of science would have nothing to say . . . Scientific views according to which I am a moment of the world are always naïve and hypocritical, because they imply, without mentioning it, this other view, that of consciousness, by virtue of which in the first place a world disposes itself about me and begins to exist for me.' Maurice Merleau-Ponty, *Phrnomenologie de la Perception* (Paris: Gallimard, 1945), ii–iii.

15 'All that I have written seems like straw compared to what has now been revealed to me.' Cited in J. Weishepl, *Friar Thomas D'Aquino* (New York: Doubleday, 1974), 322.

16 Cf. *Being Given*, 367.

17 'The New Testament is unintelligible except as the flowering of the
    Hebrew tradition and the asking of the creation question that became
    central to the Jewish Bible.' Herbert McCabe, *God Matters: Contemporary
    Christian Insights* (London: Mowbray, 2000), 42.
18 Cf. Te Velde, *'Divine Science' of the Summa Theologiae,* 161.
19 'If it is true then that Marion's phenomenology is not or does not intend
    to be in any straightforward way, a theology it is also true that his
    theology and phenomenology inform one another more or otherwise
    than Marion himself might allow, for the former already operates in
    a quasi-phenomenological manner, and the latter in fact accepts the
    understanding of revelation set out in the former to the exclusion of other
    historically actual, and therefore possible understandings of revelation.'
    Carlson, 'Introduction', *The Idol and the Distance,* xv.
20 Isaac Newton, *The Columbia World of Quotations* (New York: Columbia
    UP, 1996), n.41419.
21 S. Hawking and L. Mlodinow, *The Great Design* (London: Bantam Books,
    2010), 117.

Bibliography

Anselm, St. *Prosologion,* trans. A. Mc Gill. London: Macmillan, 1968.

Aquinas, Thomas. *De Ente et Essentia.* Paris: Roland-Gosselin edn, 1948.

— *De Substantiis Seperatis.* Turin: Marietti, 1954.

— *In librum Beati Dionysii de Divinis Nominibus.* Turin: Marietti, 1950.

— *In librum Boethii de Trinitate Expositio.* Turin: Marietti, 1954.

— *In librum de Causis Expositio.* Turin: Marietti, 1955.

— *In XII libros Metaphysicorum Aristotelis Expositio.* Turin: Marietti, 1964. (*Commentary on the Metaphysics of Aristotle,* trans. J. Rowan. Chicago: Henry Regnery, 1961.)

— *In libros Peri Hermeneias Aristotelis Expositio.* Turin: Marietti, 1964. (*Aristotle on Interpretation: Perihermeneias,* trans. J. Osterle. Milwauke: Marquette UP, 1962.)

— *In VIII libros Physicorum Expositio.* Rome: Leonine edn, 1884.

— *Quaestiones disputatae de malo.* Turin: Marietti, 1965.

— *Quaestiones disputatae de potentia.* Turin: Marietti, 1965.

— *Quaestiones disputatae de veritate.* Turin: Marietti, 1964.

— *Quaestio disputata de virtutibus cardinalibus.* Turin: Marietti, 1965.

— *Quaestiones Quodlibetales.* Turin: Marietti, 1949.

— *Scriptum super IV libros Sententiarum,* ed. P. Mandonnet and P. Moos. Paris: Lethielleux, 1929–47.

— *Summa Contra Gentiles.* Turin: Marietti, 1967. (English trans. *Summa Contra Gentiles, On the Truth of the Catholic Faith,* 5 vols, trans. A. Pegis, J. F. Anderson, V. J. Bourke and C. J. O'Neil. New York: Doubleday, 1955–7.)

— *Summa Theologiae.* Turin: Marietti, 1952–62. (*Summa Theologiae,* trans. English Dominicans. London: Eyre and Spottiswoode, 1964–74.)

Aristotle. *Metaphysica,* trans. W. Ross. Oxford: Clarendon Press, 1928.

Augustine, St. *De Trinitate.* Paris: Bibliotheque Augustinienne, 1955.

Baghramian, M. and A. Ingram, ed. *The Philosophy and Politics of Diversity.* London: Routledge, 2000.

Barth, Karl. *Credo,* trans. J. S. McNabb. London: Hodder and Stoughton, 1936.

— *Dogmatik im Grundriss.* Munich: Kaiser, 1947.

— *The Epistle to the Romans,* trans. E. Hosykns. London: Oxford UP, 1933.

Beyer, C. 'Edmund Husserl', online. *Stanford Encyclopaedia of Philosophy.* Stanford: Stanford UP, 2007.

Bonaventure, St. *Itinerarum Mentis in Deum.* Rome: Quaracchi edn, 1891.

Bouillard, Henri. *Karl Barth,* 3 vols. Paris: Aubier, 1947.

— *The Logic of the Faith,* trans. M. Gill. Dublin: M.H. Gill and Son, 1967.

Bowker, John. *The Sense of God: Sociological, Anthropological and Psychological Approaches to the Sense of God.* Oxford: Oxford UP, 1973.

Candler, Peter and Conor Cunningham. *Transcendence and Phenomenology.* London: S.C.M. Press, 2007.

Caputo, John and Gianni Vattimo. *After the Death of God.* New York: Columbia UP, 2007.

Caputo, John and Michael Scanlan. *God the Gift and Postmodernism.* Bloomington: Indiana UP, 1999.

Chambon, Roger. *Le monde comme perception et realite.* Paris: Vrin, 1974.

Collins, James. *The Emergence of Philosophy of Religion.* New Haven: Yale UP, 1967.

Connell, Desmond. *Essays in Metaphysics.* Dublin: Four Courts Press, 1996.

Davies, Brian. *An Introduction to the Philosophy of Religion*, 3rd edn. Oxford: Oxford UP, 2004.

Descartes, Rene. *A Discourse on Method, Meditations, and Principles*, trans. J. Veitch. London: J.M.Dent, 1912.

Diller, Kevin. 'Karl Barth and the Relationship between Philosophy and Theology', *The Heythrop Journal*, vol. LI (2011), 1035–52.

Dondeyne, Albert. *Contemporary European Thought and Christian Faith*, trans. Ernan McMullin. Pittsburgh: Duquesne UP, 1958.

Dumery, Henri. *The Problem of God in Philosophy of Religion,* trans. C. Courtney. Evanston: Northwestern UP, 1964.

Fackenheim, Emil. *The Religious Dimension of Hegel's Thought.* Bloomington: Indiana UP, 1967.

Farrer, Austin. *Finite and Infinite.* London: Westminister Press, 1943.

Faulconer, James E., ed. *Transcendence in Philosophy and Religion.* Bloomington: Indiana UP, 2003.

Feuerbach, Ludwig. *The Essence of Christianity*, trans. George Elliot. NewYork: Harper and Row, 1957.

Gilson, Etienne. *Le philosophe et la theologie.* Paris: Fayard, 1960.

Hawking, S. and L. Mlodinow. *The Great Design.* London: Bantam Books, 2010.

Hegel, G. W. F. *Berliner Schriften.* Hamburg: Meiner, 1956.

— *Lectures on the Philosophy of Religion*, 3 vols, trans. E. Spiers and J. Sanderson. London: Routledge and Keegan Paul, 1895.

— *Lectures on the Philosophy of Religion*, 3 vols, ed. Peter C. Hodgson. Oxford: Oxford UP, 2007–8.

— *On Christianity: Early Theological Writings*, trans. T. Knox and K. Kroner. New York: Harper Torchbooks, 1961.

— *The Encyclopaedia of the Philosophical Sciences*, trans. W. Wallace. Oxford: Oxford UP, 1873.

— *The Phenomenology of Mind*, trans. J. Baillie. New York: Harper, 1967.

Heidegger, Martin. *Basic Problems of Phenomenology*, trans. A. Hofstader. Bloomington: Indiana UP, 1982.

— *Basic Writings from Being and Time (1927) to The Task of Thinking (1964)*, ed. David Farrell Krell. London: Routledge, 1978.

— *Identity and Difference*, trans. Joan Stambaugh. Chicago: Chicago UP, 2002.

Hick, J., ed. *The Existence of God*. London: MacMillan, 1964.

Hick, J. and A. McGill, *The Many-Faced Argument*. London: Macmillan, 1968.

Husserl, Edmund. *Cartesian Meditations*, trans. D. Cairns. The Hague: Martinus Nijhoff, 1968.

— *Ideas*, trans. W. Boyce Gibson. New York: Collier, 1962.

— *The Paris Lectures*, trans. Peter Koestenbaum. The Hague: Martinus Nijhoff, 1967.

Isaye, G. *La theoriede la mesure et l'existence d'un maximum selon Saint Thomas*. Paris: Beauchesne, 1949.

James, William. *The Varieties of Religious Experience*. London: Collins, Fontana Library, 1960.

Janicaud, Dominique, Jean-Francois Courtine, Jean-Louis Chretien, Michel Henry, Jean-Luc Marion and Paul Ricoeur. *Phenomenology and the 'Theological Turn' – The French Debate*, trans. B. Prusak and J. Kosky. New York: Fordham UP, 2000.

Johnson, K. *Karl Barth and the Analogia Entis*. London: T&TClark, 2010.

Kant, Immanuel. *Critique of Practical Reason*, trans. T. Abbott. London: Longmans, 6th edn, 1909.

— *Critique of Pure Reason*, trans. Norman Kemp-Smith. London: Macmillan, 1933.

— *Religion within the Limits of Reason Alone*, trans. T. Greene and H. Hudson. New York: Harper Torchbooks, 1960.

Kearney, Richard. *Anatheism: Returning to God after God*. New York: Columbia UP, 2010.

— *Strangers God and Monsters*. London: Routledge, 2003.

— *The God Who May Be*. Bloomington: Indiana UP, 2001.

Kenny, Anthony. *Reason and Religion*. Oxford: Blackwell, 1987.

Laeur, Quentin. *Hegel's Concept of God*. New York: SUNY Press, 1982.

Leask, K. and E. Cassidy, eds. *Givenness and God*. New York: Fordham UP, 2005.

Levinas, Emmanuel. *En decouvrant l'existence avec Husserl et Heidegger*. Paris: Vrin, 1967.

— *Totality and Infinity*, trans. A. Lingis. Pittsburgh: Duquesne UP, 1969.

Little, Arthur. *The Platonic Heritage of Thomism*. Dublin: Golden Eagle Books, 1949.

Luther, Martin. *Lectures on Genesis*, ed. J. Pelican. St Louis: Concordia Publishers, 1958.

Mc Cabe, Herbert. *God Still Matters*, ed. Brian Davies. London: Continuum, 2007.

McPherson, Thomas. 'Finite and Infinite', *Mind*, vol. 66 (1957), 370–85.

Marechal, Joseph. *Le point de depart de la metaphysique*. Bruxelles: Lessianum, 1949.

Marion, Jean-Luc. *Being Given: Toward a Phenomenology of Givenness*, trans. Jeffrey L. Kosky. Stanford: Stanford UP, 2002.

— *Cartesian Questions: Method and Metaphysics*, trans. and ed. Jeffrey Kosky. Chicago: Chicago UP, 1999.

— *Dieu sans l'etre*, trans. Jeffrey L. Kosky. Paris: PUF, 2002.

— *God without Being*, trans. Thomas Carlson. Chicago: Chicago UP, 1991.

— *The Idol and the Distance*, trans. and intro. T. Carlson. New York: Fordham UP, 2001.

— *The Visible and the Revealed*, trans. Christina Gschwandtner and others. New York: Fordham UP, 2008.

Matczak, Sebastian. *Karl Barth on God*. New York: Alba House, 1962.

Masterson, Patrick. *Atheism and Alienation: A Study of the Philosophical Sources of Contemporary Atheism*. South Bend: Notre Dame UP, 1971.

— 'La definition du fini implique t-elle l'infini?' *Revue Philosophique de Louvain*, t.62 (1964), 39–68.

— *The Sense of Creation: Experience and the God beyond*. Aldershot: Ashgate, 2008.

Meillassoux, Quentin. *After Finitude: An Essay on the Neccesity of Contingency*, trans. Ray Brassier. London: Continuum, 2008.

Merleau-Ponty, Maurice. *Eloge de la Philosophie*. Paris: Gallimard, 1958.

— *Phenomenologie de la Perception*. Paris: Gallimard, 1945.

— *Sens et non-sens*. Paris: Gallimard, 1961.

Moran, Dermot, ed. *Phenomenology – Critical Concepts*. London: Routledge, 2004.

— *The Routledge Companion to Twentieth Century Philosophy*. London: Routledge, 2008.

Nagel, Thomas. *The Last Word*. New York: Oxford UP, 1997.

— *The View from Nowhere*. New York: Oxford UP, 1986.

Newton, Isaac. 'Quote n. 41419', *The Columbia World of Qoutations*. New York: Columbia UP, 1996.

Papineau, David. *Reality and Representation*. Oxford: Blackwell, 1987.

Patterson, P. and J. Pugh, eds. *Analytical Thomism: Traditions in Dialogue*. Aldershot: Ashgate, 2006.

Plato. *The Dialogues of Plato*, trans. B. Jowett. London: MacMillan, 1982.

Pontifex, Mark and Ian Trethowan. *The Meaning of Existence: A Metaphysical Enquiry*. London: Sheed and Ward, 1953.

Ricoeur, Paul. *De l'Interpretation*. Paris: Seuil, 1965.

— *Philosophie de la volonte*. Paris: Aubier, 1960.

Roland-Gosselin, M. Dd. 'Dela connaissance affectif', *Revue Scientifique de Philosophie et Theologie*, t.27 (1938), 1–25.

Searle, John. *The Construction of Reality*. London: Penguin, 1955.

Smart, Ninian. *The World Religions*, 2nd edn. Cambridge: Cambridge UP, 1998.

Smith, John. *Experience and God*. New York: Oxford UP, 1968.

Sweeney, Leo. 'L'infini quantitative chez Aristiote', *Revue Philosophique de Louvain*, t.58 (1960), 505–28.

Thibaut, Henri. *Creation and Metaphysics: A Genetic Approach to Existential Act*. The Hague: Martinus Nijhoff, 1970.

Turner, Denys. *The Darkness of God: Negativity in Christian Mysticism*. Cambridge: Cambridge UP, 1995.

Vancourt, Roger. *La pensee religieuse de Hegel*. Paris: Fayard, 1960.

Van Riet, Georges. *Philosophie et Religion*. Paris: Nauwelaerts, 1970.

— 'Le Probleme de Dieu chez Hegel: Atheisme ou Christianisme?' *Revue Philosophique de Louvain* t.63 (1965), 354–418.

Warthall, Mark, ed. *Religion after Metaphysics*. Cambridge: Cambridge UP, 2003.

Weisheipl, James. *Friar Thomas D'Aquino*. New York: Doubleday, 1974.

Index